Philosophical Probings:
von Wright's Later Work

Other interview books from Automatic Press ♦ VIP

Formal Philosophy
edited by Vincent F. Hendricks & John Symons
November 2005

Masses of Formal Philosophy
edited by Vincent F. Hendricks & John Symons
October 2006

Political Questions: 5 Questions for Political Philosophers
edited by Morten Ebbe Juul Nielsen
December 2006

Philosophy of Technology: 5 Questions
edited by Jan-Kyrre Berg Olsen & Evan Selinger
February 2007

Game Theory: 5 Questions
edited by Vincent F. Hendricks & Pelle Guldborg Hansen
April 2007

Legal Philosophy: 5 Questions
edited by Morten Ebbe Juul Nielsen
October 2007

Normative Ethics: 5 Questions
edited by Thomas S. Petersen & Jesper Ryberg
November 2007

Philosophy of Mathematics: 5 Questions
edited by Vincent F.Hendricks & Hannes Leitgeb
January 2008

Epistemology: 5 Questions
edited by Vincent F.Hendricks & Duncan Pritchard
September 2008

Complexity: 5 Questions
edited by Carlos Gershenson
September 2008

Mind and Consciousness: 5 Questions
edited by Patrick Grim
February 2009

See all published and forthcoming books in the 5 Questions series at
www.vince-inc.com/automatic.html

Philosophical Probings: von Wright's Later Work

edited by

Frederick Stoutland

Automatic Press ◆ $\frac{V}{|}$P

Automatic Press ♦ $\frac{V}{I}$P

Information on this title: www.vince-inc.com/automatic.html

© Automatic Press / VIP 2009

This publication is in copyright. Subject to statuary exception
and to the provisions of relevant collective licensing agreements,
no reproduction of any part may take place without
the written permission of the publisher.

First published 2009

Printed in the United States of America
and the United Kingdom

ISBN-10   87-92130-20-8   paperback
ISBN-13   978-87-92130-20-4   paperback

The publisher has no responsibilities for
the persistence or accuracy of URLs for external or
third party Internet Web sites referred to in this publication
and does not guarantee that any content on such
Web sites is, or will remain, accurate or appropriate.

Typeset in $\LaTeX 2_\varepsilon$
Graphic design by Vincent F. Hendricks

To Elizabeth von Wright

"Love's not Time's fool"
(Sonnet, 116)

Contents

Contributors   v

Preface   vii

Introduction   1
   Frederick Stoutland

Part 1. Rationality, Goodness, and Action

von Wright on Normative Rationality   17
   Alberto Emiliani

What is the Order among the Varieties of Goodness?
A Question Posed by von Wright   35
   David Wiggins

von Wright's Compatibilism   61
   Frederick Stoutland

Kantianism and von Wright's Compatibilism   83
   Martina Reuter

von Wright and the Logic of the Practical Syllogism   93
   Krister Segerberg

Logical Determination and the Principle of Bivalence   111
   Dag Prawitz

Part 2. Logic and Philosophy, Then and Now

Logic and Philosophy in the Twentieth Century   139
    Georg Henrik von Wright

A note on von Wright's Lecture on Logic and Philosophy in
the Twentieth Century   159
    Nuel Belnap

Logic and Philosophy in the Century That Was
    Johan von Bentham   163

The Demise of Modern Logic?   169
    Sven Ove Hansson

The Place of Logic in Philosophy   177
    Eva Picardi

von Wright on the Future of
            Logic and Philosophy   185
    Soren Stenlund

Logic and Philosophy in the Twenty-First Century   199
    Timothy Williamson

Contributors

Nuel Belnap, Jr. is Alan Ross Anderson Distinguished Professor of Philosophy, professor of history and philosophy of science, and fellow of the Center for Philosophy of Science at the University of Pittsburgh. His present interests lie principally in philosophical logic, with other interests in metaphysics, the philosophy of the social sciences, and computer science.

Johan van Benthem is University Professor at the University of Amsterdam, Professor of Philosophy at Stanford University, and Visiting University Professor at Zhongshan University in Guangzhou, China. His research interests include temporal logic, logic and philosophy of science, logical structures in natural languages, model theory of modal languages, and dynamic logics.

Alberto Emiliani is Docent in Philosophy at the University of Helsinki and teaches at the Gymnasium in Faenze, Italy. His philosophical interests center on Wittgenstein, and he has published a number of papers on von Wright.

Sven Ove Hansson is Professor and Head of the Department of Philosophy and the History of Technology at the Royal Institute of Technology in Stockholm. He is editor of the journal *Theoria*. His interests include the assessment of various kinds of risk (for example, foods, chemicals, and nuclear fuel), philosophy and technology, and environmental policy.

Eva Picardi is Professor of the Philosophy of Language and Director of the Doctoral Program in Mind, Logic, and Language at the University of Bologna. Her interests are in contemporary philosophy of language and the history and philosophy of logic, with special emphasis on Frege.

Dag Prawitz is Emeritus Professor of Theoretical Philosophy at the University of Stockholm. He taught previously at the University of Lund and the University of Oslo. His main areas are logic (principally, proof theory), the philosophy of logic and mathematics, and the philosophy of language.

Martina Reuter is Academy Research Fellow at the University of Helsinki. Her main interests are in the moral psychology of Catharine Macaulay and Mary Wollstonecraft, the phenomenology of Husserl, Merleau-Ponty, and Hannah Arendt, and feminist philosophy.

Krister Segerberg is Emeritus Professor of Theoretical Philosophy at Uppsala University. He was previously Professor of Philosophy at the Åbo Academy University and at the University of Auckland in New Zealand. His main interest is philosophical logic, including the logic of action and belief revision.

Sören Stenlund is Emeritus Professor of Theoretical Philosophy at Uppsala University. His interests include the philosophy of language, of logic, and of mathematics; the nature and history of philosophy, and the philosophy of Wittgenstein, particularly his philosophy of mathematics.

Frederick Stoutland is Emeritus Professor of Philosophy at St. Olaf College in Minnesota and Permanent Visiting Professor at Uppsala University. His main interest is philosophy of action and its connection to moral psychology, philosophy of mind, and philosophy of language.

David Wiggins is Wykeham Professor of Logic Emeritus at Oxford University and Fellow of New College. He was previously Professor of Philosophy at Bedford College, London, and Birckbeck College, London. He has published works on logic, metaphysics, ethics, the philosophy of language, moral and political philosophy, and the history of philosophy.

Timothy Williamson is Wykeham Professor of Logic at Oxford University. He has taught at Trinity College, Dublin, and was Professor of Logic and Metaphysics at the University of Edinburgh. His main research interests are in philosophical logic, epistemology, metaphysics, and philosophy of language.

Preface

This volume originated in a conference held in May, 2006 to honor the memory of Georg Henrik von Wright who died in June of 2003. The conference took place at the Åbo Akademi University, of which von Wright had been a long-time supporter and sometime Chancellor. Although fluent in Finnish (as in English and German), Swedish was his mother tongue, and it was, therefore, especially fitting that the conference meet in Finland's Swedish-speaking university. The language of the conference was English, however, and participants came from six countries, reflecting von Wright's wide circle of international colleagues and friends.

Part I of this book consists of six papers that are revised versions of ones read at the conference. All deal directly with the philosophical work von Wright published after his Gifford Lectures in 1959 and 1960, and they are arranged roughly in the chronological order of the publications they discuss: *Norm and Action*, *The Varieties of Goodness*, *Explanation and Understanding* and related works on action, and, finally, his discussion of future contingents in *Truth, Knowledge and Modality*.

Part II contains the Inaugural Lecture von Wright gave at the 11th Congress of Logic, Methodology and Philosophy of Science in Uppsala in 1991. Entitled "Logic and Philosophy in the Twentieth Century," it surveyed the history of logic since Aristotle and its post-Fregean relation to the foundations of mathematics, considered the expansion of logic into various types of modal logic, and reflected on the interconnection of logic and philosophy in analytical philosophy. It concluded that formal logic would not have a prominent role in philosophy in the 21st century, because, having become a science, it had ceased to be philosophy, and because its central role in 20th century philosophy reflected "a belief in progress, fostered by scientific and technological developments...

[which] is giving way to a somber mood of self-critical scrutiny of the achievements and foundations of our civilization."

The lecture was a magisterial survey of a complex topic, but it was controversial, especially among analytical philosophers that regard the techniques and achievements of formal logic as essential to good philosophical work. Six distinguished philosopher-logicians have, therefore, been asked to comment on it. They all disagree with it in greater or lesser degree but from different points of view and for diverse reasons. Taken together the comments make a rich feast of reflection on the role logic might play in philosophy in the 21st century.

The conference in Åbo was organized by Lars Herzberg, who was Professor at Åbo, and Lilli Alanen, Professor at Uppsala University. It was attended by a large number of von Wright's colleagues and friends, as well as by his two children and their families and his widow, Elisabeth, to whom this book is dedicated. Thanks are owed to the Åbo Akademi University, to those who organized and facilitated the conference, to all the participants, and to those who attended.

In the editing of this book, I have received significant counsel, assistance, and support from Krister Segerberg, and Lars Herzberg, Dag Prawitz, and Lilli Alanen have been helpful and supportive. Vincent F. Hendricks and **Automatic Press** ♦ $\frac{\vee}{\mid}$P agreed to be its publisher, and he has most efficiently moved things along. The work of editing was done at the Philosophy Department at Uppsala University, and I am appreciative of the various kinds of aid I received there. A special note of thanks is owed to the Anders Karitz Stiftelse for a generous stipend that encouraged the publication of the book and will help make it more widely accessible. The contributors to Part I have been most cooperative in revising the papers they read at the conference, and the contributors to Part II have written excellent comments at relatively short notice. I am very grateful for this cooperation, support, and help, all of which has made this book possible.

Frederick Stoutland
Uppsala
August 2008

Introduction

Frederick Stoutland

1. Georg Henrik von Wright was born in Helsinki in 1916 and, apart from two years in Brooklyn as a very young lad and one year in the Tyrol when he was twelve, he spent his youth there. He cultivated his interests in literature, history, and mathematics at home and at school, and then studied philosophy and history at the University of Helsinki. He settled on philosophy for graduate work at the University, where his supervisor was Eino Kaila, a brilliant and charismatic philosopher who was connected with the Vienna Circle, had brought its new philosophy and logic to Finland, and encouraged von Wright in that direction. Because of the conditions on the continent, however, von Wright went instead to Cambridge in 1939 to study with C.D. Broad, and there he met Wittgenstein and Moore, who, together with Kaila, became the major influences on his philosophical development. He returned to Helsinki after a year and in 1941 received the Ph.D. for his thesis on *The Logical Problem of Induction*.

During the war, he was for a time in the Finnish Defense Forces Ballistic Laboratory and then in the Governmental Information Department. He married Elisabeth von Troil in 1941, and they had two children, one in 1943 and the other in 1945. After the war, von Wright was appointed Professor of Philosophy at the University of Helsinki, but he soon returned to Cambridge as a lecturer, and in 1948 he was appointed to the Chair of Philosophy in Cambridge, which Wittgenstein and, before him, Moore had held. In 1951 he resigned to return to Helsinki and resume the Professorship to which he had been appointed in 1946. In 1961 he was appointed to the Academy of Finland, which at the time comprised twelve persons from diverse fields whose lifetime membership in the Academy freed them to do their own work.

He later was instrumental in reorganizing the Academy so that it supported general research in Finland, but he retained his lifetime position.

Helsinki continued to be his home even while he taught and lectured around the world, notably as Professor-at-Large at Cornell, in giving (among others) the Gifford, Tarner, Woodbridge, Tanner, and Leibniz Lectures, and in engaging philosophers from many countries in philosophical conversation on topics of mutual interest. He was also active in numerous cultural and intellectual institutions in Finland and abroad, for example, as long term President of the Philosophical Society of Finland, as President of the International Union of the History and Philosophy of Science, and as one of three executors of Wittgenstein's estate, charged with overseeing the publication of his *Nachlass*.[1]

von Wright published his first philosophical paper in 1938 (in *Theoria*: "Der Wahrscheinlichkeitsbegriff in der modernen Erkenntnisphilosophie") and published continuously until his death sixty-five years later. Risto Vilkko's bibliography lists 527 papers and books (which does not count many of the translations of those works into other languages) plus 33 works that he edited.[2] Although most of the works deal with philosophical topics, von Wright also wrote essays about people, history, literature, politics, and more, works that were philosophical in character in the wide sense of the term. I will not – I cannot – survey this impressively large and consistently high quality body of work on so many subjects. What I will do is give a brief account of the stages of von Wright's philosophical work, together with an account of his changing views about the spiritual and humanistic context of philosophy.

The latter involve what von Wright called the "*Weltanschauung* aspects of philosophy," and he recognized that such matters are often regarded as integral to philosophy itself. But he found them "difficult to cultivate in the climate of the new 'exactitude' demanded of philosophy by logic and the advanced scientific thinking of the century, " and hence they found in his case "an outlet

---

[1] An excellent supplement to this brief sketch is Risto Vilkko's biographical account in the *Journal for General Philosophy of Science* (2005) 36: 1-14. For further biographical details, see von Wright's "Intellectual Autobiography" in P. A. Schilpp and L. E. Hahn, eds., *The Philosophy of Georg Henrik von Wright* (Open Court, 1989) and his personal autobiography, *Mitt liv som jag minns det* [My Life as I remember it] (Uddevall: Bonniers, 2001).

[2] *Journal for General Philosophy of Science* (2005) 36: pp. 155-210.

in writing of an essayistic nature without either scholarly or otherwise academic pretension."[3] This meant, not that such writing did not aspire to or meet high standards of excellence, but that meeting those standards did not call on the distinctive competence of a professional philosopher. He thought philosophy really was a profession, writing that "whereas there are good examples of successful amateurs in the sciences, I cannot think of any in philosophy."[4] He, therefore, kept a fairly strict line between his professional philosophical work and his writings on the spiritual and humanistic dimensions of life and society, though the line became less distinct in his later writings. They were never, however, separated in his own mind or life, just as they were never so separated, he noted, for Kaila or Wittgenstein. Although I will not discuss von Wright's essayistic writings on these matters, they are among the best things he did, and a grasp of the point of view he expressed in them is essential to comprehending his achievement as a philosopher.

2. The first stage of von Wright's philosophical work was on induction and probability, an interest that brought him to Cambridge and that lasted until the late 1940's. His doctoral dissertation in Helsinki[5] was about the canons of induction that Bacon and Mill used to ascertain causes and effects, which von Wright replaced with the notions of necessary and sufficient conditions in order to reformulate the classical canons. This was extended, corrected, and related to probability theory in a number of papers and then in his *Treatise on Probability and Induction*, written in 1948 but not published until 1951.[6] In the early 1940's C. D. Broad wrote a series of articles for *Mind* (England's leading philosophical periodical) on von Wright's results in this field, and the result was that von Wright became famous in the wider philosophical world. This no doubt contributed to his being elected to the Chair of Philosophy at Cambridge in 1948, although by that time he had come to know Moore and Wittgenstein, both of whom he had greatly impressed.

The next stage of von Wright's work was logic. His aim was not a contribution to logic in the style of Russell, Gödel, Tarski,

---

[3]Von Wright, *The Tree of Knowledge and Other Essays* (Leiden: E.J. Brill, 1993), p. 2. This is the best collection of these writings in English.
[4]Schilpp and Hahn, p. 53
[5]*The Logical Problem of Induction* (Helsinki: Acta Philosophical Fennica, 1941; 2nd revised edn., Oxford: Blackwell, 1957).
[6]London: Routledge & Kegan Paul, 1951.

or Church but a philosophy of logic and a philosophical logic. He took the task of logic generally to be to describe and systematize the principles used in argumentation, inference, and proof, the aim of his own work being philosophical reflection on those principles and the concepts they involve. In the course of that work, a new aim emerged: to extend the application of logic as it had developed since Frege, to subject matters which traditionally made no explicit use of logical symbols and methods.

The focus of this work was the concept of logical truth, which he began to investigate by considering how far the Tractarian notion of logical truth as tautological could be extended to quantificational logic. He showed that this could be done for simpler quantificational structures, and in so doing invented "distributive normal forms." This work led to such related topics as conditionals, entailment, negation, and the logical antinomies, on which von Wright wrote clarifying and stimulating papers.

While working on the quantifiers, he noticed a parallelism between the structure of 'some', 'none' and 'all' and that of the modal terms 'possible', 'impossible', and 'necessary.' Just as the negation of 'Some S are P' is equivalent to 'No S are P', so the negation of 'P is possible' is equivalent to 'P is impossible', and just as the negation of 'Some S are not P' is equivalent to 'All S are P', so the negation of 'Not-P is possible' is equivalent to 'P is necessary', and so on. A little later, he noticed an analogous parallelism for the deontic modal terms 'permissible', 'forbidden' and 'obligatory.' His project was to articulate these modalities in logical systems analogous to propositional and predicate logic, which would have precise rules for well-formed formulae and valid inferences, enable exact determination of what a claim entailed and what it contradicted, and permit investigation of meta-logical issues like consistency and completeness. His ideas on how to do this for the strict modalities were written in 1950,[7] while his proposals for deontic modalities appeared in his "Deontic Logic" in *Mind*, 1951.

"Deontic Logic" is his most famous paper, for it created a new subject that was his own in a special sense. It showed how to symbolize various normative claims and precisely determine their logical interrelations, and it opened up new claims and relations that may not be noticeable outside a logical system. This "logic of norms" was of great interest to legal philosophers who wrestled

---

[7]Published in *An Essay in Modal Logic* (Amsterdam: North Holland Publishing Co, 1951).

with such questions as whether two laws are mutually consistent or whether, and in what sense, a system of laws may be consistent or complete.

Von Wright's interest in the logic of norms was sustained by its connection to issues about truth. He had since his youth been committed to a "deep conceptual gap separating the world of facts from that of norms and values," and he continued to hold to that gap in its radical form as the view that normative judgments are neither true nor false. This raised the problem of how a logic of norms is even possible, for such a logic assumes that there are logical relations between norms and that there are disjunctive and conditional norm sentences, and those assumptions appear to require that norm sentences have truth value.

won Wright discussed this problem a number of times, perhaps foremost in *Norm and Action*. In dealing with it, he appealed to the distinction between sentences which *give* a norm, and thus are *prescriptive*, and those which *state* that a norm has been given, and thus are *descriptive*, which yields two possibilities for constructing a logic of norms without assuming that normative judgments are true or false. The first is to have a logic, not of norms as such, but of the sentences which describe given norms and thus have truth values. The second is to have a logic of norms proper but do not require that logically complex sentences with logical interrelations must have a truth value, so that "Logic has a wider reach than Truth." von Wright changed his mind more than once on which of these ways is better,[8] and finally suggested a third possibility, which is that deontic logic is "neither a logic of norms nor a logic of norm-propositions but a study of conditions which must be satisfied in rational norm-giving activity."[9]

3. These two stages of von Wright's work were largely done by someone who was a believer in the "spirit of scientific rationality." He became such a believer in his youth, inspired above all by the Cartesian mathematics and physics that had also inspired Eino Kaila and the logical empiricists, the new logic, and analytic philosophers generally. Although never believing whole-heartedly, as many analytical philosophers did, that scientific rationality

---

[8]Cf. *Norm and Action: A Logical Inquiry* (London: Routledge & Kegan Paul, 1963); *An Essay in Deontic Logic and the General Theory of Action* (Amsterdam: North-Holland Publishing Co., 1968); *Truth, Knowledge, and Modality: Philosophical Papers*, vol. 3 (Oxford: Blackwell,1984).

[9]Cf. *Six essays in Philosophical Logic* (Helsinki: Act Philosophica Fennica, 1996). This is the topic of Alberto Emiliani's paper below.

would result in inevitable progress – even his youthful "aesthetic humanism" was strongly affected by Spengler's pessimism – he was a believer in the ideal of philosophy as one of the exact sciences.

This attitude changed when his professorship in Helsinki required that he teach moral philosophy, and under the influence of Werner Jaeger's *Paidea*, he abandoned "aesthetic humanism" for an individualistic "ethical humanism" that recognized a practical rationality on a par with the rationality of the exact sciences. This point of view, implicit in *Norm and Action*, became explicit in *Varieties of Goodness*, his main work in moral philosophy. Its central claim is that *moral* senses of "good", and of "right" or "duty," are dependent on and derive from non-moral uses of the terms. It is a conceptual inquiry, which aims at making "fixed and sharp that which ordinary usage leaves loose and undetermined," but since it denies that there is any clear distinction between ethics and meta-ethics, its inquiries into how to improve our moral concepts are also meant to be inquiries into what moral point of view we ought to adopt. It assumes that there can be "a philosophical pursuit deserving the name 'ethics', which shares with a common conception of 'meta-ethics' the feature of being a *conceptual investigation* and with a common concept of 'normative ethics' the feature of aiming at *directing our lives*."[10]

The book is Aristotelian in its classification of the varieties of goodness, in its taking seriously the notion of virtue, in its taking the human good to be more basic than duty, and in its commitment to there being such a thing as *practical* rationality that is not inferior to the rationality of the exact sciences. These notions are not rare today, but they were audacious in 1963, and it is understandable that von Wright regarded *The Varieties of Goodness* as the best argued of all his works and the most fun to write.

The individualistic humanism that had nourished *The Varieties of Goodness* was shattered in 1967 by the Vietnam War, which affected von Wright deeply and which he protested in eloquent and effective ways and that brought him to think about the human condition in social and political terms. The result was the "social humanism"[11] to which he remained committed the rest of his life, and which he expressed in interviews and powerful essays

---

[10] *The Varieties of Goodness* (London: Routledge & Kegan Paul, 1963).

[11] The terms for these various kinds of humanism were coined by von Wright himself.

on the threat to human life of the very scientific rationality which inspired his early efforts in philosophy. The ideal of scientific rationality, he argued, had played a major role in creating social and technological conditions that both threaten the natural environment and inspire irrational and unjust ways to try to meet the threat. This argument made him Scandinavia's most prominent public intellectual, but it made him controversial, for he attacked both the Left for failing to see that continued expansion of the welfare state puts an unsustainable burden on natural resources and the Right for failing to note that this was particularly burdensome to the poor countries of the world.

These changes resulted in a significant shift in his conception of philosophy, and although he returned now and again to logical matters he had discussed earlier, his books from now on expressed new thoughts, and while typically written in an analytical idiom, they articulated views that often ran counter to analytical philosophy and connected with continental philosophers and Wittgenstein. He had come to think of philosophy not as an exact science but as a critical reflection on the underlying assumptions of our thinking, judging and acting, assumptions that are embedded in social institutions and traditions and hence require that philosophical reflection inevitably scrutinize the foundations of society.

4. The philosophical books written during this final stage of his work are on philosophy of action and philosophy of mind. His best-known book on the former is *Explanation and Understanding*, but others are equally important, in particular, *Causality and Determinism* and *Freedom and Determination*.[12] This work began with an attempt to get a symbolism adequate to distinguish various kinds of action – to distinguish, for example, what agents do (either by bringing something about or preventing something) from what they do not do (either intentionally or by simply doing nothing). It struck him that such distinctions could not be expressed without a symbolism for different kinds of *change*, and hence he worked at embedding a logic of action in a logic of change, for instance in *Norm and Action*.

Broader issues about action became explicit in *Explanation and Understanding*. It argued that explanations of intentional action are distinct from explanations in the natural sciences because the latter appeal to causal laws while the former invoke conceptual

---

[12] *Causality and Determinism* (New York: Columbia University Press, 1973); *Freedom and Determination* (Helsinki: Acta Philosophica Fennica, 1981)

connections between an agent's reasons and his actions. Explanation of action is, therefore, necessarily connected with practical reason (and the practical syllogism),[13] and the intentional attitudes whose contents function as reasons should be seen, not as internal states with causal powers, but as ways of understanding and articulating what agents *mean* by their behavior. He connected this view with the Aristotelian tradition, contrasting it with the Galilean tradition that assimilated explanation of action (and historical events) to the law-based model of the natural sciences.

Explanation and Understanding reinforced this view by arguing that the concept of cause is inseparable from the concept of (experimental) intervention in nature, and hence inseparable from, indeed derivative from, concepts of action and agency. This implied that the kind of determinism that threatens to undermine the possibility of genuine human agency is self-defeating. Determinism became a core interest of his, which he expressed partly in investigations of issues like knowledge and truth about the future and kinds of necessity,[14] partly in discussions of explanation and free will,[15] partly in criticisms of the way determinism encourages a "reified conception" of people and social institutions as governed by universal laws.

Von Wright first encountered philosophy as a youth through the mind-body problem, but he published little about philosophy of mind until his Tanner Lectures, "Of Human Freedom" in 1984,[16] when reflection on the relation of neuro-physiological explanation to explanation of action led to some remarks on psychophysical parallelism. He then began to write extensively on philosophy of mind, the best of which is published in *In the Shadow of Descartes*,[17] which has papers on the relation of physiological and action explanation, on the concepts of quality and thing, and on perception and sensation (with special attention to sounds). The papers do not form a unity and do not discuss current literature and controversies (of which von Wright was by no means ignorant), but they manifest an intense effort to get clear on some of

---

[13] Cf. *Practical Reason: Philosophical Papers*, vol. 1 (Oxford: Blackwell, 1983).
[14] *Truth, Knowledge, and Modality: Philosophical Papers*, vol. 3 (Oxford: Blackwell, 1984).
[15] *Causality and Determinism*.
[16] Now in *The Tree of Knowledge*.
[17] *In the Shadow of Descartes – Essays in the Philosophy of Mind* (Dordrecht: Kluver, 1998).

the most difficult and fundamental issues in philosophy of mind, and they contain a wealth of distinctions and observations which may prove productive.[18]

One other dimension of von Wright's work must be noted, work that went on for many years, namely his involvement with the Wittgenstein papers. He knew Wittgenstein well, was named as one of his literary executors, and devoted enormous time and effort to his large and extraordinarily complex *Nachlass*. He searched for lost material, interviewed persons who knew Wittgenstein, organized and indexed the papers, and edited several volumes of Wittgenstein's correspondence and manuscripts. While he wrote relatively few papers on Wittgenstein's thought, they include some splendid studies, which have been published (along with his moving "Biographical Sketch") in his *Wittgenstein*.[19]

5. One way of evaluating the achievement of a philosopher is to consider which of his works will be read and learned from in, say, the next century. Although von Wright's rank in 20th century philosophy was not that of Wittgenstein, Heidegger, or similar notables, his works had virtues that suggest they are more likely to endure than those of philosophers who were simply first-rate. In particular, they combined outstanding competence in using the methodological resources of analytical philosophy with a notably imaginative, probing, and broad-ranging discussion of central philosophical issues. There are philosophers who are skilled at drawing distinctions, constructing arguments, and making use of logic and other technical achievements, but who fail to reflect on the philosophical assumptions of their claims or to consider their historical context or wider philosophical implications. There are others who write on broad philosophical issues and draw on the history of philosophy, but who are imprecise in their assertions and methodologically careless. Von Wright had both extraordinary methodological competence and an acute sensitivity to the philosophical assumptions and consequences of his work. He was, on the one hand, expert in logic, knew the intricacies of probability theory, decision theory, and other scientific achievements, and he was careful and precise in drawing distinctions and giving arguments. On the other hand, he drew on a careful reading of the

---

[18]For an example, see Alberto Emiliani's "On Mind and Sensations: G. H. von Wright's last Philosophical Journey" in I. Niiniluto and R. Vilkko, eds., *Philosophical Essays in Memoriam: Georg Henrik von Wright* (*Acta Philosophica Fennica*, vol. 77, 2005).

[19]Oxford: Blackwell, 1982.

history of philosophy from the pre-Socratics through Descartes and Leibniz and beyond, his work was imbued with scholarship and literary and historical allusions, and he was acutely aware of the larger intellectual, social, and political world in which he worked.

In spite of these virtues, it is difficult to predict which, if any, of his works will be known and read in a hundred years – for three reasons. One is that he wrote on such a large and diverse range of philosophical topics: philosophical logic and the philosophy of logic, ethics, epistemology, philosophy of action, of law, or mind, the history of philosophy, and more. He also wrote a great deal on an equally diverse range of topics that he took to be outside his distinctively philosophical competence. All of these works were superbly crafted, creative and penetrating, and they were rich with illuminating insights and unexpected observations. But they were not unified by an overarching philosophical theory but simply by having been written by von Wright, who brought to all his work a distinctive and recognizable way of thinking and writing. That means that what often motivates persons to read a philosopher, namely his general theory of truth, reality, goodness, or what have you, will not motivate persons to read von Wright. It also means that what person read will depend on their special interests, interests that are diverse and may not survive into the next century.

Another reason is the nature of his writing, which demands a great deal of the reader if his insights and claims are to be adequately understood and used. Although he shared with Wittgenstein an aversion to superficial, careless, or pretentious writing, and wrote in a lucid and unconvoluted style that was perfectly suited to his subject and to himself, some of his best philosophical work (again like Wittgenstein's) will seem obscure and irrelevant unless one is prepared to do the hard work of thinking along with him. Doing that yields rewards in extending one's horizons, getting at the root of problems, and seeing new ways of resolving them. But it is arduous work because the point of an argument, an observation, or a whole passage may not be obvious until one has come to feel for oneself the problem von Wright was wrestling with, and thereby come to see how he would resolve a problem that is also one's own. It may be that very few are prepared to give von Wright's work that kind of attention.

A third reason it is difficult to predict the fate of von Wright's work is that it is so closely tied up with him as a person. What is most impressive about von Wright is his work *together with* the man, and for those who knew him at all, these are not easily separated. I have noted how the unity of his work depends on *his* having written it, which means it was written by a man who combined impressive intellectual gifts with enthusiasm and energy, kindness and attentiveness, and great personal charm. These features lay back of all his work, but they are not easily detected in it by those who did not know him, while for those who did, they give it a special verve and import. The writings alone, separated from his person, as they must now be, may be less likely to be read and valued.

In any case, what is read and valued will depend on the point of view of the reader. Analytical philosophers will value most his early work. They might consult his work on induction and probability, though very likely only for historical reasons. If they read his philosophical logic, it will be to see the origins of work that has been developed in numerous ways, while his work in the philosophy of logic will be relevant for his analysis of concepts like entailment and contradiction. His work on norms will, I believe, continue to be of interest to legal theorists in places like Latin American. But none of these works will figure prominently in the philosophical canon of the 22nd century.

If any of his works do so figure, it is likely to be his later works like *The Varieties of Goodness*, *Explanation and Understanding*, and *In the Shadow of Descartes*. None of these works fares very well in the current climate of philosophical opinion, which is dominated by an analytical metaphysics that is largely physicalisitic. But that is a philosophical fashion that will not endure, any more than the idealistic metaphysics that the early analytical philosophers took as their target. Von Wright's work is not beholden to any fashion, and it may – I believe it will – survive the current one.

These later works are not finished systematic treatises but open-ended discussions of very basic philosophical issues, which one reads to be free from philosophical orthodoxy and dogmatism, to lay bare the difficulties of a problem, to suggest directions in which to go, to avoid fruitless projects and dead ends. I think of them as lying between analytical philosophy, on the one hand, and Wittgensteinianism, on the other – two philosophical points of view from which von Wright learned much without, in his later work, begin committed to either.

Von Wright's early work was certainly in the tradition of analytical philosophy, and he remained in some sense an analytical philosopher all his life: he did not repudiate the tradition out of which he came, he felt at home with its idioms and he practiced its virtues of making clear distinctions and giving arguments, stating matters in intelligible prose, being as precise as possible, and so on. But in important respects he ceased to be, in his later work, an analytical philosopher. He there made explicit his view that the formal logic developed in the 20th century belongs to science rather than to philosophy, and although he worked at philosophical logic off and on, he regarded neither it nor his contribution to it as philosophically central. What was central was the philosophical issues it involved, which he discussed in works that show the influence of two other traditions, namely hermeneutic philosophy and what he called "praxis-relevant philosophy." Although he did not regard them as unconnected with analytical philosophy, he took their insights to be distinctive and essential, and he accepted their critique of scientific rationality. He also made clear that his use of the term "theory" did not mean that theory building was an aim of his work. "The inspiration for my thinking," he wrote, "has come from literature and history, and from accumulated experience and impressions of 'the world around me.' This self-characterization partly accounts for the fact that I have never tried to offer a theory about how the phenomena which were the objects of my thinking should be explained or interpreted."[20]

This rejection of scientific rationalism and theory-building should remind one of Wittgenstein, but many who consider themselves Wittgensteinians think of him as a paradigm analytical philosopher and hence reject his work for the same reasons analytical philosophers have prized it: he constructed theories, he invented formal vocabularies in the attempt to get a kind of ideal language, he wrote systematic treatises on various topics, and so on. I maintain that this characterization of von Wright is mistaken, but that does not mean that he was a Wittgensteinian. He was, however, much closer to the spirit of Wittgenstein's work than is generally recognized. Here is the way he put it himself.

> As far as the 'content' of my philosophic thoughts goes, I think I learnt and continue to learn most from Wittgenstein. He molded my conception of what philosophy is. He made me realize that

---

[20]The Tree of Knowledge, p. 4.

one cannot hope for 'final solutions' in that subject. Many things which philosophers say, naively simplifying matters, I could never say, having learnt from Wittgenstein to appreciate the conceptual multiplicity of the situations with which the philosopher has to cope. The insights which I acquired from him were essentially negative: I am still struggling to transform them into something positive as he successfully did himself. But my way will have to be different.[21]

6. I will conclude by saying a few things about von Wright's sense of himself as a public figure and then something about his persona.

von Wright was a notable public figure in a number of ways. He wrote (and spoke) a good deal about socio-political issues. He discussed the politics of higher education and scientific research, he called for global responsibility, and he attacked nuclear power. As I noted earlier, he forcefully criticized the scientific rationality that had inspired him as a youth for encouraging social and technological conditions that threaten our environment and burden the poor. Most important for me personally was his moving and powerful protest against the Vietnam War, which was being waged by a country of which he was fond.

Von Wright was hesitant, however, about taking public stands on specific policies and actions or seeking to influence those who were in a position to make necessary changes. Although this was a disappointment to some, his failure to make such activity an integral part of his philosophical work was not a betrayal of his calling. He was more active in various public causes than most philosophers and was as reflective about his society and the times in which he lived as anyone I know, but he had no illusions about possessing special philosophical insight on matters of politics and human life. He never confused activism and reflection of that kind with philosophical work, and whenever he was asked to comment on such issues, he insisted that he did so as a citizen and not as a philosopher. His vocation was that of a philosopher, which he carried out by writing papers and books of the highest quality, by being a responsive colleague to philosophers around the world, by being the soul of the Helsinki department (for instance, by leading a weekly research seminar whose discussion he always opened with a philosophically intriguing question no matter how bad the

---

[21]Schilpp and Hahn, p. 16.

paper may have been), *and* by participating in public life when it promised to be useful and did not compromise his vocation as philosopher.

I have written these remarks as a friend of von Wright's – one friend among numerous others. That he had so many friends – was a friend to so many – was in part because he was such a likable person: a superb conversationalist on almost any topic and an attentive listener, with an easy sense of humor and a terrific memory, somewhat of a hypochondriac, but never complaining or self-important. But it was also because he *cultivated* friendships in an uncommon way, as would be attested by men and women from around the globe to whom he wrote letters over many years, invited to his home or, occasionally, made phone calls. His capacity for friendship was the virtue those who knew him would mention first, and one is tempted to say that his distinction as a philosopher was matched by his distinction at being a friend for so many. It meant that he was loyal, that he cultivated the relationship, that he was discreet and did not gossip. But he was also straight-forward in his evaluations of people and happenings – frank without being unkind. He was not a complicated man, and there are no deep, dark secrets about his life. He was an admirable man, who is missed by all who continue to find his work instructive and stimulating, and by the many who loved him and who remember with gratitude his unforgettable presence.

Part 1

Rationality, Goodness, and Action

von Wright on Normative Rationality

Alberto Emiliani

Preliminary

Von Wright's article "Deontic Logic", published in 1951 and soon followed by publications by Becker and Kalinowski on similar topics, inaugurated a new field.[1] The aim of the article was to apply the techniques of modern logic to an analysis of normative discourse. However, the conclusions reached in this article were unsatisfactory in several respects — as von Wright remarked later. *Norm and Action*[2] is in fact von Wright's attempt to solve some puzzles that "Deontic Logic" left open and to organize the results of his ongoing research about norms into an extensive theoretical body.

Since 1963, deontic logic has been significantly discussed and developed in several ways, becoming an established field of investigation and research. As we shall presently see, some of the most powerful criticisms against the approach endorsed by *N&A* were put forth by von Wright himself in his subsequent writings — I shall especially mention "Norms, Truth and Logic"[3] and "Is there

---
[1] Oskar Becker, *Untersuchungen über den Modalkalkül* (Meisenheim am Glam, 1952); Georges Kalinowski, "Théorie des propositions normatives," *Studia logica*, 1 (1953), pp. 147-182; G. H. von Wright, "Deontic Logic," *Mind*, 60, 1951, 1-15. Repr. in *Logical Studies* (London and Kegan Paul, 1957), pp. 58-74.
[2] *Norm and Action. A Logical Enquiry* (Routledge and Kegan Paul, London, 1963). Henceforth: *N&A*.
[3] "Norms, Truth and Logic," in *Philosophical Papers, vol. I, Practical Reason* (Blackwell, Oxford, 1983), 130-209. Henceforth: *NTL*.

17

a Logic of Norms?"[4] However, *N&A* is a classic in that it puts crucial conceptual distinctions and a number of central problems under sharp focus.

The significance of *N&A* can be evaluated from several angles. Von Wright builds a system of deontic logic that rests on a logic of action, which in turn presupposes a logic of change. All of them are designed, discussed and completed in *N&A* — an enterprise that also requires a fair amount of technical work. But *N&A* is also a work in the philosophy of right, with conspicuous connections with moral philosophy and the philosophy of politics. Eventually, *N&A* is a study in logic and, in a way, a study about logic. It marks a turning point in the development of von Wright's conception of the nature and aims of deontic logic: two very different approaches coexist in it, one of which subsequently defeated and superseded the other. My aim is to examine the conflict between these approaches as well as the problems from which they arise.

Norms and truth value

In 1983, twenty years after the publication of *N&A*, von Wright remarked that the development of his views on deontic logic is characterized by his attempt to solve a fundamental philosophical problem, which I shall call *the philosophical problem of norms* (cf. *NTL*). The problem consists in the fact that norms do not have a truth value — they constitutively differ from descriptions. Let us deal with this a bit more.

Consider a sentence that can be used to express a norm (a prohibition, a permission): in accordance with *N&A*, we call it a *deontic sentence*. Many such sentences manifest a typical ambiguity. Take e.g. the deontic sentence "it is forbidden to throw objects out of the windows." It admits of two interpretations, that is, it can be used in two different ways. On the prescriptive interpretation, it is a *normative formulation*,[5] that is, the *expression of a prescription*. The sentence is used to prohibit throwing any objects out of the window: therefore it is roughly equivalent to "don't throw anything out of the window!" On the other hand,

---

[4]Is there a Logic of Norms?, *Ratio Juris*, 4 (1991), 265-283; repr. In Georg Henrik von Wright, *Six Essays in Philosophical Logic* (Helsinki, Acta Philosophica Fennica, 1996). Henceforth *ILN*.

[5] I follow the terminology of N&A: 20 years later von Wright used "normative formulation" to mean more or less the same as "deontic sentence".

the same deontic sentence can be interpreted as a *normative statement*[6], that is, as a sentence saying that such and such a norm is in force. Sentences of this kind are used to inform someone about the existence of a norm.

Admittedly, the distinction between normative formulations and normative statements is a case of fuzzy borderlines. In fact we frequently come across deontic sentences used both to inform us about the existence of a norm and to re-issue it as it were. At any rate, the conceptual distinction is clear: to promulgate or to issue a norm, so that it is in force, is one thing; to assert that there is such and such a norm is another. Think of two thieves talking about the laws against burglary: whenever they state a law, they do so to complain against it, to make jokes about it, or to inform one another about the existence of the law – but hardly in order to enforce it or to prescribe something by means of it.

According to N&A, normative statements express *norm-propositions*. Some words are in order about von Wright's use of the term "proposition", which he discussed in his fine paper "Demystifying Propositions."[7] Shortly put, what is true is not a string of signs, a sentence as such, nor a Platonic entity; it is a sentence in use, a sentence viewed in the role it plays within a language, especially in connection with the possibility of occurring after "that" in a that-clause. Thus, a norm-proposition is not an entity in a Platonic sky, even if one could say that it is the *content* of a normative statement.

Norm-propositions have a truth value: they are true if and only if the described norm exists. But no question of truth and falsity can arise, according to von Wright, about norms themselves (i.e. about the prescriptions which are expressed, but not described, by normative formulations).

From truth value to compatibility, hence to logic

How does this bear on the *logic* of norms? At the time of N&A von Wright thought that the fact that norms don't have a truth value puts the very possibility of a logic of this kind in jeopardy. Two related groups of problems arise.

First, it is clearly impossible to construe molecular norms as truth-functions of other norms, whereas the possibility of joining propositions by means of truth-functional connectives is pivotal to

---

[6] N&A, p. 106.
[7] In *Truth, Knowledge and Modality* (Oxford, Basil Blackwell, 1984).

propositional logic. To be sure, one can try to reinterpret truth-functional connectives in such a way that they (partly) change their meaning and can be used to construct molecular norms. This will eventually be von Wright's choice in *NTL* and later. Reinterpretations of this kind are discussed at length also in *N&A* (VIII).

The analysis of the negation of a norm is especially interesting (*N&A*, VIII, sections 4, 7 and 8). For example, consider the deontic sentence "you ought to open the window". There are at least two candidates for the position of the negation of this sentence understood as a normative formulation (a prescription): the prohibition to open the window and the permission to leave it closed. In addition to these, according to von Wright, "You ought not to open the window" could mean that no norm or order (of any kind) about the window has been given to you (meaning more or less the same as "You are not expected to open the window") – this sentence would thus express the absence of norms and therefore it could hardly be regarded as a normative formulation (the expression of a prescription). In this case, negation would therefore turn a prescription into a description.

Von Wright's analysis eventually led him to put forth a definition of the negation of a norm as another norm having opposite character (permission vs. order) and internally denied content (production vs. forbearance): thus, e.g., the negation of an order to open the window is a permission to leave it closed. The resultant notion of negation significantly resembles an intuitionist notion in that it need not be the case that either a norm or its negation are in force.

However, even if a prescriptive (re)interpretation of logical connectives is possible in some relevant cases, this is to a large extent a matter of setting new definitions – a matter of tentatively marking out sharp limits where we have but faint borderlines. The definitional choices that we take may have several reasons – a need for symmetry, for structural analogy between the prescriptive and the truth-functional use of logical connectives – but their effect is not so much to chart an existing territory as to form it. In the second place, it is by no means clear whether the application of logical connectives to normative formulations will produce other normative formulations in all cases.[8] Thus, at the time of *N&A*,

---

[8] In 1981 ("Problems and Prospects in Deontic Logic. A Survey", in E. Agazzi (ed.), *Modern Logic. A Survey*, Dordrecht, Reidel, 1981, 399-423) von Wright still inclined towards a descriptive interpretation of disjunctive deontic

von Wright did not regard the prescriptive reinterpretation as the winning strategy.

Second, if deontic sentences are interpreted prescriptively, that is, as normative formulations, the notions of compatibility, incompatibility and implication between norms become problematic: for, according to von Wright, the most natural way of understanding such notions is in terms of truth.[9] Consider the sentences "John opens the window" and "John does not open the window". They are incompatible (more correctly, the propositions they express are incompatible). What does their incompatibility consist in? A natural answer is that John cannot both open and not open the window at the same time: that is, the two propositions cannot be true at the same time. Now, whereas it is impossible that incompatible propositions are true at the same time, it *is* possible that norms prescribing the production of incompatible states of affairs exist at the same time. It is possible that some normative authority issues a norm according to which John is allowed to open the window while another authority prohibits him to do so: and it is even possible that one and the same legislator issues "incompatible" norms of an analogous kind.

The quickest solution would be to give up the notion of incompatibility between norms, but a choice of this kind would instantly annihilate the logic of norms. If no norms were incompatible with any other norms — if no possible set of norms were inconsistent – there would be no logic of norms. Implication between norms requires incompatibility: a set of norms S implies another norm N if and only if the negation (in some not truth-functional sense) of N is incompatible with the norms belonging to S.

In fact we think that one who has issued some given norms is bound not to issue certain other norms *qua* incompatible with the former; that she is bound to acknowledge other norms *qua* entailed by the former, etc. In other words, we recognize the existence of logical relationships between such norms as "Everyone ought to open the window" and "John ought to open the window", and between the latter and "John is allowed not to open the window". To drop the logic of norms is to think that our talk of compatibility, incompatibility or implication between norms is disorganized and arbitrary, similar in nature to a reaction to a kind of food.

---

sentences: but in *NTL* he gave a thoroughly prescriptive interpretation of the logical connectives that occur in "molecular norms."

[9] *NTL*, 7.

The nature of the compatibility between norms is the kernel of the philosophical problem of norms mentioned above.

> I wish I could make my readers see the serious nature of this problem. (It is much more serious than any of the technicalities of deontic logic.) It is serious because, if no two norms can logically contradict one another, then there can be no logic of norms either. There is no logic, we might say, in a field in which everything is possible. So therefore, if norms are to have a logic, we must be able to point to something which is impossible in the realm of norms. But that we can do this is by no means obvious. [N&A, 148]

Thus, it is a bit surprising that von Wright did not perceive the difficulty at all in his first writing in deontic logic (the 1951 article). But he soon realized the problem. In the Preface to his *Logical Studies*[10] he said that deontic logic would be an extension of logic beyond the realm of truth; but it is in *N&A* that we find a direct attempt to meet this difficulty.

The first strategy: a logic of norm-propositions. Objections

We actually find *two* such attempts. In the chapters of *N&A* devoted to the construction of the system of deontic logic, von Wright proceeds in accordance with two different strategies that appear to be interconnected as far as *N&A* goes but are in fact independent. He works out a *logic of normative statements* (expressing norm-propositions); but he also puts forth a conception of *normative rationality* that entirely differs from it. While the latter strategy subsequently led him to a refined and profound account, the former was gradually abandoned: yet it is one of the characteristic features of *N&A*, and we shall start from it.

The former strategy is essentially an attempt at outflanking the problem. Normative statements ("such and such a norm exists") have a truth-value. Therefore, it is possible to construe truth-functions and to define consistency, compatibility and implication in relation to *them*. We would thus be enabled to grasp the logic of norms, not so much in the norms themselves as in the normative statements that describe them – that mirror them.

---

[10]London, Routledge & Kegan Paul, 1957.

Does this work? Is it possible that a logic of normative statements grasps the special features of the logic of norms? One of such features is, e.g., that an order to produce a certain state of affairs implies the permission to produce it and is incompatible with a permission to forbear to produce it. The crucial point is: are we really sure that normative statements, being descriptive in nature, are not *merely* in accordance with the logical laws of ordinary propositional logic? Are we sure that they obey additional logical laws that are peculiar to norms? We would certainly not be content with a logic of normative statements if it merely collapsed onto propositional logic. Thus, to be sure, it is necessary (but not sufficient) for a definition of norm-incompatibility that a normative statement is incompatible with its negation. That is to say, to state that a norm exists is incompatible with denying that it exists. This is something that the logic of normative statements has in common with propositional logic. But we need more: incompatibility between order to do and order or permission to forbear, etc. This is not an easy task. An analysis of the compatibility of, say, two different orders often requires insights into the special logical features of norm, action and change. For example, an order to open a window

(1) $$Od(pT \sim p)$$

is not incompatible with a permission to close the same window

(2) $$Pd(\sim pTp)$$

because the two ordered actions have no common condition of application (in order for me to be able to open a window, it must be closed; but it must be open if I am to close it).

The following case can shed some light on von Wright's former strategy. Suppose we want to develop a logic of chess. It is evident that a chess move does not have a truth value, but it is evident that a *description of the fact* that such and such a move has been made does have a truth value. Thus we could decide to bypass the difficulties of a logic without truth values and develop, instead of a logic of chess, a logic of the descriptions of the moves of chess. Would this work? To a certain extent, it obviously would: for example, our logic of chess-descriptions would regard the two sentences "a pawn has been moved from e2 to e4" and "a pawn has not been moved from e2 to e4" as incompatible – like any instance of p and $\sim p$. But the logic of chess-descriptions would soon come up against the peculiarities of a logic of chess. Moves that the rules of chess would exclude as illegal would not be automatically struck off as illegal by our logic of chess-descriptions. Moving a pawn from e2 to e5 is in fact illegal in chess — it is chess nonsense — but the description "a move of the white pawn has been made from e2 to e5", far from being inconsistent, could even be *true*.

There is an escape. We could argue that talking about a *legitimate* chess move of a pawn from e2 to e5 is in fact nonsense, and thus the description above could be struck off as ill-formed. We have merely to replace all the occurrences of "move" with "legitimate chess move". Thus, through the notion of a *legitimate chess move*, the whole logic of chess would as it were be inherited by the description of chess, even if one could retort that a heavy load is placed upon the notion of a *legitimate chess move* – that this notion is doing all the hard work and that its implicit logic is all we ought to be interested in. To this we shall presently return.

An analogous strategy is at work in *N&A*. At the time of *N&A*, von Wright thought that the logical peculiarities of norms would somehow be reflected onto norm-propositions expressed by normative statements, which would thus inherit them.[11] The true key of this strategy is in the notion of an "existent norm", that is, a norm that has been issued and is in force. Since norm-propositions are true if and only if the norms they describe are in force, the incompatibility between two norm-propositions can be traced back to the (ontological) impossibility that such norms coexist; implication between norms (e.g. between the prohibition to throw objects out of the windows and the permission not to throw objects out of the windows) can be traced back to the fact that the existence of a norm (or set of norms) implicitly enforces another norm (thus calling it into existence) etc. Implication is thus understood in terms of the necessary existence of certain norms, *given that* other norms exist. Thus, the notion of existence comes to play a primary role: *N&A* actually deals very much with the *ontology* of norms.

Von Wright's approach allowed him to develop and refine deontic logic to a remarkably high degree. His logic is a powerful analytical tool that enabled him to shed light on several topics that are fundamental in a philosophical investigation of norms. However, his appeal to a logic of normative statements (norm-propositions) has profound flaws. I shall not deal with the fact that the crucial notion of existence of a norm is obscure and to

---

[11] *N&A*, VII, 2; VIII, 16: *NTL*, 8.

a certain extent fuzzy. Assume it is not. Von Wright's plan was to reach the incompatibility between norms by means of a notion of incompatibility between norm-propositions. But, as we argued above, incompatible norms *can* in fact coexist: two opposite orders *can* be given (even if orders of this kind would in the long run entirely distort and change our activity of giving orders). Much more plausibly, a vast system of norms can have general norms whose implications contradict one another in certain cases etc.

This is where von Wright introduces his second strategy – the appeal to normative rationality, which we shall presently deal with. For the moment, suffice it to say that, according to von Wright, two incompatible norms can be issued and can coexist, but this should *be regarded as irrational*. The case somehow resembles that of chess. The notion of a legitimate chess-move was introduced in order to guarantee that the only moves we are concerned with are legitimate – in order to exclude our having to deal with mad chess-players moving pieces at random on the chessboard. Now, the notion of a rational norm-giver is introduced in order to guarantee that the existence of norms faithfully follows the logical relationships between norms and makes our logic of norm-propositions (that are true if and only if the described norms exist) congruent with the logic of norms prescriptively understood. However, the appeal to a notion of normative rationality, instead of supporting von Wright's first strategy, is an implicit acknowledgment of its failure. The coexistence of two incompatible norms is claimed to be irrational; but this – the very notion of two coexisting and incompatible norms – *presupposes that norm-incompatibility is independent of possibilities of existence of norms.*

In order to emphasize the kernel of the difficulty, let us make things easier by assuming that incompatible norms can*not* in fact coexist. Then, a situation in which the norms "it is compulsory to open the window" and "it is permitted not to open it" are both in force cannot occur. Such a situation would be described by the following normative statement: "A norm exists that prescribes opening the window and another norm exists that permits not opening it". According to our assumption (that incompatible norms cannot coexist) this statement is *inconsistent*. Its inconsistency would be understood in *N&A* in terms of existence; that is, in terms of the impossibility for the two norms to coexist. It is of essential importance to emphasize that, in order to have a case of proper inconsistency, the non-coexistence of the two norms must not merely be a matter of fact, it must be of a *logical* nature. But to say that the inconsistency of the norm-proposition above depends exclusively on the logical impossibility that the two described norms coexist is but a longish and roundabout way to say that it depends on the incompatibility of the norms themselves. In other words, from a merely truth-functional point of view, the fact that two incompatible norms do not coexist is not of a logical nature: it cannot be anything more than actual non-coexistence. Thus, we do not have *a form of incompatibility based on truth and existence* that mirrors an incompatibility between norms: we have only one kind of normative incompatibility, which is concerned with the peculiar features of norms. Why not then turn directly to the logic of norms? What is truly relevant is not the (alleged) inconsistency of the normative statement: it is the incompatibility of the described norms. (Similarly, if the pivot of our logic of chess is in the notion of a legitimate chess move, our true interest is in the notion of legitimacy that is implicit in it, and we have failed to reinterpret the logic of chess in truth-functional terms.)

The second strategy: normative rationality

Von Wright's second strategy in *N&A* (the one based upon normative rationality) directly addresses these issues. As we mentioned above, von Wright's view[12] is, briefly, the following. That two norms exist that respectively order and prohibit, say, the production of a certain state of affairs, is possible, but it is *irrational*. We would not regard as rational a legislator who issued norms aiming at obtaining incompatible results. The logic of norms rests on the fundamental assumption that we have views about what a rational (or reasonable, or coherent) legislator should and should not do — views about the limits that bind the activity of a rational legislator. But according to what has been argued above, such bounds and limits are neither founded upon nor justified in terms of a truth-functional logic.

Thus von Wright's second strategy is in fact entirely independent of his former strategy — the logic of normative statements and propositions. This explains why the development of a conception of normative rationality eventually superseded the views

---

[12] *N&A*, VIII, 7.

of *N&A*.[13] In spite of its seeming simplicity, von Wright's conception has in fact far-reaching consequences. I shall first examine some "internal" consequences concerning the structure of deontic logic, then some consequences about the philosophy of norms and, especially, about the relations between norms and logic.

First, the incompatibility of two or more prescriptions is not *absolute*; it is instead related to a rational normative will and to a model (or ideal) of rationality. The logic of norms applies to a *corpus*, that is, to a set of norms issued and enforced by a single normative authority ("will" or norm-giver).

Second, the conception of normative rationality paves the way for a logic of norms — not merely a logic of normative statements or norm-propositions. The possibility of reformulating the concepts of consistency, compatibility and implication between norms in relation to a rational normative authority makes an appeal to the existence of norms redundant. Assume that two or more norms are inconsistent: this is not so *because* at least one of the propositions that assert their existence is necessarily false; nor *because* their coexistence is impossible: they are inconsistent because we regard as irrational that one and the same norm-giver should issue such and such norms. For example, in the case of orders, a set of norms is consistent if and only if "the conjunction of their contents is a doable state of affairs".[14] Such a definition can easily be extended to permissions.[15] On this basis, instead of saying that a norm "is entailed" by a set of norms, we should formulate our point in terms of the rational commitment of a norm-giver to accept a certain norm whenever its negation is inconsistent with the set.[16] Thus, the true aim of deontic logic is to specify in a clear and orderly way the forms of normative discourse that express *our conception* (or ideal) of normative rationality.

Yet one could wonder what the important point is. If the only alternative to our model of normative rationality were a model according to which law-givers systematically prescribed and prohibited the same actions, or they prescribed producing incompatible states of affairs, could *that* be regarded as a model of rationality at all?

---

[13] In *NTL* von Wright remarks that the conception of normative rationality that we find in *N&A* was substantially correct: his main criticism is for not having drawn the appropriate conclusions from it.
[14] *ILN*, 39.
[15] *ILN*, 39-40.
[16] See *NTL* and *ILN*.

To this we reply that, in the first place, even if no viable alternative to our model of rationality could be imagined, still von Wright's emphasis is on the fact that norm-compatibility, norm-implication etc. – the logic of norms – are constituted in relation to an ideal of a rational norm-giver (rather than in relation to "laws of the existence" of norms).

In the second place, the alternative model of normative rationality (or rather, irrationality) mentioned above is by no means the only possible one. Other models could be characterized by sporadic conflicts arising on special and uncommon occasions. If the legislator and the community did not regard such cases as serious inconsistencies affecting the harmony and stability of the corpus but merely as inconsequential incidents to be taken care of locally (e.g. on the basis of wisdom and common sense), we would have here a model that we could be inclined to accept as rational, although significantly different from ours. A different case would be that of a model of relaxed or slackened normative rationality. In such a model, the logical relationship between a general norm applying, say, to all the citizens, and instances of it prescribing specific actions to individual citizens, is weakened, so that the step from the general to the individual case is by no means automatic. On the contrary, there is wide communal agreement about the fact that an automatic and, as it were, inexorable application of a general norm to the individual cases would be too rigid, cruel and even unreasonable. The accepted practice is, instead, that the application of the norm to individual cases must take into account other "imponderable" elements that cannot be exhaustively listed once and for all. Such a community would end up with an ideal of normative rationality that is even less than "loose", since the borderline between rationality and irrationality would be basically blurred.

Von Wright's conception of normative rationality has a crucial relevance for the philosophy of norms and the relationship between logic and rationality. Before *N&A*, the aim of von Wright's deontic logic was to provide a logical foundation for normative rationality: to show that logic reaches up to an area that is beyond truth and falsity. Thus, for example, he tried to find the logical laws that *make* a certain normative behaviour inconsistent (and so, irrational). The spirit of such an enterprise basically belongs to the great philosophical tradition initiated by Frege, Russell and the Wittgenstein of the *Tractatus*. I don't mean that Frege and the young Wittgenstein would approve of deontic logic

— the contrary is true. What I mean is that von Wright's first investigations in deontic logic share a fundamental premise with Frege and Wittgenstein. Such a premise can be sketchily formulated by saying that there are fundamental logical laws that are independent of the opinions of the speakers, of the cultural contexts and even of the actual existence of human beings; these laws determine which thoughts are logically well formed and which are valid. Even more sketchily, rationality has a logical *justification*.

N&A is the turning point. It partly subscribes to this view, but the conception of normative rationality brings about a revolution – a thorough reversal of this perspective. Our aim is not a self-standing logic of norms: it is a clarification of the notion of normative rationality that emphasizes its articulation and net of commitments.[17] The logic of norms does not *justify* normative rationality. The fact that the same thing cannot be ordered and be prohibited is not a requirement that deontic logic superimposes on a rational norm-giver. The converse is true, that the notion of a rational norm-giver superimposes some minimal requirements on the notion of consistency in deontic logic. The norm-giver's commitment to act in accordance with the laws of deontic logic is there only if the norm-giver aims to be rational — and if there is agreement about the meaning of normative rationality. Hence the label of "nihilist" that von Wright explicitly attached to his logic of norms in *NTL*. I think that this label might, on the whole, be misleading, because von Wright's goal is not to undermine the notion of normative rationality or to show that deontic logic is illusory. His claim is instead that the roots of normative rationality are not to be found in foundations of a logical nature. Such roots are instead in basic attitudes concerning actions, norms and their relationships – attitudes that define the meaning of such notions together with their syntactical relationships. Thus, the other label ("anti-rationalist") that von Wright suggests in *NTL* for his conception of deontic logic seems, on the whole, more to the point.

Against this, one could retort that von Wright is in fact trying to provide a pragmatic foundation for normative rationality, one in terms of communal agreement about the actions by which we apply norms, promulgate them, react to them etc. But that objection would not do justice to the fact that von Wright's conception, far from replacing one kind of foundation with another, leads us towards the basic contention that there is no logical room for a foundation or a justification of norms. His goal is not to

---

[17]Cf. *N&A*, VIII, 7.

provide a justification of normative rationality in terms of communal agreement about the actions by which we emanate norms and react to them. Any agreement *about* the conditions of compatibility, implication etc. between norms – about the accepted model of normative rationality – in fact presupposes a practice of giving norms and applying them, and thus it presupposes a basic network of relationships between norms. Communal agreement about norms is not to be regarded as a set of social facts in terms of which normative rationality is defined; mutually related norms acquire definition and identity within a network of normative actions but not on the basis of it. Thus, if communal agreement plays a major part, it is an *agreement in* actions, rather than *about* them.[18]

These remarks lead us towards themes and views that characterized the later Wittgenstein, especially in *On Certainty*. I don't know if one could correctly say that von Wright was in any direct sense influenced by Wittgenstein. What is sure is that he was engaged in close, almost uninterrupted, reflection on and even struggle with Wittgenstein's works. At first sight, von Wright's logical investigations (to which *N&A* belongs) bear very little similarity, at least in form and style, with the investigations of the later Wittgenstein. On the other hand, von Wright's fundamental revolution in his approach to deontic logic pervades the investigations of *N&A* in many more respects than the conception of normative rationality. Von Wright's research seems to be guided throughout by the implicit assumption that the nature of the logic of norms depends on our basic attitude to them, on our ways of acting and of thinking in relation to them, and on our substantial agreement *in* attitudes, actions and thoughts. Thus, according to von Wright, some problems concerning the validity of certain logical principles don't have a solution, not so much because we have failed to discover it up to now, as because the fabric of conventions, actions, ways of living and of understanding that would establish the validity of those principles is still too thin, weak and ambiguous. *N&A* provides many examples of this kind: see e.g. the discussion of the principle *nullum crimen sine lege* (V, 14); of a definition of permissions in terms of obligations (V); of the

---

[18]This subject is complex and profound. It has to do with the primacy of action in logic, the asymmetry between agent and observer and several more topics, including scepticism. I am presently working on this.

principle that Ought entails Can (VII, esp. sect. 6); of the question whether there are norms that exist necessarily (VIII, 8), and many more.

One could object that von Wright's stance is an admission of defeat: a defeat in the search for a precisely articulated and defined foundation of deontic logic. But the absence of a logical *foundation* does not entail lack of logical *articulation*. On the contrary, the goal of deontic logic is to perspicuously grasp the principles of normative discourse and to clarify the relations between norms and other norms, as well as between norms, action sentences, descriptions of changes and descriptions of states of affairs. This can be done in the most orderly way with spotless formal equipment. But the formal apparatus is meant as a set of tools used to clarify the normative segment of ordinary language by way of overlap and comparison rather than as a means for grasping and describing the hidden logical essence of norms.

To sum this up, it is correct to call von Wright's conception "anti-rationalist"; it is perhaps misleading to call it "nihilist"; it would certainly be wrong to call it "irrationalist". Von Wright emphasizes that normative rationality does not have a logical justification. But this, far from being an inescapable element of irrationality in the logic of norms, is a constitutive aspect of the rationality of norms.

Appendix

A previous version of the present paper was published in December 1988 as an introduction to the Italian translation of *Norm and Action*. I sent a copy of it to Georg Henrik von Wright, who replied after a few days. For almost twenty years, that reply has been a source both of pleasure and of uneasiness to me, because I felt that some of the ideas which he seemed to like so much should be made known to a wider public. Thus, von Wright's old letter (dated 1 February 1989) may explain my decision to write a new version of my article in English. Moreover, his letter contains remarks on logic and on Wittgenstein's influence that are of some interest of their own. Therefore, I have resolved to reproduce the part of the letter concerning my paper in its entirety.

> Your Introduction I have read and I hasten to reply in case the Publisher becomes impatient and you wanted to hold up publication until you have

heard from me. My reply is shorter than it perhaps otherwise would have been and will not contain anything which gives reason for changes. In short: I am very, very grateful for what you have written. It is seldom that I have read anything about my ideas which so well captures what I think myself is their essence. In fact, I have got to understand myself better through reading your paper. (As you may remember, there is a volume in preparation about "my philosophy" in the series Library of Living Philosophers. It is now ready for publication and will probably appear later this year. I cannot help thinking: what a pity that your essay is not included in that book!)

It is quite right that there are two "philosophical strategies" implicit, but not clearly distinguished, in N&A, viz. "una logica degli asserti normativi [a logic of normative statements]" and "una concezione della razionalità normativa [a conception of normative rationality]". In my book the two strategies are "mixed" in a confused and confusing way. Therefore you are also entirely right when you say that "the major flaw in N&A is perhaps in mixing a 'logic of norms' with a 'logic of normative propositions'".

Later, my work in deontic logic has been increasingly oriented toward the "rationality strategy" without perhaps an entirely clear recognition of its philosophical peculiarities. You connect this with my "neowittgensteinianism" of Explanation and Understanding and myself have not seen these connections clearly before. Implicitly, I am of course immensely influenced by Wittgenstein but when working I practically never "think about Wittgenstein" and I could myself say what you say: "I don't know if one could correctly say that von Wright was in any direct sense influenced by Wittgenstein."

As you indicate, this change from the one "strategy" to the other may have great consequences for our view of logic. To which extent I shall myself be able to explore them, is uncertain.

I shall not do much more work in logic in this life myself; and whenever I start thinking about something I tend to "relapse" in (my) old, more "traditional" ways of thinking. Other logicians will have the same difficulty – or just simply continue in the old grooves without reflecting much on the more philosophical questions. I am sure that my last writings on deontic logic, in particular, will not encourage others to follow in the same direction where I ended.

Alchourrón has made an attempt to build deontic logic without recourse to the notion of truth. The idea is that one can define a concept of "logical consequence" which is broader than the traditional one. This may be true – but also this attempt, if philosophically sound, will take us to considerations about rationality.

What is the Order among the Varieties of Goodness? A Question Posed by von Wright

David Wiggins

---

1. We attribute all sorts of goodness to all sorts of objects. This variety and heterogeneity, almost if not uniquely proprietary to good, were recognized by Aristotle with no other sceptical outcome than the rejection of Plato's unitary Form of the Good. See *Nicomachean Ethics* I.6 and *Eudemian Ethics* I.8. Aristotle though was a very sober thinker. In modern times we are more precipitate. Once we know the temptation to think of "good" as a word that can be used to predicate almost anything of almost any kind of thing, it seems we reach immediately for the idea that all there is to a thing's goodness is its provoking approval (A. J. Ayer, C. L. Stevenson), or its lying within the range of a sincere universal prescription (R. M. Hare), or its answering to some relevant interest to be specified from the context (Paul Ziff),[1] or its having properties that provide reasons to respond in certain ways to it (Thomas Scanlon).[2] As we shall, see there is a grain of truth in each of these proposals, but in each case the truth in question lacks the metaethical significance commonly attributed to it.[3]

Is the great variousness and plurality of goodness really the chaos that it appears?

---

[1] Paul Ziff, *Semantic Analysis* (Ithaca N.Y.: Cornell University Press, 1960), Chapter Six.

[2] This last is the so-called 'buck-passing' theory. See Thomas Scanlon, *What We Owe To Each Other* (Harvard University Press, 1998), pp.95-100.

[3] Or so I should claim. See *Ethics: Twelve Lectures on the Philosophy of Morality*, (Harvard University Press and Penguin Press, 2006), chapters 11 and 12. See also pp.176-7.

Let us try to enumerate the varieties of goodness, to understand each variety and to discern order among them.

2. In the first chapter of *The Varieties of Goodness*,[4] Georg Henrik von Wright sets out the distinct varieties into which he proposes to partition all good or goodness. There is the *instrumental* variety, the goodness of things seen as instruments for purposes, their suitability or effectiveness for those purposes. (Consider von Wright's sundry examples "good knife", "good horse", "good house", "good harbour", "good way of making a bed", "good way of unlocking a door") There is the *technical* variety (consider "good orator", "good carpenter", "good navigator"). There is the *medical* variety. (Consider "good heart", "good eyes", "good hearing", "good eyesight", "good memory".) There is the *beneficial*. (Consider the fact that exercise "is good for" the healthy, that lubrication is "good for" an engine, that institutions of a certain kind are "good for" a country. See p.10.) Then there is the larger category of which von Wright says that the beneficial is a sub-category, the larger category that he calls (without specifically Benthamite intent) *utilitarian* goodness. By way of illustration of the need for the more inclusive category, consider in parallel with the beneficial the collateral varieties of goodness within which one finds a plan or an opportunity or a piece of luck which is good by being advantageous and/or favourable for some given or contextually particular purpose, or a virtue which it is good for its possessors to have (p. 42) because it prepares them to face danger (say) or protects them (as von Wright asserts) from the temptations to idleness or excess. Then there is the *hedonic* good. (Consider a "good apple", a "good wine", a "good dinner" or a "good holiday", and the goodness of things which are in some way "pleasant".)

3. There is much more to say about the adjective "good". But what about the substantival use of the word? Von Wright says that sometimes it denotes "anything which is an end of action or object of desire or want or need" (p. 10). But sometimes "the good" stands for what von Wright calls "the good of a being". This last von Wright compares with "das Wohl" and identifies as that being's welfare. Welfare is one of the three eminently important concepts (he says) which regard "man as a whole". The other two are health and happiness. "[Welfare] can be called, somewhat solemnly, the good of man", von Wright said in his

---

[4]London: Routledge & Kegan Paul, 1963.

summation of his whole position.[5] Then he said "The things which promote [welfare] are called beneficial, those which detract from it harmful. All things inclusive of their consequences which a man treasures for their own sake are parts of the whole which is his good or welfare. Health, one could say, is the basis of welfare and happiness its crown or flower".

4. In the early 60s, some linguistic philosophers might have objected that von Wright's search for system was crowding out the pulsating multifariousness of the phenomena. But he was ready and waiting to add yet more varieties. He adds for instance that

> There are the uses of "good" which refer to matters of conduct and character. A man can be good and do good. Good is usually done to somebody. When a man does good to some being, his acts or deeds are frequently, though not always, called good as well. An act can be done from a good motive or with a good intention. There is a feature of benevolence and a preparedness to act called a good will... (p. 11).

Indeed there is at least one other variety which I should have urged von Wright to mark somewhere, namely *goodness in a calling*. A further candidate might be aesthetic goodness, the goodness that consists in the beauty of a thing. *Varieties* is wide open to such suggestions. We shall come in due course to "good man" and "good act". But we shall begin with those that von Wright first anatomized.

5. From the opposite side, there is another sort of objection von Wright might have encountered. In the 60s, when few analytical philosophers had got beyond the thought that J.L. Austin had put about by remarking that, even where it stands alone, the adjective "good" is usually substantive-hungry (or "attributive" as P.T. Geach preferred to say[6]), philosophers who looked for system might have questioned whether von Wright really needed to recognize so many varieties. They might have claimed that instrumental goodness, technical goodness and all the rest could be unified in a simple category of goodness of a kind: "Where the

---

[5]See page 35 of the intellectual autobiography that he wrote for *The Philosophy of Georg Henrik von Wright*, edited by P.A. Schilpp and L.E. Hahn (Open Court, 1989).

[6]See "Good and evil", *Analysis* 17 (1956), pp.33-42.

word "good" holds open a place for a substantive, all the semantic differences that result from the collocation of the adjective and a particular substantive can be traced to the substantive. On a proper theoretical understanding, there is no reason to suppose that the contribution of the adjective "good" itself needs to vary. Let us not postulate more varieties of goodness than we need".[7]

In response to all this, let us refer to Chapter Two of *Varieties*. In that chapter, von Wright is ready to allow that "by calling something "good" in the instrumental or in the technical sense we often... say that this thing is *good of its kind*". So far, this is in line with the claim made by his imaginary critic, the univocist. Take "good knife". Simply to understand what a knife is

---

[7] Von Wright would have been suspicious of the assumption I am imagining the semanticist making of a simple and self-evident parallelism between a putative variety of kinds of goodness and a putative variety of senses of "good".

The starting point for any mediation between von Wright and the semanticists is the evident need to supplement von Wright's rather restricted idea of ambiguity (cp. page 14) and to make room for the thought that a good dictionary should afford just as many different readings of a given word as are needed (neither more nor fewer than are needed) to explicate its contribution at each and every one of its occurrences. So far I should side with the semanticists against von Wright. The measure of polysemy – the measure of "ambiguity" in this lexicographical sense (or of "homonymy" in the sense which, by transposing from the material to the formal mode, we derive from Aristotle's at *Categories* 1a1-3) – is the number of different headings/sub-headings a good dictionary needs to award to the word and to specific constructions involving the word in order for the dictionary to gloss the meanings of all sentences involving the word.

From this point onwards matters are less straightforward. The test for ambiguity just proposed would be easy to apply if it were (or could be) the business of lexicography to furnish a perfect analysis or a set of perfect analyses for each word in the dictionary. But there are good reasons why this was never to be expected. (See my "Three moments in the theory of definition or analysis: its possibility, its aim or aims and its limit or terminus", *Proceedings of the Aristotelian Society*, Vol. CVII (2008).) That is the reason why in stating the criterion of ambiguity I had recourse to the contestability-inducing verb "gloss". Where glossing is concerned, do we want austere economy of means or do we also want generous illumination?

In practice – and now I am inclining to von Wright's cause – the anatomizing of the varieties of goodness has to proceed without looking for decisions concerning the number of entries an authoritative and theoretically perfectly parsimonious dictionary could allow itself. Decisions of *that* sort must come at the end, not at the outset. Only at the end can it be determined how many different things are meant (at the level of reference/Bedeutung) by the word "good" – and how many different varieties to recognize. Meanwhile let us anatomize varieties without keeping count of varieties or senses.

is to grasp the idea of a standard for knives. So much seems right, but how general is the good-of-its-kind proposal? One doubts how well it can work with "good fortune", or "good outcome" or "good act". Are there standards of excellence for outcomes or acts such as we have for knives or watches or cars? (Cp. *Varieties*, page 44.) It may be that goodness of a kind will need to play a larger part in the philosophy of goodness than von Wright expected (lexicographers certainly invoke this category), but substantive-hunger or attributivity explains less than the univocist hopes for. Even where it is most apposite, not everything is straightforward.[8]

6. In the face of this defence of von Wright, his critic may be tempted to deploy Ziff's idea that the goodness of a thing depends only on its answering to the interest that is relevant in the context. "Focus on the varieties of context and of interest," the critic may say, "not on varieties of goodness." But now there are other difficulties. Consider von Wright's category of medical goodness, the goodness of organs or faculties or the soundness of limbs. After a bicycle accident in which I break my left leg, I can refer to my right leg as my "good leg". The critic may think that this option is a product of the context. In opposition to that, von Wright would adduce his separate category of medical goodness. He could agree that it takes a context to activate or trigger the medical reading of "good [such and such]." But context cannot account for everything here, he might say. Suppose Ziff were right and just any old interest relevant to the context would suffice.

---

[8] At page 19, von Wright points to a difference that he marks by distinguishing "*x* is as a K good", which implies that *x* is indeed a K, from "*x* is good as a K", which only implies that (whether or not *x* is a K) *x* "can be used to advantage in the way Ks are normally used or performs well enough in the way characteristic of Ks". A knife with a solid heavy handle can be good as a hammer even though, not being a hammer at all, it is not a good hammer. Not everything which is good for some purpose also belongs to some kind which is essentially associated with that purpose. Will not every theory need then to distinguish instrumental and useful goodness? In further explanation of that distinction, see *Varieties* page 43-4:

"Even a poor knife can, under circumstances, be useful. It is useful whenever the use of this knife is a good thing. But this usefulness of the knife does not necessarily mean that it is a good *knife*....[Consider] the difference in meaning between the phrases "be good for a purpose" and "serve a purpose well". To say [the former] ordinarily means that it *can be used* to serve the purpose. If [at time t] we are in pursuit of the purpose in question, then this thing is useful [at t], a good thing to have at [t]. But ....*instrumental* goodness [of a knife] is typically an *excellence* or ....a *rank* and *grade*, whereas usefulness [at this or that juncture] is not."

Then we should have the following result. At the next phase in the history of my accident, where the hospital consultant wants a broken leg to demonstrate to his students and that is the relevant interest, an assistant could whisper to him as the great man hurries into the anatomy theatre, "the patient's left leg is the good leg" meaning that the left leg is the one the consultant needs to demonstrate to the students. That's what he could whisper if Ziff were right. But the assistant can't say that. For the good leg is the other one. It's the right leg, despite the fact that this leg is of no relevant interest. Relevant interest is powerless against the way in which the importance and salience for human life of the healthy or unimpaired has imposed itself on the language we speak and the thoughts that we have. Its imprint is the provision for a separable medical reading of "good", ready and waiting for the summons of any speaker who would call upon it. (This is the subject of von Wright's Chapter Three, sections 7-12.) No doubt the assistant could remark "David's left leg is a good leg for the consultant to demonstrate to his students." But this could not show that my right leg was not the good leg. Nor would such a rewriting be of any help to the thesis propounded by the critic whom we have imagined objecting to von Wright's enterprise. For there is no such substantive as "leg for the consultant to demonstrate to his students".

7. So much then for resistance deriving from the taste for antisystematic profusion (section 4) and so much for an objection coming from the side of philosophical semantics in blinkers (sections 5 and 6). But in response to the second kind of resistance, I want to supplement the record with a word more about "goodness of a kind" and then to offer a general remark about the whole project of distinguishing varieties.

Unlike instrumental goodness, technical goodness (as in "good orator", "good carpenter", "good navigator") looks as if it would have been highly amenable to being subsumed within goodness of a kind. With technical goodness, there is a real plausibility in the claim that anything that acts or operates well under some head will belong to a kind that is associated with that mode of doing, acting, or operating. This gives the simple univocity theorist at least one part of what he wanted. But it doesn't release us from the necessity to recognize the technical as a distinct variety of goodness. What, after all, *is* a carpenter or orator? One only qualifies as such by being passably good or passably skilful at working wood or being well enough capable of persuading others by public speech. Or, as von Wright puts the point: "an attribution of technical goodness of its kind is a secondary valuation. Its basis, the primary valuation, is a judgment to the effect that this being is *good at* something" (*Varieties*, p. 33, von Wright's italics).[9]

General remark. Having come so far with von Wright, let us pause to distinguish three different tasks.

(1) There is the task of delimiting and distinguishing different varieties of goodness. See sections 3-7 above and sections 10-11 below. (A small beginning upon a large assignment.)

(2) There is the task of discovering what can be said about goodness as such – about the general or undifferentiated property of which the varieties of good are determinations. See sections 18-20 below.

(3) There is one more enquiry we ought to pursue. Of each particular variety of goodness identified in the execution of (1), we may ask: (a) are things that fall within this variety of goodness best called by a predicate that is proprietary to the variety (or to a sub-variety of the variety), "just" (say) or "brave" or "skilful" or "favourable" or "sharp" or ...? (b) are things that fall within the given variety to be described by some construction proprietary to this variety (cf. "good" + "at", as it figured in the possibility that appeared in the second paragraph of this section)? (c) may the things that fall within the given variety be called or described by the word "good" taken as standing not for undifferentiated good but for the particular variety of good that is in question? In illustration of this last possibility consider "[medically] good" as predicated of limbs or organs that are not harmed or impaired (cf. section 6); or consider "[aesthetically] good" as predicated of the legs of a film-star who insures them for a million dollars or as predicated of the fine bearing or beautiful face of some poet or poetess or hero or heroine or other person singled out for attention; or consider "[vocationally] good" as predicated

---

[9] One who restricts the univocity thesis in order to salvage some fragment of it will want Von Wright's assumptions to be spelled out here as they regard the relationship between "good" in "good at" and "good" in "good carpenter" – and then generalized. But at this point let us wrestle no more with an imaginary opponent and wait to hear from him.

This is the moment to make the obvious remark that in further studies of the varieties of goodness it will be necessary to attend much longer and harder to the syntax and semantics of all the varieties of grammatical construction built on the pattern: "is" + "good" + preposition...

of the practitioner of a humane calling (see section 14) or "[ethically] good" as predicated with the meaning either of benevolence (see section 15) or of inclusive moral goodness (see section 15).

8. Enough said about von Wright's project, his method, and the prima facie merits of his provisional and incomplete typology of the divers varieties of goodness. We now arrive at the chief question of this paper. In Chapter One of his book and in advance of everything else, von Wright raises the question of the unity and the order that persist amid this variety:

> The unity in the variety [of goodness]...is not that which a genus gives to the species falling under it. Nor does it appear to be a unity of the sort for which analogy or family resemblance can be held responsible....The meaning pattern of "good" is peculiar and puzzling. It is worth more attention than it has received on the part of philosophical semanticists. It is not however my plan to discuss these aspects in the present work. (Varieties, p. 17.)

In the face of a similar question about the meaning-pattern of "good", Aristotle was more forthcoming. He made two positive suggestions:

> There is no common account to be had of that which constitutes the goodness of honour, the goodness of wisdom or understanding and the goodness of pleasure. Even in the case of things that are good in themselves, there is no common Form. How then is it that we call each of these things good? It is no mere accident surely that each of these things answers to the word "good".[10] This is no chance homonymy. Can it be that all the things that answer to "good" contribute in some way or other to some single thing or derive from a single thing? There is also another possibility: is some principle of analogy at work here? What sight is to the body, intellect is for the soul and so on. Nicomachean Ethics 1096b 24-29[11]

---

[10] Compare also NE 1129a30 to which we shall return.

[11] On these sentences, see Heda Segvic, "Aristotle on the Varieties of Goodness", *Apeiron* 37 (2004), 151-176. See also Christopher Shields, *Order*

I agree with von Wright in finding simple analogy insufficient for the explanatory task (even if, as we shall see, it has some subsidiary usefulness). But what about Aristotle's first idea, which von Wright lets pass? Suppose we single out one primary or central sense of "good" as the original or focal sense. Then how many of von Wright's other and mutually distinguishable ways of reading "good" can we arrange around its focus and account for by showing how they build out from that central sense? That is the question I shall try to answer.

Aristotle figures in what follows because it is his suggestion that I press into service. But it is present-day conceptions not Aristotelian conceptions of the various varieties of good which will concern us – our own conceptions as I shall try to read them, in agreement or occasional disagreement with von Wright. In so far as Aristotle enters here, that is not in the cause of our interpreting him but in order for us to make use of his thoughts.

9. Aristotle's most celebrated deployment of the first of the two strategies he mentions for finding order or system within homonymy – the *focal* strategy, as Aristotelians might call it – is in connection with the multiplicity of *be*. The thing which *is* (or has being) in the primary or central or focal sense is a substance, a man, a tree, God etc. Then, in radical dependence upon substances, there are other things which *are* (have their being) in related but distinguishable senses of "is" or "are". These other things *are* by virtue of how some substance is qualitatively – *white*, say, or *healthy* – or by virtue of the size it is – *six foot tall*, say. Others have their being in other ways. Acts, for instance, *are* by virtue of what a substance does – *run*, say, or *walk*. See *Metaphysics* 1028 a20.

The metaphysically problematic character of Aristotle's proposal about being must not detract from the beautiful plainness of the parallels that he adduces. Consider "healthy" as it occurs

---

in multiplicity: homonymy in the philosophy of Aristotle, Clarendon Press, Oxford 1999. For discussions I have myself attempted of them, see "On sentence sense, word sense and difference of word sense", in D. Steinberg and L. Jacobovits, *Semantics: an interdisciplinary reader* (Cambridge University Press, 1971). See also pages 249-253 of my "Replies", in *Essays for David Wiggins: Identity, Truth and Value*, eds. Sabina Lovibond and Stephen Williams (Blackwell, 1996), p. 249. And see equally Stephen Williams's essay.
    Aristotle's theory of focal meaning was clarified and made fully available to 20th century philosophy by G.E.L. Owen. See his *Logic, Science and Dialectic* (London: Duckworth, 1986), especially Essay 10 (dating from 1957).

in "healthy person", "healthy exercise", "healthy food", "healthy coat" (viz. the glossy, health-evincing coat of a prize dog or cow), or (as per Aquinas' happy addition) "healthy urine". Here are five occurrences of "healthy" requiring no less than five different explanations. Yet one has only to relate each sense to one and the same focus, namely the condition of the person or animal that is healthy. Urine, for instance, is healthy just if it is such as a healthy animal would pass. It is *indicative* of health. Exercise is healthy just if it *promotes* health, and so on. "Everything that is healthy is somehow related to health, by preserving health or producing it, or being indicative of it or being receptive of it." (*Metaphysics* 1003 a34-b1.) [12]

That which follows will chronicle the effort to do for "good" that which Aristotle does for "healthy". In advance of the chronicle, let me say that, in the process of applying Aristotle's idea to the phenomena, we score a handful of successes, but then optimism falters. The multiplicity of the phenomena stretches and complicates the simple focal hypothesis and then confronts it with cases that lie outside its range. Yet that which this failure reveals will not be a scene where all you can say is that "good" is the most general adjective of commendation. Nor will it remain dark why the peculiar character of "good" makes it an insecure basis for scepticism concerning value properties, as well as a singularly odd place to begin upon a general study of the sense and the reference of the great generality of value-predicates.

10. How shall we apply the focal strategy to the meaning pattern of good? The most obvious way to proceed seems to be to take as our focus what von Wright calls *the good of a being*, always bearing in mind the case which is especially interesting to us, namely the well being or the faring well of the human animal.

It is a strange thing that, once one decides to proceed in this way, one finds von Wright as if anticipating it – despite his supposed postponement of these questions. Prominent among such anticipations is his treatment of the capacious category *utilitarian goodness* and its several sub-varieties. See pages 42-3:

> In the case of useful things which are also called beneficial, that to which the useful is favourably

---

[12] Note that Aristotle doesn't mean by 'somehow' 'just anyhow related'. For reasons of its own or of its speakers', the language settles upon some ways and refuses semantic recognition to other possibilities. (A medical professor who lectures on health and preventive medicine is not for that reason a healthy professor.)

> causally relevant... may be characterized as the
> good of some being. ... Physical exercise, for in-
> stance, is beneficial because good for the health.
> "Health" is another name for the good of the
> body. The good of the human body is an as-
> pect of the good (welfare) of man. Thus to say
> that exercise is beneficial is to say that it affects
> favourably, immediately the good of the body,
> and ultimately the good of man... [So] every-
> thing which is beneficial favourably affects the
> good of some being... [A] thing which affects
> the good of some being protectively rather than
> promotively we call (merely) useful rather than
> (also) beneficial... [V]irtues are protective rather
> than promotive of [the] good [of a being] ... Any-
> thing which is an end of action [is] a good. A
> thing is useful when it is favourably causally rel-
> evant to some good [in the sense of "a good" just
> explained] ... [It] is beneficial when it is promo-
> tive of that peculiar good which we call the good
> of a being....

Such claims are ready and waiting to enter into a focal or Aristotelian answer to the order in variety question, the answer organized around the central notion of the good of a being. But before we go any further at least three points need immediate attention.

First, some might object that pace von Wright virtues are not always or necessarily protective of the person's good, the welfare of the being that he or she is;[13] and object further that virtues represent other kinds of goodness beside that of being protective (cp. Aristotle *Nicomachean Ethics* 1097b2-4). We shall come back to these matters in sections 15 and 17.

---

[13]With this contrast come tangled issues. See Philippa Foot, *Natural Goodness* (Oxford University Press, 2001), chapters 5 and 6. See also *Varieties* p.151: "It is of some importance for educationists of a certain bent of mind to remember that virtues are no ends in themselves but instruments in the service of the good of man, and important for educationists of a certain other bent of mind not to lose sight of the fact that it is only by being aware of harmful consequences of yielding to passion that man has a rational ground for aspiring after virtues. For, be it observed in this connexion, we do not commonly and naturally call the virtues "beneficial". This is significant. The virtues are *needed;* absence of virtue is a bad thing for us. The goodness of the virtues is that they protect us from harm and *not* that they supply us with some good."

Secondly, von Wright says that anything which is an end of action is *a good*. Compare his earlier remark: "By "a good" ... one can also understand anything which is an end of action or object of desire or want or need" (p. 10). Things are less straightforward here than they were with beneficial goodness. We shall have to say that such an end of action or "object of desire, want or need" counts as a good only by virtue of its appearing to the agent or subject in question under the aspect of contributing either causally or constitutively to the good of some being who is of concern to that agent or subject.

Thirdly, a word about von Wright's example "lubrication is good for an engine". Supplementing the focal strategy with a generous helping of analogy, are we to suppose that artefacts which are dear to us come to concern us in such a special and affectionate way that we cannot help thinking of them as if they had a good of their own? (Compare p. 50.) Better surely to recognize that the way in which lubrication is good for an engine is that it prevents the deterioration or destruction of the engine, thereby preserving a good, namely the good that consists in its working, where *that* good can appear under the aspect of contributing to the good of beings.[14]

11. We need to fill out the larger picture within which explanations based on the "good of a being" are to operate, but it serves well enough to quote that which von Wright says (pp. 86-7):

> Of the being who does well we also say that it flourishes, thrives or prospers. And we call it happy. If health and well being primarily connote something privative, absence of illness and suffering; then happiness and well-doing again primarily refer to something positive, to an overflow or surplus of agreeable states and things.

These sentences are the cue to bring into the picture medical and hedonic goodness.

The focal account of the goodness of organs and faculties which are not defective will refer their particular goodness to the particular ways in which organs and faculties normally serve the good of the being. There is a great deal more to say about what those ways are (*Varieties* surveys some of this ground); but, here as everywhere, the important thing for purposes of the Aristotelian project is not the old ideal of strict definition but that

---

[14]Peter Hacker made this second suggestion to me.

the explication and elucidation of each semantic variation upon good should need to make a non-gratuitous circuit through the idea of the good of a being. At least under this head, and in its application to medical goodness, the focal hypothesis survives well enough.

12. Next then hedonic goodness and the goodness of pleasant experiences or of the pleasures of a life comprising divers enjoyable activities (a life whose circumstances are liked by the one who lives the life). Can we account for their goodness in the same sort of way? These subjects are notorious for their intractability. I begin upon them with von Wright's characteristic contention (p. 62), no less memorable than that last quoted, to the effect that, just as there is a positive notion of health which involves consciousness of fitness or strength, so there is a positive notion of [well being] which "has a primary conceptual alliance with pleasure. Of the being who enjoys this aspect of its welfare [well being] we say that it is happy. Happiness could also be called the flower of well being".

Let us embark upon the goodness of that which is enjoyable or pleasurable with the case that is easiest, namely the goodness of pleasures whose enjoyability is well captured in Aristotelian terms by describing them in terms of unimpeded activity. Such are the pleasures (i.e. activities) von Wright has in mind when he speaks (pp. 64-5) of things one is keen on doing, enjoys doing or likes to do[15]. (See *Nicomachean Ethics*, book VII.) Surely the goodness of such pleasures does indeed derive in part from the way in which they can heighten an animate being's however indistinct awareness of its own "good of a being", even as that awareness enhances the pleasures themselves. Pleasures of this sort must have some conceptual alliance with happiness conceived in the way in which von Wright conceives it. Yes. Imprecise though it is, so much seems worth saying. But not all pleasures, nor yet all pleasure, fall very aptly within the ambit of Aristotle's unimpeded activity theory or under the good-of-a-being theory. Consider the mode of attention whose goodness as pleasure is owed to the aesthetic goodness or beauty of its perceptual object. What on earth does that sort of goodness have to do with the good of a being?[16] The

---

[15]On these, see G.E.L. Owen "Aristotelian Pleasures" *Proceedings of the Aristotelian Society*, 72, 1971-2, pp.135-52.

[16]It is not to be denied that some pleasures of this sort do make reference to the goodness of a being, but not all do. For a case where there is a connection of sorts, see David Hume, *Enquiry into the Principles of Morals*

pleasure that engages with such an object feeds or nourishes the good of a being (the subject of experience) – yes, so much can be allowed – but it does so by putting the being into relation with another and antecedent kind of goodness. Cognate difficulties will occupy us later. Meanwhile, before I babble, I pass onward to the next task.

13. So far, not without some difficulty, we have treated utilitarian goodness, beneficial goodness, medical goodness, and hedonic goodness. Next let us try to bring in instrumental goodness. Examples of this are "good house" or "good way of changing a tyre". Confronting this variety of goodness, the friend of focal meaning will want to say that, once joking and irony are put aside (as in "a good way of cutting off one's nose to spite one's face"), we normally confine our attributions of instrumental goodness to classes of things which second the kinds of aim or purpose that von Wright calls 'ends of action' – where an end of action qualifies as good only under the aspect of contributing (or so it is hoped) either causally or constitutively to 'the good of a being'.

Something similar applies to technical goodness. If someone is a good orator or a good carpenter, it is clear that there must be all sorts of occasion on which his or her knowledge and skill can secure that which will appear there, in that context, as a good – and appear thus under the aspect of contributing instrumentally or constitutively to the good of a being. By contrast, we are less happy with "good assassin" or "good counterfeiter". Here the focal theorists must say that such uses rest on bare analogy. (We shall return to analogy.) In defence of that claim, let me commend an experiment. Say to yourself the words "good highwayman". Do they not prompt you to think of a highwayman on the side of the good of beings who are poor or oppressed – of Robin Hood, say, rather than of some pitilessly expert predator upon travellers on the road? With "good highwayman" we do not listen (it seems) for a technical sense of "good". Unless we belong to the criminal world or we are lexicographers or spectators interpreting expressions of the admiration in which that world holds certain criminal expertises, we wait to hear some sense akin to that of "helpful", "benevolent" or "good [person]".

VI.1, Selby-Bigge, pages 243-4: "... the view [i.e. spectacle] of [happiness], whether in its causes or effects like sunshine or the prospect of *well-cultivated plains* ..., communicates a secret joy and satisfaction" (italics added).

14. This is a proper moment for me to say why one might think that, over and above technical goodness, von Wright should recognize goodness in a calling. Consider being a doctor. As is pointed out at *Varieties* (p. 37), there is more to qualifying as a good doctor than technical goodness: "[For] most so-called professions... [pure] technical goodness is secondary to instrumental goodness." This understates the point, however. One who is skilled in healing but decides to redeploy that skill however marvellously well by writing medical textbooks may in that way (as von Wright puts it) "serve the ends and purposes of men and institutions". (The phrase is from the same page of *Varieties*.) But even this falls short of that which is required in the calling of doctor. The bad temper or misanthropy of someone who is skilled in healing but fears to betray the strong aversion he has recently discovered in himself to the close presence of other human beings surely stands in the way of his being fully or unqualifiedly a good *doctor*. Being a good doctor depends upon more than skill and more than the biomedical knowledge that goes into writing textbooks. It depends inter alia upon a particular formation of character and will and a distinctive sort of concern with the good of beings. May it be that there is here a separable variety of goodness, one with its own relation to the good of a being? At this point, another thing we come to anticipate is the possibility of an ambiguity in the claim "x is a good doctor", an ambiguity that has nothing to do with any ambiguity in "doctor". Minimally, "x is a good doctor" may mean that x is diagnostically or in other ways technically adept. But its further meaning is that, beyond his or her undoubted technical mastery, x follows the humane vocation of doctor.

There are other vocations, but rather than pause to narrow or to refine the proposal, let me try to say how full or plenary goodness in a calling such as a doctor's relates to our semantic focus, *the good of a being*. Like this perhaps: one who follows such a calling leads a life that is centred upon concerns special to one with a particular insight or understanding directed at a humane purpose. In a way which these define, persons of this sort have to be ready at any instant of night or day to recognize the claims that the good of a being can make upon their capacities and their will.[17] In respect of the provision of the things that flow

---

[17] An objector may say: "This all sounds very nice, but what about "good henchman"? What about the good and faithful servants of an evil master. Remember that they too have their vocation, as well as certain skills

from his or her having that vocation, such a person puts himself or herself *at the beck and call* of the good of a being.

15. So far so good – but only so good – for the focal hypothesis. Now though we must treat some of the other varieties that von Wright mentions.

What shall we say about "good man" or "good person"? Would that von Wright had said more about it. In the event, all we have are his brief remarks at Chapter Six, section 12. Their gist may be conveyed in his own words as follows:

> When the phrase "a good man" is used, not in the sense of instrumental or technical goodness but with a moral tinge, it is related to the notions of doing good and of having good intentions. But it has no clear and distinct relationship to these notions .... I think it is true to say that, when the phrase "a good man" is used with a so-called moral meaning, it is related to our idea of a benevolent man.

In explication of "you're always so good to me", as of "you are always too good to me", an ordinary dictionary will lend support to the last suggestion. But, as von Wright anticipates, we shall certainly want more. Can we not put "good person" into some definite relation with "good act" and "good intention"? And, at the same time, must we not make a proper allowance for the thought that a properly good person will not allow their benevolence to trump their sense of justice?

At the outset – because von Wright does so and not because we expect this to issue in an Aristotelian outcome – let us go back to Aristotle. To judge from *Nicomachean Ethics* I.7 and II.6, Aristotle thinks that the *arete* or goodness of a man, depends on how he carries out the *ergon* that is proper to man. *Ergon*

---

or expertises. They too have a particular formation of character and will. They too work to no set hours. The elucidation of goodness in a vocation or calling simply does not need the sort of detour which your project has enforced upon you through the notion of the good of a being."

I acknowledge the difficulty. But I submit that there is only a faint resemblance between vocations of the sort I have been concerned with and the roles of henchman or mobster's bodyguard. This is not to deny that one who is outside the Mafia can acknowledge that there is an analogy. But the need to deploy this sort of explanation draws attention to the huge distance at which certain strained occurrences of "good" lie from the focus *good of a being*. In section 19, we shall draw out the significance of the question of nearness or distance.

is commonly translated as 'function'. Man is to his *ergon* as a flute-player is to flute playing, a builder to building, an eye to seeing, a hand to the things we do with a hand, a foot to walking or running. The trouble is that, as explained in terms of function, none of these analogies is very illuminating. It is not as if Aristotle is party to the thought that man is to be compared with a cog or spindle in a machine, or compared with a limb or an organ that serves some larger organism. Aristotle is no more party to such thoughts than we are. Nor yet can one model the goodness of a human being on the functional or technical goodness of a craftsman or musician. You can't be a builder without possessing some training, skill or aptitude. But you can be a human being or *anthropos* without having any particular skill or aptitude at all. (Cp. *Varieties*, p.133.)

At this point, since von Wright has carried us here, let us make an experiment. Taking our cue from Richard Bentley, restoring the initial digamma to *[w]ergon,* and seeing the English and Greek words reveal one and the same Indo-European root, let us start afresh with the idea of work. As rational beings with the nature that we discover we are blessed or encumbered with, what work do we assign to each other or to ourselves? Then think of *man* as akin to *Mensch* or *homo* and think of *homines* as each and all candidates to be recognized as partaking in the solidarity of a community of persons or *the party of humankind* (as Hume might call it). Think of the party of humankind as the community whose members recognize one another by the human form and hold to one another (in so far as they do hold to one another) in the causes of solidarity, reciprocity and mutual protection under the constraints and requirements of natural virtues such as benevolence and artificial virtues such as fidelity or justice. A good human being is one who serves these ends and fulfils in these particular ways the watching brief which he or she holds on behalf of the good of a being, that is on behalf of human beings.[18]

This is miles from von Wright and miles more from Aristotle. But it does prepare the way to treat "good act" and "good intention" in a quasi-Aristotelian way by saying that a good intention is the sort of intention we expect of a good person and a good act the sort of act we expect a good person to undertake.

---

[18] A watching brief. The good person need not be a busybody. As likely as not, one part of his/her originary motivation is the sense of the *badness* of disregarding the harm that will result if *no-one* seeks to protect or defend the good of human beings.

What is more, this whole proposal leaves us free to explore the chance a good person has of happiness (or to compare and contrast their chance of true felicity and the chances of other kinds of people) without confusing the goodness or virtue of a human being (their *eu zen* taken in the sense one explains by reference to ethical virtue) with the good of a being as understood in the sense of the good *for* a human being (or *eu zen* in the sense of welfare or happiness). It lays bare the openness for us of that question.[19]

16. When we conjoin this proposal with the focal hypothesis, there are two kinds of doubt.

First doubt. By this account, "good act" or "good intention" is scarcely a simple derivative from the "good of a being" in the way in which "healthy food" or "healthy urine" is derivative from "health" or "healthy animal". It depends on the intermediation of something which has itself to be explained focally. So, "good intention" or "good act" is an offshoot from an offshoot from "good of a being", namely "good person". That is in the spirit of the original hypothesis, but let us not omit to record this development.[20]

A second and graver doubt goes back to the originary notion of the good of a being from which we tried to arrive at "good person"? In thinking about the good of (for) human beings politically and socially gathered together, a good person has not only to attend to the welfare towards which a good person directs his or her benevolence – that was the good of a being as we understood it when we were concerned with instrumental, utilitarian, beneficial, medical etc. goodness –, not only to attend to the solidarity of the human qua human and the absolute prohibitions that defend human beings from one another, but to attend also to certain special and further necessities, namely those in the providing for which the collectivity creates and defends the arrangements through which trust is concerted and expectations are made dependable.[21] This is the province of Hume's artificial

---

[19]In so far as Aristotle's own conception of a good (*agathos* or *spoudaios*) person (*anthropos*) fails to close the question – that issue does not concern us here – there are then at least two different ways for it to be open.

[20]I make a similar proposal for the linkage holding between the different senses of the adjective "just". See *Ethics: Twelve Lectures on the Philosophy of Morality*, (Harvard University Press and Penguin Press, 2006), p. 290.

[21]See my *Twelve Lectures,* op.cit., chapters 8,9 and my *Lindley Lecture,* "Solidarity and the Root of the Ethical" (Lawrence, Kansas: University of Kansas Philosophy Department, 2008).

virtues. Once these are brought into the picture, however, we can no longer think of the good for a human being as simple benevolence conceives it or characterize the full goodness (virtue) of a human being simply in terms of benevolence. Indeed the plenary goodness of a human being will require under some circumstances that he or she *oppose* that good-benevolent disposition within him or herself (along with the aggregative propensities to which that may give rise) by dispositions that exclude that which solidarity prohibits or that demand the agent's attachment to justice or fairness or fidelity. The upshot is this. Even as we seek to connect the varieties of goodness to the unitary focus of the good for a being, the focus transforms itself. As a result, the good of (for) a being seems to comprise or contain within itself two or three distinct varieties of good of (for) a being. A focal theorist must be ready to separate the good for a being that we ask of benevolence, the good for a being that consists in the solidarity of fellow beings with him or her, and the good for a being which it is the office of fidelity, fairness or justice to defend and to maintain.

17. Very soon we must review the prospects for the focal theory. First though let us go back to the very beginning and engage in our own way with the claims that Aristotle makes at NE 1096b23-26: 'there is no common account to be had of that which constitutes the goodness of honour, the goodness of wisdom or understanding, and the goodness of pleasure. Even in the case of things that are good in themselves, there is no common Form or Idea.' Straying from Aristotle to any extent that we need, what account should we ourselves give of these several goodnesses?

Pleasure has its own relation to the good of a being, as we have seen, but it has already directed us toward varieties of goodness whose goodness seems to resist being represented as deriving from the good of a being. (See section 12 above.)

Honour is the tribute, the recognition pleasing to the receiver, that befits his or her virtues or achievements. In a non-degenerate case, the recipient receives such honour as a good in itself, not as a means to some further or alien benefit. What qualifies honour so conceived to count as a good? It is accorded to the recipient by those who know him or her, accorded freely, and accorded on the basis, as Aristotle notes, of the recipient's *aretê* – their bravery perhaps, or their endurance, or their love of the polis, or their artistry ... or, as (as we might insist) their moral virtue or personal goodness. Such honour confirms and assures the recipient in his or her possession of something that s/he can value for what it is in itself.

On the supposition that so much is correct about honour, it seems that, without von Wright's encouragement[22] but in tandem with that which the idea of honour discovers to us, we are filling out our account of other things too. Not least, we are enlarging that account of the goodness of a good person (section 15) with an account of the goodness *for them* of attaining to the goodness of a good person. Suppose we conclude that the attainment of ethical virtue is an end in itself and a good for the possessor of that goodness. How then to explicate what we must mean in saying this? Stealing a turn of phrase from *Eudemian Ethics* 1218b4-7 ('... one good is *prakton* another not. The good which is *prakton* is the sort of good which is a thing-for-the-sake-of-which *(hou heneka)*')[23], we might interpret ourselves as saying that ethical virtue is a thing-for-the-sake-of-which and something we might seek not only for the sake of its beneficiaries, but also for its own sake and for what it is in itself. That surely amounts to saying that being a good person is a *constituent* of the practical good. But then we have to ask: have we not added yet one more variety of good to the varieties which are comprised in the good of a being?

A cognate question arises about the distinguishable goodness that I take third, the goodness of wisdom or understanding. This wisdom would still be a practical good, something we might strive for and a thing-for-the-sake-of-which, even if we did not depend on its instrumental contribution to our welfare. But how can this further goodness that we attribute to it be completely subsumed under the good of a being that we took to be our focus in explaining either the good/goodness of the varieties of goodness we were mostly concerned with in section 5-7 and 10-14 or in explaining focally the good/goodness of benevolence and of ethical virtue more generally?[24]

18. It is time to ask how much can be achieved by persevering so single-mindedly in the line of enquiry that we began upon in section 8. If we want to answer von Wright's question about the

---

[22] For von Wright's own view of the virtues see the citation in section 10 and note 11.

[23] For her explanation of the import and importance of this sentence, I am indebted to Heda Segvic, op. cit. page 155.

[24] In section 22 we shall touch on one further difficulty about the goodness of wisdom.

("peculiar and puzzling") meaning pattern of "good" then Aristotle's focal hypothesis will scarcely give us an account of "good" with the simple beauty, perfection and apparent completeness of Aristotle's account of "healthy". It is true that by allowing the idea of the good of a being constantly to develop, then arranging in some way for different varieties of good to be related to different aspects of that good and allowing focal explanations to be nested within focal explanations (see section 16, paragraph two), we might regain some ground for the focal theory. But further progress will also depend, or so it appears, upon integrating that which can be achieved in this way into some larger strategy. What shall that be? The only obvious candidate is a speculative, quasi-historical or reconstructive account of the whole history of the English word "good" (or a corresponding word in any other language) set out in a narrative hospitable to focal explanations, hospitable to the differentiation of the different aspects of the good of a being, and structured also in divers other ways.

If that possibility seems obvious now, then why did it not figure at all in our deliberations in section 8, or in Aristotle's or von Wright's deliberations? Well, it is exposed to a doubt that the focal proposal need not provoke. Would an account of the long and complex history of "good" and its immediate cognates such as "well" (cp. German "gut" and "wohl", French "bon" and "bien") be an account of any well-made single however capacious idea? This is a more than purely theoretical doubt. On a recent visit to Stockholm (May 2008), I encountered Swedish-speakers who asked how readily von Wright could have translated the name of his own book into his native language. Raising similar questions about Russian, they asked why I was so sure that there was some overarching goodness whose varieties von Wright had enumerated. If these interlocutors were not teasing me and if their doubts about Swedish are well considered, does that mean that other languages have greater expressive power? Or do languages such as Swedish subvert the pretensions of languages whose speakers take themselves to grasp some generic determinable as wide as that which "good" appears to stand for?

Prescinding from the particular question about Swedish, let me state the best case that I can for the existence of some large undifferentiated idea whose several or many determinations can be unfolded as the varieties of goodness.

19. I start on this from a subordinate question. When one says that something is a good *in itself,* which variety of goodness is that?[25] It seems that one cannot dispense with the thought that the good in itself invokes the same property whose determinations will be recorded and brought into intelligible relation with one another by the lexico-cultural narrative that reconstructs and explicates the history of the word "good".

A second question. In his first chapter von Wright says:

> We may feel astonished at the fact that a smell as well as a general, rainfall as well as lungs, can be good. It may, that is, be astonishing to consider how diverse good things can be. But we should not hesitate to call the pleasant or the skilful or the useful or the healthy forms of the good. (Page 17.)

What are we to say about the last occurrence of "good"? It may indeed seem astonishing, where good has such a variety of significations, that von Wright can say this. Yet it seems evident that he can.

If it seems evident that von Wright can say this, how can he? Well, a parallel may be useful. At the beginning of Book 5 of *Nicomachean Ethics* Aristotle warns us that "just" is homonymous. But this is no random homonymy, he says. Transposing Aristotle's use of the term into ours, I redeploy and paraphrase freely the observation he makes at this point:

> [where] homonymy is close, it does not trouble us in the way it does where the denotata are too far apart and the mutual incongruity is as evident as it is with kleis meaning the collar bone of an animal and kleis meaning the thing one uses to lock the door. Nicomachean Ethics 1129a26-31.

It would be absurd for a Greek speaker to declare himself astonished at the variety of *kleides* (keys). Door keys and collar bones, like money banks and river banks, have only an analogical-cum-etymological connection. Such things themselves really don't belong together. By contrast, the varieties of justice do belong together, even if you have to be careful when you try to generalize about all these justices taken together. In various ways they all help to preserve some thing, a political constitution, a *res publica*, a joint concern... that partners hold in common (cp. *Eudemian Ethics* 1241b13-16).

---

[25]Similarly, when we ask what is so good about something or someone we precisely don't specify in advance which variety we are enquiring about.

If the varieties of justice belong together, why shouldn't the varieties of goodness? Of course, they will not belong together if we try to count as good everything that is called good on the basis of *merely* analogical or etymological connection. (See section 13, also note 17.) But let us insist that all analogical widenings of the extension of "good" be validated and validated strictly on their merits.[26]

All right, but what then *positively assembles* the far-flung various varieties of goodness and justifies counting them together as varieties of "goodness"? What is the principle? Things get more difficult now, but I shall make a suggestion. Like undifferentiated justice, undifferentiated good is an irreducible category of our thinking. It cannot be identified by a biconditional equivalence. But that need not prevent it from possessing certain marks (in Frege's sense of "mark"). A strong candidate for consideration is this: in one way or another, everything that falls under goodness in general relates somehow to a thing-for-the-sake-of-which, a thing (such as health, security, knowledge, understanding...) worth acting to secure, to care for, to safeguard, to achieve.... What the philosophical lexicographer recapitulates under "good" is the history of our constant interrogation of the life that we lead and the place where we lead it, our constant interrogation of things that concern us or might concern us or ought to concern us.[27] The philosophical lexicographer's work needs to be all of a piece with this constant engagement on the part of human beings.

20. We now have three further questions.

First, do we grasp the good in general by abstracting it from its determinations? That is implausible. Or do we begin with the good in general and then learn its determinations. That is even more implausible. The answer I prefer is that, at the beginning, we are striving to achieve, secure, care for, safeguard... all sorts of things and we are subsuming these things under various

---

[26]To call the collar-bone *kleis* was an admirable piece of linguistic invention. But it fell short of investing the putative determinable *kleides* with more than etymological interest. Too much was lost in the transposition – a key as something lost or found, a key as leading inwards or onwards to something else that is to be kept safe... a key as something with which we lock, unlock and lock again at will. No sufficient semantic *interest* or *point* could attach to the putatively serious general attribution *kleis*.

[27]In their several ways, Ayer, Stevenson, Hare, Ziff and Scanlon all see this. . How much more they see needs to be determined author by author.

categorizations which it will become possible at a later stage, after countless refinements, to understand as varieties of goodness. But the full or proper grasp of the undifferentiated good and its determinations must be simultaneous.

Secondly, will a large property such as the one I have tried to characterize have room within it for all the varieties of goodness? That will be the subject of section 21.

Thirdly, what understanding does the schema encapsulate of goodness as such? That will be the subject of section 22.

21. With the second question, let us start upon what may appear as one of the hardest cases, cosmological goodness (as one might call it). Consider from among the early verses of *Genesis* the following:

> 1.3 And God said let there be light; and there was light and God saw the light, that it was good ...

> 1.10 And God called the dry land Earth and the gathering together of the waters he called the Seas and God saw that it was good....

> 1.31 And God saw everything he had made, and behold it was very good.

Whatever the word's etymological history, we now hear these occurrences of "good"/"tov" as carrying a resonance not well explained by hearing them as variants upon "well-made" or "the product of God's technical goodness" or "God's provision of that which would minister to the good of beings (not least human ones)". Someone may say that the goodness spoken of in *Genesis* is not worth bothering with – is either unintelligible or at best the product of idle analogizing; still less, they may say, can it qualify as a thing-for-the-sake-of-which or as an end of human concern or endeavour. Yet I believe that pre-theoretically we understand it.[28] I note further that, when Thomas Hill, Jr. asks what we

---

[28] Nor, once you look long and hard enough, is this sort of good unintelligible to Aristotle (who does not assert that all *agathon* is *prakton*). See *Metaphysics* XII, chapter 10:

"We must consider also in which of two ways the nature of the universe contains the good or the highest good, whether as something separate by itself or as the order of the parts. Probably in both ways, as an army does. For good is found both in the order and in the leader, and more in the latter; for he does not depend on the order but it depends on him. And all things are ordered together somehow but not all alike – both fishes and fowls and plants;

are to think of someone who uproots his whole front garden to make a concrete parking lot for three cars and a tool shed, we can ask why the beauty of grass, flowers and shrubs was not for him a thing-for-the-sake-of-which-*not*, namely not to lay waste the goodness of the world. Why suppose that everything we can care about – every thing-for-the-sake-of-which – is something we ourselves create or *confer* goodness upon, or is something that *owes* its goodness to the fact that it contributes to our good?

22. On this basis, it may seem that the characterization we offer of the undifferentiated good accommodates within it not only cosmological good, but also the aesthetic good that troubled us in section 12. By the same token, it seems there is room within the good for that which is interesting or beguiling or beautiful among the concerns of wisdom or understanding. It is by ministering to these concerns that wisdom or understanding qualifies as a constituent of the good of our being. (This by way of supplement to section 17.) Now, however, having followed this line, we come to the third of our three concluding questions.

What understanding do we achieve of the goodness of the kinds of good last mentioned by showing how they bear upon the good of a being? The fact that they can become things-for-the-sake-of-which shows something important about human beings and their susceptibilities. But this fact need not show very much about these varieties of good. The interesting or beguiling or beautiful nourishes the good of human beings, but precisely by coming to us from without. It is an *antecedent* sort of goodness which impinges upon us. It will be topsy-turvy for the focalist to try to trace this antecedent goodness itself to the good of a being. Let the lexico-philosophical reconstructors of the evolution and of the meaning of "good" not confuse the fact that theirs is an inquiry into the human scale of values with the utter falsehood that the human scale of values is a scale exclusively of human values.[29] It is a human scale of human *and* non-human values – of both. The narrative must make room for this, as well as for

---

and the world is not such that one thing has nothing to do with another, but they are connected. For all are ordered together to one end."

[29] Compare Bernard Williams "Must a concern for the environment be centred on human beings?" *Making Sense of Humanity* (Cambridge University Press, 1995), p.243; David Wiggins, "Nature, respect for nature, and the human scale of values", *Proceedings of the Aristotelian Society*, New Series Vol. 100 (1999-2000), section V. (The proper text of this address is given only in the Society's own bound *Proceedings*, published in 2000. The text in the Society's autumn 1999 instalment is not the published text.) On cognate

much else that it is hard to understand.³⁰ Even on an optimistic view, the focal theory can aspire to engage with only one however large subclass of the phenomena.

---

matters, see also my "Sufficient reason: a principle in diverse guises, both ancient and modern," *Acta Philosophica Fennica*, Vol. 61, 1996, pp. 119-132.

[30] For comments and suggestions I owe a particular debt to Peter Hacker, Roger Crisp (and to his article "Goodness and Reason: Accentuating the Negative", *Mind 2008*, 117), Roger Scruton and Åsa Wickforss.

von Wright's Compatibilism

Frederick Stoutland

There are different versions of compatibilism. One is the Hume-Mill version, which regards all explanation of events as a matter of causal law, accepts the determinist thesis that all events are instances of causal laws, and contends that this is compatible with human agents being able to act other than they do. The compatibilist argument is that the explanatory causes of action – desires, beliefs, volitions, etc. – do not coerce the action, but enable agents to do what they want or will to do, which is not undermined by their wanting or willing also being caused.

Kant called this a "wretched subterfuge" and offered his own version, whose essential point was that there are two distinct types of explanation of human behavior. One explains it by citing the causal laws that govern its occurrence in the empirical world, thereby embedding it in a deterministic structure and ruling out free action. The other explains it in terms of features our will and intention endow it with, which renders determinism irrelevant and hence allows for autonomous agency. Determinism and freedom are compatible because they belong to distinct types of explanation and hence to distinct ways of understanding and being. Our autonomy as rational agents is not compromised by any causal explanation of the effects of our acting.

Von Wright's compatibilism is Kantian. I begin by laying out his point of view, which I reformulate in terms of the distinction between nomological and rational explanation, his claim being that determinism is relevant only to the former. His main compatibilist claim is, then, that the same behavior can be explained by both a nomological (neuroscientific) and a rational explanation. I next consider how to account for the congruence between what is explained by each of these types of explanation, the answer I propose raising anew the issue of compatibilism, which now concerns the "completeness of physics." On that point I conclude that we should be incompatibilists.

1. Von Wright claimed that "Determinism is compatible with action *in the sense* that every change in the world which results from the action of an agent, i.e. is imputed to agency, might also have resulted from another change which is its causally sufficient condition."[1] To understand this some background is needed.

Von Wright distinguished between the *consequence* and the *result* of an action. The former is what an action *causes*, the latter is the *criterion* for an action having been performed – an occurrence that is logically necessary to the action and hence not something it causes. A consequence of Jane's opening the door is that fresh air goes in; the result of her opening it is that the door opens. The cause of the latter is not Jane's opening the door but the act *by which* she opens it, for instance, turning the handle. Results and consequences should be thought of not as constituents of actions but as two ways of describing them.

But the door might have opened 'by itself' (because of a sensor like those at grocery stores), in which case it is not true that *Jane* opened it. Here the action "'shrinks' to those things by which he meant to perform his action."[2] Even if Jane turned the handle at that very moment, *she* did not open the door because what caused it to open was an external mechanism: the door would have opened even if she had done nothing. In this case, because there was a causally sufficient condition of the *result* of the (attempted) action of opening the door, the *agent* did not open it.

Opening the door von Wright calls a *non-basic* action because we do it *by* doing something – by turning the handle. When we try but fail to perform such actions, they 'shrink' to the action *by which* we try. *Basic* actions, by contrast, are actions we do not do *by* doing something: they are typically moving our body or limbs. Jane did not turn her hand *by* doing something more basic. Turning our hand usually is a basic action, but if our hand were injured, we could turn it by using our other hand, in which case it would not be basic.

---

[1] *Causality and Determinism* (Columbia University Press, 1974), p. 133. Henceforth C&D.

[2] *Explanation and Understanding* (Routledge and Kegan Paul, 1971), p. 127.

The *result* of a *basic* act (as of all action) is the *criterion* that it was performed. The result of raising my arm is that my arm goes up, but raising it does not *cause* its going up. Let us consider a very special case where my arm goes up just as I intend to raise it but in fact goes up because of a mechanism arranged by a mischievous scientist. If this were a *non-basic* act, it would not be true that I raised my arm since it went up 'by itself,' and the act would 'shrink' to the act *by* which I *tried* to raise it. But this is a *basic* act and no shrinking is possible since there is no act *by which* I raise my arm. Do we say that since the *result* of the (attempted) action of raising my arm is caused by a mechanism, I did not raise it? That would, it seems, to be deluded – to think I was raising my arm when I was not, because a mechanism caused it to go up.

Von Wright argues that we need not say that. This is a case where the bodily movement "takes place, as intended, but still cannot rightly be said to result from our action. Such cases are rare indeed... but they can be imagined and they sometimes occur." He continues:

> Someone thinks he gets up from his chair. At the very same time some (to him invisible) agent, or perhaps the operating of a hidden mechanism, lifts him from the chair. Did he then not get up, i.e. must we say that he did not raise himself.
>
> The answer would depend on the circumstances of the case. Assume the agent has been ill and for some time too weak to raise himself from the chair (in which one has seated him). He is getting better and makes efforts to raise himself. Suddenly he thinks he has succeeded—but, alas, he is mistaken: it was in fact the invisible agent who helped him to get up. We can tell him this and perhaps make him realize it by asking him to get up on an occasion when we know there is no-one to help him.
>
> Assume, however, that the agent is in perfect health and has no reason to doubt that he can get up from the chair. He gets up, and when asked why he does this answers, e.g., that he is going to leave the room. If it is then pointed out to him that he was in fact lifted from the chair at that very moment—and thus would have been

raised in any case—he could retort: "How strange it should have happened at the very moment I rose." Neither he nor we would say that he was under an illusion, but would regard the operation of that peculiar cause of the result of his action as simply a coincidence.

Thus in the case of basic actions too, it is not the existence of a cause of the result of an action which shows that the agent is deluded in thinking that he acts. What would show that he is deluded is, for example, the existence of good reasons for holding that, although the result materialized, the agent is temporarily or permanently disabled from doing an action of the kind in question, or that he has not yet learnt to perform the action properly. The existence of a cause of the result is, in fact, immaterial to the characterization of the action as an "illusion."

But what if the "invisible" agent or cause were always there to help us do what we do? Would not the constant coincidence between the performance of the action and the operation of this hidden thing be very strange indeed? So strange that we should have to modify our view of an agent's freedom—even if it would not be right to label his acting "illusory" ?

To this it should be said that the coincidence, as we now imagine it, would still be subject to some restrictions. Sometimes the cause operates when the agent does not act, and produces what would have been the result of his action had he acted. And sometimes the cause fails to operate when he sets himself to act, and therefore vitiates the accomplishment of his action. These are normal and familiar phenomena—to any one of us. If cases of the first kind were very frequent, we should feel unsure whether there is an opportunity for our action and thus unsure when we can perform it. And if there were very many cases of the second kind, we should doubt whether we master the action at all. So our idea of acting, of being able to do certain things, others not, depends upon the not too frequent occurrence and non-occurrence respectively of such discrepancies between causes and actions. That this requirement is satisfied is a contingency. But it is nothing to be surprised at. For, it is a condition which the world must satisfy if we are to entertain our present notions of action and agency. [C & D, 130f.]

A cause "*always*" there to help us" can be conceived if we take the hidden mechanism to be our brain and nervous system, whose operation is in some sense sufficient to cause the movements of our body and limbs.[3] This raises two issues that von Wright discussed on a number of occasions. One is how to understand what I call the *congruence* between what an agent does intentionally and the non-intentional movements of her body and limbs, which von Wright refers to as a requirement on our "idea of acting, of our being able to do certain things, others not." The other is how to understand the *compatibility* between our intentionally moving our body and limbs and those movements being caused by neural events. These two issues are closely linked, and I shall discuss them both.

2. I would rework von Wright's treatment of these issues in three ways. First, I would give a different account of the *individuation* of action. Let me use Anscombe's famous example. A man 1) moves his arm 2) in pumping water 3) to replenish a water-supply 4) to poison the inhabitants of the house, and 5) unknowingly does other things like wearing down his shoe leather. On von Wright's view, the man is doing five things that are individuated by five *results*: his arm moves, the water gets pumped, the water supply is replenished, etc., each of which (except the first) is a *consequence* of a *previous* action. If the man fails because the pipe is broken and no water gets to the house, then his action shrinks to moving his arm and pumping water. It would shrink further if the pump went up and down by itself, in which case his moving his arm up and down would be idle. But the latter is a *basic* act and hence cannot shrink, which means that even if the sufficient cause of his arm movements is a neural mechanism, he may be

---

[3]Conceiving this possibility is not as easy as von Wright suggests since it raises difficult issues about the wider context – biological and otherwise – of the brain and nervous system.

intentionally moving his arm up and down. This illustrates von Wright's claims about both the congruence and the compatibility between a man's intentionally acting and the neural causes of the result of his acting.

A main difficulty with von Wright's view of individuation is that it suggests that basic acts are a distinctive kind of action, as if one could sometimes act basically and at other times non-basically. But every act is basic in that no matter how complex it is, doing it requires doing something *not by* doing something, for otherwise there would be an infinite regress of our not being able to act until we had already performed another act. To resolve this, I recommend Anscombe's view that the man acts only once, though what he does in so acting is multiple, that is, has many descriptions. To be action, it must be intentional under at least one description (action is *essentially* intentional), but it may be intentional under many (depending on how successful the agent is) and not intentional under many more.

On this view, what von Wright called the result of an action individuates, not a distinct action, but one of the several things an agent does in a single acting. If the man does intentionally all the things mentioned, then his acting has the complex description: "poisoning the inhabitants by replenishing the water supply by pumping water by moving his arm up and down," a description that is true of his acting because his acting caused the pump to go up and down, which caused the water supply to be replenished, which caused the inhabitants to be poisoned. But there was a *single* acting because having moved his arms up and down, he does nothing more (if conditions are right) to pump the water, replenish the water supply, poison the inhabitants, and whatever else his movements cause. What is basic or non-basic is not his acting but the things he does in acting, which are specified in the descriptions of his acting. That is to say, the concept of a basic act is intensional: whether an act is basic depends on how it is described. To describe his acting as replenishing the water supply is to give it a *non-basic* description since he does that *by* doing something. To describe it as his moving his arm is to give it a *basic* description because he does not do that *by* doing something.

Secondly, I would alter von Wright's use of the term "cause." When he referred to causes, he always meant "Humean causes," which he took to be grounded in universal laws with necessary force. This is the root of his idea that causal claims are founded on our ability to intervene in nature in order to bring about an effect: the point of intervention is to obtain evidence that the occurrence of an event of one kind is lawfully connected with the occurrence of an event of another kind. On his view, rational explanations of action – explanations in terms of the agent's reason for acting – are not causal because they are not grounded in law-like generalizations.

This sense of "cause" invites misunderstanding, for it suggests that to explain an action as intentional is not to explain why an agent acted but only to describe what her action was or was intended to be. Von Wright occasionally spoke of rational explanations as limited to "a set of conditions under which the conduct of an agent has to be interpreted or understood in a certain way,"[4] which suggests that they do not aim to explain *why* the agent acted but to understand *what* she did – that they belong, as Sellars put it, to the intentional rather than to the real order – in which case they are surely not causal. But that was not what von Wright meant, for he always treated reasons as explaining *why* an agent acted as he did. To act, he wrote, "is to interfere with the course of the world, thereby making true something which would not otherwise ... come to be true of the world at that stage of its history."[C&D, 39]

I would argue that the generic sense of "explain" is "render intelligible", which can be done in different ways in different situations. Any explanation that renders intelligible *why an event occurred* is plausibly called *causal*, and since acting is an event, an explanation of why someone acted intentionally is plausibly called *causal*. This sense is not ruled out by von Wright, who granted that reasons were causes in *some* sense of "cause,"[5] and because this wider sense is less prone to misunderstanding, it is the one I will use.

Thirdly, I would recast von Wright's distinction between intentional actions and bodily movements. He makes this in a number of ways, in particular by distinguishing between "the behavior which can be explained teleologically as action" and the behavior which can "be explained causally as movement."[6] By the first, he means an explanation of behavior as what the agent intended it to be, which is what it *is* if she succeeded, and otherwise is what she

---

[4]"On So-called Practical Inference" in G. H. von Wright, *Practical Reason* (Basil Blackwell, 1983), p. 32.

[5]*Explanation and Understanding*, p. viii.

[6]P. A. Schilpp and L. E. Hahn, eds., *The Philosophy of Georg Henrik von Wright* (Open Court, 1989), p. 808.

tried to do. It is a *rational* explanation because it aims to render the performance of an action intelligible by specifying what the agent takes to be a reason for her acting. As I would formulate it, this puts behavior in the *logical space of reasons*, where items are related to each other by normative standards such as correct, favoring, obligatory, or permissible.

The contrary is *the logical space of laws,* to which explanations in the physical sciences characteristically belong in that they put phenomena in the context of natural laws. Such explanations exclude terms with normative significance, even when we express them by saying, for instance, that the *reason* for an eclipse of the sun is the natural laws governing the solar system. We use "reason" here because the explanation makes the eclipse intelligible, but since this is nomological intelligibility, "reason" is not used in a normative sense. No contemporary scientist would claim the solar system *favored* an eclipse, found it appropriate, correct or justified, for this type of explanation has been excluded from the physical sciences since the demise of Aristotelian physics.

I would, therefore, take von Wright's distinction between actions and movements to be between the logical space of reasons and the logical space of laws,[7] and hence construe the issues of congruence and compatibilism as a matter of the relation between these two logical spaces. This means that I am using "causal" to denote causal *explanations* and not causal *relations,* which was also the way von Wright used the term. Causal explanations, like explanations generally, are *intensional*: explanations are always of phenomena under some description. Causal relations hold between particular events no matter how described, so that their ascriptions are *extensional.* My claim is that rational explanations are causal explanations *in the logical space of reasons* and hence are not, as von Wright put it, Humean or law-like. This cannot be a claim about causal relations, for they hold no matter how described and hence belong to no particular logical space. Nor do they necessarily yield an explanation of phenomena since they may be true even if the cause and effect are described in terms

---

[7]This distinction originates with Wilfred Sellers in his *Empiricism and the Philosophy of Mind* in H. Feigl and M. Scriven eds., *Minnesota Studies in the Philosophy of Science*, Vol. 1 (University of Minnesota Press, 1956) It has been modified, most notably by John McDowell.

with no explanatory value and, consequently, do not render the occurrence of an event intelligible.[8]

3. The defining feature of explanations in the *logical space of laws* is that they *exclude* terms with normative significance. There is a further essential feature: they are not *first person*, by which I mean that they do not use concepts that are implicit in what is being explained. This is obvious when *what* is being explained are not agents who use concepts, but it applies also to explaining the behavior of human beings, who are concept users. An explanation of human behavior in the logical space of laws does not use concepts that belong to the commonsense conception of ourselves and our world, but concepts that require expert knowledge and skill.

This second feature of nomological explanations means that they aim at something like "a view from nowhere" – at an understanding and explanation of the world that is accessible to any expert. It is crucial to note that the *normative* significance of the world as providing reasons for an agent's acting is *not* thus accessible because situations present themselves *as* normatively significant only to persons who occupy a specially relevant point of view in virtue of their culture, practical competencies, their needs, sensibilities, and so on. This means that, although the normative significance a situation has for an agent is accessible to others, it is not accessible to them "from nowhere" but only if they understand the agent's own point of view and the way the world presents itself to her. The two features are, therefore, interrelated: because nomological explanations exclude first person concepts, they are not normative, and vice versa.

Explanations in terms of natural laws presume precise generalizations whose formulation is very difficult, requiring that we abstract from real life situations, simplify complexities without distorting them, and create experimental situations that isolate processes from interfering factors. To do that we must abandon, or at least radically alter, our commonsense concepts of action and psychological states in favor of technical concepts that belong to a theory that enables mathematically formulated generalizations and inferences.

It is only against this background that determinism is a live option. Given a range of phenomena that can be characterized in

---

[8]These points have been developed by Davidson, for example, in his "Causal Relations" in *Essays on Actions and Events* (Oxford University Press, 1980), p, 149-162.

terms of concepts that (being neither normative nor first person) permit such precise generalizations, it is possible to formulate natural laws that govern that range of phenomena, so that (in the words of one definition of 'determinism') "given a specified way things are at a time t, the way things go thereafter is fixed as a matter of natural law."[9] Since at least the 16th century, many have thought that the motions of bodies in the solar system constitute such a range of phenomena so that the way things go in the solar system has been fixed for millions of years as a matter of natural law. Determinism as a general thesis would be the claim that *all* phenomena are thus fixed.

4. The defining feature of explanations in the *logical space of reasons* is that they appeal to reasons for action, that is, to considerations that *favor* an agent's acting in a certain way. A consideration may favor acting in the strong sense of requiring it (for example, on moral grounds), but more often in the weaker sense of rendering it appropriate, beneficial, justified, etc. Of course, rational explanations frequently appeal to considerations that do not *actually* favor the action. Saul gave money to a beggar because she is poor, but she may in fact be rich, her begging being a kind of theatre. The reason he gave the money did not actually favor his doing so, but it nevertheless explained it, something we came to know by understanding his point of view – how the situation presented itself to him, namely as a poor woman who needed money.

This explanation presumes no generalizations, even such a cautious one as, "Whenever persons of a certain type encounter, in these circumstances, a beggar they take to be in need, they give her money." We may be able to *predict* that Saul would give a beggar money because we've seen him doing so many times, but that rough generalization does not *explain* why he does so, certainly not why he gave money to *this* beggar. What explains it is that she, as he saw it, needed money. That is the reason for his having given – its cause, I would say, but not its necessitating cause.

Reading Anscombe convinced me that causes need be neither nomological nor necessitating. That C caused E on this occasion does not entail that when C occurs again, E must, as a matter of law, also occur – even if the situations are the same. The claim that C was sufficient for E means that C was *enough* for E – that

---

[9]Carl Hoefer, "Determinism" in *Stanford Encyclopedia Online*.

it was a sufficient condition in *that* sense – but it need not be a sufficient condition in the logico-philosophical sense of *whenever* C occurs, then E occurs. 'Sufficient condition', Anscombe wrote, "sounds like 'enough', and one certainly *can* ask: 'May there not be *enough* to have made something happen – and yet it not have happened?'"[10] Rational explanations are like that: the presence of a beggar was sufficient (enough) reason for Saul to give her money – it explained why he did so – but it doesn't follow that if he were to encounter a beggar again, he would give her money, even if the circumstances were the same.

Because rational explanations are not nomological or necessitating, the question whether all or only some of them are deterministic is moot. Determinism is not relevant to explanations in the logical space of reasons, but only to those in the logical space of laws.

5. Indeterminist libertarians deal with non-necessitating causes in a way that seems to me mistaken. Their concern is not primarily with intentional but with *free* action, which they think can be explained by an agent's reasons only if the latter cause the action but do not necessitate it. I object, not to the latter point as such, but to their construing it as favoring an indeterministic understanding of rational explanation, one that fixes the effect probabilistically rather than universally.

This worries indeterminists, for they think it amounts to an agent's having "diminished control" over her action. If the cause of an agent's act were always followed by its effect, then she would have complete control over it. But when causation is indeterminist, she has only diminished control since the reason that purportedly explains her action may not always produce it, and the less often it produces it, the less often it explains it and the less control. This creates a dilemma since determinist causes always followed by their effects allow for full control but do not allow for free action, whereas indeterminist causes introduce an element of probability that means insufficient control for an action to be intentional.

I would reject the dichotomy, either universality or probability. A reason explains an action without a generalization of either kind connecting the reason with the action, whether directly or (as in Davidson's view) underneath. To accept the dichotomy is

---

[10]G. E. M. Anscombe, "Causality and Determination" in *Metaphysics and Philosophy of Mind* (University of Minnesota Press, 1981), p. 135.

to put explanations of action as intentional in the logical space of laws, which is a mistake since such explanations are a distinct type to which *neither* determinism *nor* indeterminism is relevant. They are not nomological, but that does not mean they are indeterminist in the sense of quantum physics.

The latter point is connected with the so-called "completeness of physics," the thesis that all phenomena can be accounted for by natural laws that are *either* universal and (hence determinist) *or* probabilistic (hence indeterminist). The latter is also a form of necessity, for in physics probability is precisely fixed by law as much as any universal generalization. The thesis is that all events can be described so that their occurrence is explained as the result of a (perhaps very complex) network of laws whose vectorial combination explains and fixes those events. The claim is that whether or not we know how those laws interact, they nevertheless operate underneath.

Indeterminists accept something like the completeness of physics: reasons that do not cause actions deterministically cause them indeterministically, which entails that agents have more or less control over their actions depending on the degree of probability of the relevant generalizations that ground the explanations. I contend, on the contrary, that rational explanations are neither deterministic nor indeterministic and hence that the completeness of physics is irrelevant to their nature. Although non-necessitating, they are not for that reason incomplete, and although presuming no precise generalizations, their explanations are not probabilistic.

6. Given the distinction between nomological and rational explanation, the question remains whether the same phenomena can be explained – rendered intelligible – in *both* ways. Can an agent's acting be explained not only *as* his doing something intentionally but also *as* movements of his body and limbs resulting from muscle contractions and neural processes? von Wright's compatibilism is essentially the claim that we can give both types of explanation, a claim he took to be established by his example of the man getting out of his chair. I find the example persuasive, although there are important complications I will discuss later.

Jaegwon Kim, however, rejects it: "A 'purposive' explanation of human action in terms of the agent's 'reasons' and a 'mechanistic' (e.g. neurobiological) explanation of it in terms of physiological mechanism must be regarded as incompatible and mutually exclusionary – *unless* we accept an appropriate reductive relationship between intentional states and underlying biological processes." His argument appeals to what he calls the 'principle of explanatory exclusion': "there can be no more than one 'complete' and 'independent' explanation for any single explanandum."[11]

We need not accept this. Let us assume that the two types of explanation are *independent* in that intentional states cannot be reduced to "underlying biological processes." Each is also *complete* in that one makes it intelligible why the agent acted intentionally as he did, the other why his (mere) bodily movements occurred as they did, even if neither explains the further factors used in the explanation. The view I defend does not violate the 'principle of explanatory exclusion' since if we manage to give two such independent and complete explanations for the same behavior, the explanations come from different logical spaces. This implies that, although we explain the same behavior, there is not, as far as Kim's principle is concerned, a single *explanandum* because (as with explanation generally) in giving an explanation of behavior, we must explain it *as* described, which in this case means *as* described in the logical space of reasons and given a rational explanation or *as* described in the logical space of laws and given a nomological explanation. These different types of description of an agent's behavior are compatible, and since explanation is of behavior *as* described, the explanations are also compatible.

7. This notion of dual explanation raises the further issue of *congruence* between the two types, which we need to clarify before returning to compatibilism. Saul gave money to a beggar because she was poor and hungry, which was the reason that explained why his arm reached out to her. Let us assume we can also explain the movement of his arm by reference to neural processes. Why should a rational explanation yield an intentional action and a neuroscientific explanation yield movements of his body and limbs that together constitute his giving money to a beggar? Why is what he did for a reason *congruent* with what occurred because of the neural processes?

Let me first mention two approaches to this question that I take to be mistaken. According to the first, once it is recognized how different neuroscientific and rational explanations are, the very notion of congruence dissolves. The first type *causally* explain why bodily movements occur, whereas the second explain

---

[11] Jaegwon Kim, *Supervenience and Mind* (Cambridge University Press, 1993), p. xiii.

what an agent's acting *means*. An agent's action does not depend on his bodily movements because, on the one hand, a wide variety of bodily movements may constitute the same action since different movements may (in different contexts) have the same meaning, and, on the other hand, the same bodily movements may mean different things depending on the context in which the agent acts. As a result, the very notion of congruence dissolves when we think through what it is supposed to mean.

This view is unsatisfactory. Although rational explanations of an agent's acting are not law-like, they are, as I argued above, *causal* in they make it intelligible not only *what* an agent did but *why* he acted as he did. Moreover, they often explain why an agent's body and limbs moved as they did: if Saul gave money to a beggar by moving his arm, then his arm moved. Here rational and neuroscientific explanations do not have unrelated explananda because each aims at explaining (although under different descriptions) why an agent's arm moved, the one because of the reason for which he acted, the other because of neural processes. At this point congruence makes its reappearance as something that cannot merely be dissolved.

The other approach is just the opposite: it contends that the difference between the two types of explanation is so vanishingly small that they can be merged, thus making possible a substantive neuroscientific explanation of congruence. This is the view of physicalists who regard an agent's reasons as her beliefs and desires, which they conceive as internal to the agent and as both reasons for her action and causes of the bodily movements involved in the action. They then argue that the causal power of beliefs and desires is grounded in natural laws, which implies that they are either reducible to or supervenient on neural states, which means their explanatory role is essentially neuroscientific.

I restrict myself to two general objections to this view. The first is that it assimilates the two types of explanation much too closely, an assimilation encouraged by defective ways of distinguishing actions from mere bodily movements. Distinguishing them in terms of the one and the many (as in the first approach) takes them to be individuated differently but leaves them on the same level. The claim that it is intentionality – their being *about* something – that constitutes beliefs and desires as mental states is characterized so broadly that it misses the really distinctive features of the mental. The fundamental distinction, in my view, is that rational explanations presume descriptions of behavior that are normative and first person, whereas neuroscientific explanations presume descriptions of behavior as "colorless movements." These two types of description cannot be assimilated within one unified explanatory theory.

The second is that this approach takes it for granted that the only alternative to the first approach is to unify the two types of explanation. There is a *third alternative*, however, which maintains that not only is *formulating* an explanation a mode of intentional action but so is *explaining* itself. Explanation is not something that exists in the nature of things, with formulation being our only contribution; it is itself something we do. We explain by making things intelligible – by fitting various factors together in a pattern that shows how or why certain things came to be, ceased to be, changed, and so on. In many cases the relevant factors are already known, the explanatory task being to fit them together to render them intelligible. In other cases, we have to discover such factors, but they have explanatory value only against the background of theories, generalizations, or interpretations that are human creations. They are not always created *intentionally*, of course – those in the rational space of reasons typically are not – but those in the logical space of laws usually are. To understand congruence we need to reflect on the relation between two ways of explaining human behavior.

8. Consider Henry, who used his right arm to pull on a string attached to a light in order to turn on the lamp. His success shows that there was congruence between his intentional acting and the mere movements of his body and limbs. We can, I contend, give an account of this congruence without resort to any theory.

In giving a rational explanation of Henry's having pulled on the string, we assume he moved his right arm in so doing. We thereby put his act of having moved his arm in the logical space of reasons, giving it a normative and first-person description as intentional. Since he moved his arm, it must have moved, the latter being what von Wright called its *result*. This means that we have also put that *movement* in the logical space of reasons, giving it a description that is normative and first-person: it can be evaluated as appropriate (or the contrary), and it is intelligible to the agent. Indeed, we can say of the *movement* that it was intentional under that description.

A neuroscientific account of Henry' behavior, by contrast, describes it as "colorless movements," which characterizes in a specialized and abstractive way (leaving out their normative and intentional dimensions) the movements that were the result of his having moved his right arm. We have assumed that we can give a neuroscientific *explanation* of those movements, and this obviously will be acceptable only if it yields those movements as thus described – movements that are non-intentional under such description.

It is evident that a substantive-theoretical account of congruence would explain why the intentional movements of Henry's right arm in his moving it were congruent with the non-intentional movements of his right arm as described in neuroscience. But there is neither need nor place for any such account of *that* because those are the same movements, although differently described – in terms of the logical space of reasons, on the one hand, in terms of the logical space of laws, on the other. If Henry moved his right arm to pull on the string, then a neuroscientific explanation of his arm movements *could not fail* to be an explanation of the movements that are the result of his having moved his right arm because the arm movements explained (in the logical space of reasons) by his moving his arm *are* the movements we explain (in the logical space of laws) neuroscientifically. The movements are described differently, but the movements described non-intentionally by neuroscience in a specialized and abstractive way *are* the intentional movements Henry makes in moving his arm in order to pull on the string.

This confirms von Wright's view that the crucial point in these matters is action described as basic. What we take to be an agent's intentional action and the non-intentional movements of his body *can* fall apart. If Henry had set out to turn on the lamp but his upper body had (unknowingly) become paralyzed, he would have been unable to move his body so as to pull on the string. But the question of congruence would then be moot, because his behavior would not be his intentionally pulling on the string, even intentionally moving his arm. It might have presented itself as having the *form* of intentional action but it could be explained *only* as non-intentional bodily movement in the logical space of laws.

Consider Henry as unable for some reason to move his right arm and hence unable to pull the string as he usually does. He would presumably then use his left arm, and a rational explanation of his acting would refer to his moving that arm to pull the string. The movements he thus made could also be described in terms drawn from neuroscience and (let us assume) be given a neuroscientific explanation. But what the latter explained would clearly have to be the same movements Henry intentionally brought about in moving his left arm. The explanations drawn from the two logical spaces would be congruent, therefore, because the movements each explained would be the very same movements differently described.

The same is true if we consider Henry as suddenly disabled so that he is unable to pull on the string with either arm. In that case he could have used his teeth, and then a rational explanation of the way he moved his body to turn on the light would explain his having clenched his teeth on the string in order to pull it by moving his head. Those movements could also have been abstractively described as non-intentional and hence explained neuroscientifically, but that would be acceptable only if *what* were explained *were* the movements, described as intentional in the logical space of reasons, Henry made in acting as he did. He managed to pull on the string in spite of the fact that he could not move his arms, and hence congruence obtained between his acting and the non-intentional movements of his limbs since both types of explanation explained the same movements, not now of either of Henry's arms, but of his teeth and head.

In explaining an agent's behavior, therefore, congruence obtains *necessarily* if the agent's behavior can be given a rational explanation. If she failed to act intentionally as expected because she could not move her limbs in the way required for *that* action but was able to act in *another* way by making different movements, then the movements that resulted from her intentionally moving her body and limbs would also be different. But so would the neuroscientific descriptions of her behavior since they describe those same movements (in neuroscientific terms), and their neuroscientific explanation would be adequate only if it yielded the movements as thus described.

9. Those who reject this account of congruence will object to my taking rational explanations as basic and requiring that neuroscientific explanations conform to them. That gives rational explanations priority over neuroscientific ones, which is unacceptable, it will be objected, to anyone sympathetic to the achievement and status of physical sciences like neuroscience.

I grant that there are contexts where the explanations of physical science have priority, for example, explaining why agents capable of intentional action exist at all. That presumes the *global* supervenience of the space of reasons on physical science: destroy the physicalistic and you destroy everything else, and not vice versa, but that has no consequences for the nature and function of rational explanations.

When it comes to action, however, rational explanations take priority because a neuroscientific explanation of the bodily movements involved in action must first *identify* the movements. When an agent acts, his body moves in all sorts of ways that are not relevant to his acting; to identify which movements are relevant, we must determine what he is doing intentionally, hence put his action in the context of the logical space of reasons and, typically, identify the reason for which he acts. It is *those* movements, the ones identified by their role in the logical space of reasons, that we aim to explain (though described differently) neuroscientifically.

Defenders of the "standard story" in philosophy of action will reply that this gets it backwards: an account of action must begin with the non-intentional bodily movements of neuroscience and add on the beliefs and desires that, by causing them in the right way, constitute them as action, thus giving neuroscientific explanation priority over rational explanation. But surely such an account is coherent only if the relevant bodily movements are identifiable independently of the actions they are involved in. This can be done for bodily movements that result from neurological defects, electric shock, artificial stimulation of the brain, etc. and hence have *only* neuroscientific explanations. But such bodily movements are intentional under no description – they are *intentionless* – and hence are quite unlike those involved in intentional action, which are intentional under some description. Intentionless movements are the movements of diseased, degenerate, or disabled bodies and limbs, and hence their neuroscientific explanation is at best indirectly relevant to explaining the movements of healthy bodies and limbs. To explain the latter, we must first identify the actions in which they are involved.

The basic reason rational explanations are fundamental is that it is essential to the *nature* of our bodies and limbs to move intentionally (under a description) but not to move intentionlessly. The latter are the movements of bodies and limbs that are defective in some way, but the former are the movements of bodies and limbs that are healthy and hence expressive of their nature. An unhealthy body is a defective form of a healthy body; a healthy body is not a healthy form of an unhealthy body nor an unhealthy body plus something else. So intentionless movements are a defective form of bodily movements, but intentional bodily movements are not a form of intentionless movements nor intentionless movements plus something else. What is fundamental are intentional bodily movements and hence rational explanations are also fundamental.

Another way to put this point is to say that rational explanations specify *what* actions are, *why* we perform them, and *how* we do so. *What* Henry is doing is turning on the light, *why* he is doing it is to illumine the room, *how* he is doing it is by pulling on the light cord. Neuroscience plays no role in any of those claims. But we can also ask *how* Henry's arm *works* in pulling on the cord, thus asking about the mechanism that explains his arm movements. The mechanism must be in order for him to raise his arm, and we have neuroscientific accounts of what that involves, as well as of what defects in the mechanism would render him incapable of raising it.

The point is that a neuroscientific account of how our bodies and limbs work can be *applied* only if we first identify the actions, and hence the bodily movements, we want to explain in terms of a mechanism. To apply any general account, we must start with *what* is to be explained, hence start with an action as understood in the logical space of reasons, and then work backwards to the mechanism that explains the bodily movements involved in that action. We cannot begin with the movements yielded by a mechanistic explanation and then apply a rational explanation to them. We must rather begin with a particular action that has a rational explanation, and then construct a mechanistic explanation that yields the bodily movements involved in that action. Only if we already know the what, the why, and the how of an action can we identify anything whose mechanism we endeavor to specify, and that means that knowledge of the mechanism contributes nothing to the legitimacy and applicability of the what, the why, and the how of the logical space of reasons. A neuroscientific explanation is immensely significant, but the explanatory power of a rational explanation in no sense depends on it: if rational explanations were not legitimate and applicable, there would be no intentional actions and bodily movements whose mechanism we seek to specify.[12]

10. In conclusion I return to the question of compatibilism. Von Wright's discussion of the man getting out of his chair shows how rational and neuroscientific explanations of the same behavior are compatible. But in the philosophical tradition, compatibilism concerns the role of *determinism* in an account of the explanation of human action, and that is what needs discussion here.

I have argued that our concern should not be determinism *per se* but the broader thesis of the completeness of physics. The essential determinist claim that all things are fixed as a matter of natural law is not rejected by indeterminists but modified to claim, as John Dupré puts it, that "there is some quantitatively precise law governing the development of every situation,"[13] where the law can be *either universal or probabilistic*. Including the latter rules out the possibility of *predicting* the development of every situation but our interest is in *explanation*.

I have also argued that since rational explanations are not a matter of natural laws of either kind, it is irrelevant to an account of rational explanation *as such* whether one accepts the completeness of physics. But that does not mean the latter is irrelevant to the account of the *relation* of rational to neuroscientific explanation that emerged in my discussion of congruence. I maintain that an acceptable account of congruence gives priority to the former, so that it is a *criterion* for which muscle contractions and neural processes explain the agent's behavior (in the logical space of laws) that they yield behavior that (described in the logical space of reasons) is also explained as having been done intentionally. In this context neuroscientific explanations *necessarily* conform to rational.

This is the point at which the completeness of physics thesis is relevant. To accept the claim that there are quantitatively precise laws governing the development of every situation entails

---

[12]That von Wright shares this view in general is most evident in his reply to my article on his philosophy of action in the Schilpp-Hahn volume (p. 807), where he wrote that my view "hits the nail on the head" in its denying that "mere behavior is *basic* in a sense intentional action is not." Description of behavior as "mere behavior" is "a description of behavior which is 'drained' or 'stripped' of actionist connotations." It is a "new conceptualization of the situation" that presupposes a description of it "under the aspect of intentionality."

[13]John Dupré, *Human Nature and the Limits of Science* (Oxford University Press, 2001), p. 165.

that neuroscientific explanations of an agent's behavior will not *necessarily* conform to rational explanations. The reason is that, given the completeness of physics, the former appeal to factors that are not only fixed by natural law but have been so fixed from an indefinitely distant past. It may be logically possible that the factors that are so fixed will yield behavior that is also (describable as) what the agent did intentionally for a reason, but it cannot be a *criterion* for *which* neural processes explain an agent's behavior that they yield behavior that is also intelligible as an intentional action in the logical space of reasons.

Given the completeness of physics, then, explanation in terms of natural laws will have *absolute* priority over explanations in terms of reasons. This rules out what the fact of congruence clearly shows, namely, that the criterion for an explanation that renders mere bodily movement intelligible must begin with one that renders intentional action intelligible. There is good reason, therefore, to reject the completeness of physics thesis. This rejection is not grounded in reflection on our capacity to act *freely*. Acting freely requires acting intentionally but acting intentionally need not be acting freely. Whether an act is free is a question in the logical space of reasons not in the logical space of laws.

Let it be noted that my account of neuroscientific explanation is much too simple. My primary target has been the picture of neuroscience typically held by physicalist philosophers for whom the completeness of physics is a dominating motif. That picture is deficient not only in minimizing the role of the logical space of reasons but also in taking physics to be an all-embracing science. This is unfair to other sciences, biology in particular, whose explanations are often in terms of teleological factors, of the capacities – both innate and acquired – of organisms, of the role of the environment in shaping behavioral response, etc., none of which is reducible to natural law explanation. The explanations found in real neuroscience typically involve biological concepts, which means it is primarily a branch of biology rather than, as in the physicalist picture, a branch of physics, and hence, if biology is irreducible, stands as a counter example to the completeness of physics.

The latter has been attacked by philosophers of science in recent years for presenting an idealized picture of physics itself, one that confuses models of the phenomena with the actual workings of nature. Scientific models are abstractions, either theoretical structures or experimental set-ups constructed by investigators, of which neuroscientific accounts of human behavior are an example. Natural laws may apply with great exactness to these models, but they do not apply in any straightforward way to the real life behavior they model, even if we add numerous *ceteris paribus* conditions. While the laws of nature are indispensable to explaining phenomena in the logical space of laws, it is empirically unjustified to assert that all such phenomena can be explained by them. John Dupré puts the point forcefully:

> ...Far from knowing that these laws [of Newtonian mechanics] are universally true, we know that they are generally false. The assumption that the laws of Newtonian mechanics are, in some sense, carrying on regardless under the overlay of increasingly many interfering and counteracting forces is not merely sheer speculation, but actually of dubious intelligibility. What are these laws supposed to be doing, given that the objects, subject to such diverse other influences, are not behaving in any sense in accord with them? Certainly this can hardly be a good empirical ground for the alleged universality of microphysical laws.[14]

This means that although there are no *a priori* limits on *where* nomological explanations will run out or be inapplicable, there is every reason to think they are incomplete.

Von Wright wrote: "Only for *fragments* of the world *can* determinism ever become established. It is part of the logic of things here that the validity of the deterministic thesis for the *whole* world *must* remain an *open* question." [C&D,136] That is the spirit of my view, although I would reformulate it as follows: "The validity of the completeness of physics thesis for the *whole* world *must* remain an *open* question," not because the thesis might be true but because we do not know at which point it ceases to be true.

---

[14] *Human Nature and the Limits of Science*, p. 166.

Kantianism and von Wright's Compatibilism

Martina Reuter

This comment focuses on Frederick Stoutland's claim that von Wright's philosophy of action develops a Kantian type of compatibilism. The claim is philosophically interesting, not least because it touches on a broader question about the relation between Wittgensteinian philosophy and Kantian transcendentalism. Stoutland and von Wright are – at least in the texts discussed here – *not* Kantians in the sense that they defend a conception of morality based on the categorical imperative. Stoutland uses "Kantianism" to describe a conception of human action according to which an empirical world governed by causal law is compatible with autonomous agency, whereas in Kant's own philosophy autonomous agency is strictly tied to the "ought" posited by the moral law. In what follows, I shall illuminate some of the similarities as well as differences between the von Wright/Stoutland Kantianism and Kant's own point of view.

In what sense can Kant's moral philosophy be characterised as a compatibilism? As we know, Kant separated the phenomenal world governed by causality from the noumenal world of moral demand. In *Groundwork of the Metaphysics of Morals*, for example, he emphasised that as a rational being, the human being "has two standpoints from which he can regard himself and cognize laws for the use of his powers and consequently for all his actions; *first*, insofar as he belongs to the world of sense, under laws of nature (heteronomy); *second*, as belonging to the intelligible world, under laws which, being independent of nature, are not empirical but grounded merely in reason."[1]

According to Kant, the will is a cause of free action, but it is characteristically autonomous, i.e. an "uncaused cause" or "self-causing cause", and thereby something quite different from the causality of the phenomenal world. Kant wrote that *"Will* is a kind of causality of living beings insofar as they are rational, and *freedom* would be the property of such causality that it can be efficient independently of alien causes *determining* it, just as *natural necessity* is the property of the causality of all nonrational beings to be determined to activity by the influence of alien causes." [*GMM*: 52; *AK* 4: 446]

As we see from this quote, Kant conceived freedom as essentially bound to the capacity of reason. It is important to note that his concept of freedom – freedom from natural necessity – does not imply non-necessity but a different kind of necessity. The categorical imperative yields necessary demands by which the reasoned being regulates her sensuous inclinations. If humans were purely rational beings without sensuous inclination, they would follow the moral law automatically, without the need for an imperative. According to Kant the "moral *'ought'* is [man's] own necessary *'will'* as a member of an intelligible world, and is thought by him as 'ought' only insofar as he regards himself at the same time as a member of the world of sense" [*GMM*: 59; *AK* 4: 455]. Here we also see how strictly Kant's distinction between the intelligible world and the phenomenal world of sense is tied to the necessity of the moral "ought."

Kant's compatibilism thus combines two orders of necessity and ultimately two worlds: one governed by natural necessity and containing no uncaused events or autonomous causes, and the other composed of self-causing freedom and governed by reason alone. Kant struggled until the end of his philosophical life with the problem of how these two worlds are compatible, and it seems likely that the question played an essential role in the process that finally prompted him to write the *Critique of the Power of Judgment*,[2] which is concerned with the possibility of universally valid

---

[1]Immanuel Kant, *Groundwork of the Metaphysics of Morals*, ed. and trans. Mary Gregor (Cambridge: Cambridge University Press, 1998), p. 57, henceforth *GMM*; *Academie* edition vol. 4, p. 452, henceforth *AK*.

[2]See for example Paul Guyer, "Editor's introduction," in Immanuel Kant, *Critique of the Power of Judgment* (Cambridge: Cambridge University Press, 2000), p. xxii.

judgments of taste and beauty as an expression of the purposiveness of nature.

In the so called "Second Introduction" to the third *Critique*, Kant wrote that "the power of judgment provides the mediating concept between the concepts of nature and the concept of freedom, which makes possible the transition from the purely theoretical to the purely practical, from lawfulness in accordance with the former to the final end in accordance with the latter".[3] This mediating concept requires a transcendental deduction of its own, parallel to but more fundamental than the first and second deductions of the categories of knowledge and of the moral law. Kant's view is a *compatibilism* only to the extent that this third transcendental deduction succeeds and is able to combine the phenomenal and noumenal worlds in one unity.

Stoutland's elaboration of von Wright's position would appear to situate determinism and freedom in the same world and thus to be a true compatibilism. But this conclusion depends on how literally we understand the distinction Stoutland makes (following Wilfred Sellars and John McDowell) between "the logical space of reasons" and "the logical space of laws" for this metaphorical use of "space" at least seems to imply two separate worlds.

Philosophical metaphors are most often used to express what cannot be expressed unequivocally and we should note that Kant's use of "world" is as metaphorical as Stoutland's use of "logical space."[4] They both alternate between the more literal standpoint/perspective and the metaphorical world/space, and for both the argumentative role of the metaphor seems to be to emphasise the independence of the two standpoints and the two perspectives. It may be that the metaphorical "world" and "logical space" are intended to bridge two not so obviously compatible features of Kant's and Stoutland's models. This does not mean that the argument is invalid, but rather that the most interesting philosophical questions may well lurk behind the metaphor.

On the one hand, it is clear from Stoutland's presentation that descriptions of explanations according to law and those according to reason are intended to be about the *same* world. But on the other hand, they must be completely independent of each

---

[3]Immanuel Kant, *Critique of the Power of Judgment*, ed. Paul Guyer, trans. Paul Guyer and Eric Matthews (Cambridge: Cambridge University Press, 2000), 81-2. *AK* 5: 196.

[4]For a discussion of the philosophical role of metaphor, see my "The Significance of Gendered Metaphors", *NORA: Nordic Journal of Women's Studies* 14, no. 3 (2006): 151-169.

other, that is, involve different and unrelated explanations. I have difficulties grasping what this really implies, for example in Stoutland's rejection of Jaegwon Kim's critique. Stoutland writes:

> The view I defend does not violate the 'principle of explanatory exclusion' since if we manage to give two such independent and complete explanations for the same behavior, the explanations come from different logical spaces. This implies that, although we explain the same behavior, there is not, as far as Kim's principle is concerned, a single explanandum because (as with explanation generally) in giving an explanation of behavior, we must explain it as described, which in this case means as described in the logical space of reasons and given a rational explanation or as described in the logical space of laws and given a nomological explanation. [p. 73]

What really follows from Stoutland's claim? I am troubled most by what it means to speak about behaviour described and explained in one way being the *same* as behaviour described in another way: what is this *same* behaviour?

I believe that Stoutland and von Wright would both give the realist answer that the behaviour is the same because it is the same event, the same bodily movements, in the world. But how can the same movements in the same world *be* both determined and not determined? It is one thing to claim that an action can be described and explained in two ways and another to make the *ontological* claim that the action can *be* in two ways.

One way out is to claim that determinism belongs to the order of explanation and not to the world in itself, so that events as such are *neither* determined nor undetermined. Put in a more strictly Kantian terminology this would be to claim that we *cannot know* whether the event conceived as a thing in itself is subject to causal determinism (in Kant's terminology to natural necessity). This answer implies a transcendental framework: we have to conceive causality as a category of knowledge and not as a property of things in themselves. It is not evident how well this step fits with the realist intentions of Stoutland and von Wright.

Stoutland's rejection of the completeness of physics and von Wright's claim that determinism can be established only for "*fragments* of the world" both seem to broach a Kantian position regarding the necessary limits of knowledge. Both von Wright's original formulation and Stoutland's reformulation – "the validity of the completeness of physics thesis for the *whole* world *must* remain an *open* question" [p. 82] – come close to Kant's claim that our knowledge of causal relations is restricted to the phenomenal world. The completeness of physics is beyond the possibility of knowledge and can thus not be used as a basis for explanations.

Stoutland rejects the completeness of physics thesis in order to save the congruence between explanations based on reasons and explanations based on natural laws; otherwise explanations in terms of natural laws would have absolute priority over explanations in terms of reason. He writes that the completeness of physics "rules out what the fact of congruence clearly shows, namely, that the criterion for an explanation that renders mere bodily movement intelligible must begin with one that renders intentional action intelligible. There is good reason, therefore, to reject the completeness of physics thesis" [p. 81]. The structure of his argument is transcendental in taking its starting-point in "the fact of congruence" and arguing against the completeness of physics by claiming that it contradicts the conditions for the possibility of congruence.

There is an interesting similarity between the primacy Stoutland gives to the intelligibility of intentional action over mere bodily movement and the primacy Kant gave to practical reason over speculative reason. In the *Critique of Practical Reason* Kant argued that we must give practical reason primacy in order to save the integrity of both kinds of reason in relation to each other. The practical use of reason is claimed to consist in "the determination of the *will* with respect to the final and complete end"[5] and thus is very similar to Stoutland's explanations based on reasons (or the intentionality of action).

This similarity is limited[6] but quite interesting because it shows that Kant, von Wright and Stoutland all conceive it necessary to give primacy to practical and purposive reason over theoretical and merely explanatory reason. Kant concluded the section quoted above by claiming that "one cannot require pure practical reason to be subordinated to speculative reason [...], since all interest is ultimately practical and even that of speculative reason

---

[5]Immanuel Kant, *Critique of Practical Reason*, ed. and trans. Mary Gregor (Cambridge: Cambridge University Press, 1997), p. 100, henceforth *PR*; *AK* 5: 120.

[6]Kant's speculative reason is of course profoundly different from a physical description of bodily movement, but is in this context explicitly related to the realm of theoretical cognition (*AK* 5: 120).

is only conditional and is complete in practical use alone" [*PR*: 102; *AK* 5: 121]. Here Kant clearly states the primacy of purposive interest over instrumental means in a way that fits well with Stoutland's example, which describes Henry's intention to get the gate open by pulling on a bell and gives this intention explanatory primacy over the physical movements involved [p. 75].

Stoutland's appeal to congruence is able to save his realism only by using an argument based on the conditions for the possibility of congruence. Thus there seems to be a sense in which his (and von Wright's) realism rests on a claim about the conditions and limits of the possibility of knowledge. This claim differs from a strictly Kantian position because he emphasises that "there are no *a priori* limits on *where* nomological explanations will run out or be inapplicable" [p. 82]. Stoutland claims that we know *necessarily*, and thus a priori, *that* nomological explanations have limits, but not *where* these limits must be drawn.

The a priori basis of Kant's philosophy is both broader and deeper: his claim about the limits of knowledge and his distinction between the phenomenal and noumenal worlds rest on transcendental deductions, which are by their very nature synthetic a priori justifications. Kant's structure of justification requires a priori necessity in the noumenal as well as in the phenomenal realm. As we saw above, Kant's compatibilism attempts to reconcile two orders of necessity, natural necessity and the necessity of rational will that characterises human beings as members of the intelligible world.[7] Stoutland's and von Wright's compatibilism is best described as an attempt to reconcile natural necessity and contingent human intention and action. Whereas Kant's conception of the noumenal is dependent on the a priori *pre*scriptive nature of the moral law, von Wright's and Stoutland's "space of reasons" is *a posteriori de*scriptive, consisting of explanations of phenomena under some description. (It might well be that Kant's and von Wright/Stoutland's conceptions of necessity differ also in that Kant is a more faithful advocate of Newtonian physics.)

---

[7]The questions of what Kant's conception of a "necessary will" really means, how it can be simultaneously necessary and free, as well as how it can be compatible with Kant's conception of natural causal necessity, are topics that have given rise to huge amounts of interpretative and critical discussions. I will not even try to take a stance on these issues. For a competent overview of some of the most pertinent problems as well as for further references, see J. B. Schneewind, "Autonomy, obligation, and virtue: An overview of Kant's moral philosophy," in Paul Guyer, *The Cambridge Companion to Kant* (Cambridge: Cambridge University Press, 1992), pp. 328-33.

If we focus on the question of necessity, it is evident that von Wright's and Stoutland's compatibilism is *not* Kantian. When we look at the difference between them, the question of necessity is philosophically more significant than the fact that von Wright and Stoutland do not advocate a conception of morality based on the categorical imperative. The latter is in this context secondary, because contrary to Kant, Stoutland and von Wright do not need — or even want to have — prescriptive necessity in the space of reasons. (It is, of course, also secondary because they focus on a theory of action, not on ethics.)

I want to conclude by pointing at some similarities between the Kantian features in von Wright's and Stoutland's conception of action and the phenomenological reformulation of transcendental philosophy. Like Kant, Edmund Husserl takes his starting point in the question of how knowledge and experience are possible, but he substitutes Kant's transcendental deduction as a method of justification with the method he calls the transcendental reduction. According to Husserl, the task of philosophy is not to justify, but to *clarify* the possibility of knowledge. Broadly speaking he explicates what it *means* to claim that knowledge is justified. The phenomenologist studies how the world is "given" to the experiencing subject in different kinds of experience. Most significantly, this is a study of the structures of intentionality, of how human experience is directed towards the world and is "about" the world. Descriptions of experience play an essential role in phenomenology, and Husserl turned his philosophical attention from the justification of the possibility of experience to descriptions of the structures of experience. He strengthened the role of investigating the subjective aspect of experience. Whereas Kant's deduction justifies a universally valid standpoint, Husserl reveals a particular standpoint, which is dependent on how it is embedded in the world. This means that objectivity is secured by inter-subjectivity, by the coming together of perspectives, and not by universal validity as such.[8]

---

[8]See Edmund Husserl, *Cartesian Meditations*, trans. Dorion Crains (Dordrecht: Martinus Nijhoff publishers, 1960), especially § 41 for Husserl's account of the relation between Kant's and his own transcendental philosophy; for good accounts of the relation between phenomenology and Kantian philosophy, see Michael Hammond, Jane Howart & Russel Keat, *Understanding Phenomenology* (Oxford: Blackwell, 1991), pp. 84-95, 265-71; and Dan Zahavi, "Philosophy, Psychology, Phenomenology," in Sara Heinämaa & Martina Reuter (eds.), *Psychology and Philosophy: Inquiries into the Soul from Late Scholasticism to Contemporary Thought* (Dordrecht: Springer, 2008);

Husserl's critical reworking of Kant's philosophy includes a critique of the latter's concept of the a priori. In the posthumously published manuscript known as *The Crises of European Sciences*, Husserl distinguishes what he calls the "objective-logical a priori" and the "a priori of the life-world" and claims that the latter is primary in relation to the former, which is a mere abstraction from our actual experience. Husserl writes:

> The bodies familiar to us in the life-world are actual bodies, but not bodies in the sense of physics. The same thing is true of causality and of spatiotemporal infinity. [These] categorical features of the life-world have the same names but are not concerned, so to speak, with the theoretical idealizations and the hypothetical substructions of the geometrician and the physicist. As we already know, physicists, who are men like other men, know themselves as living in the life-world... Just as other projects, practical interests, and their realizations belong to the life-world, presuppose it as ground, and enrich it with their activity, so it is with science, too, as a human project and praxis. And this includes... everything objectively a priori, with its necessary reference back to a corresponding a priori of the life-world. This reference-back is one of a founding of validity [Geltungsfundierung].[9]

Kant's mistake, according to Husserl, was that he did not realise how his objective-logical a priori presupposes the a priori of the life-world, i.e. presupposes an experienced a priori [*CES*, pp. 114-18]. Husserl's a priori of the life-world radically reformulates the meaning of a priori by making it dependent on experience: we can recognise necessary a priori truths (e.g. mathematical truths) and separate them from a posteriori facts only because we are beings who experience and share a world. Husserl continues to hold that experience shows a general structure and some features that do

---

for a study of Husserl's critical reinterpretation of Kant's thought in the realm of moral philosophy, see Sara Heinämaa, "Husserl's Ethics of Renewal: Persons and Capacities", (*The Annual Review of the Phenomenological Association of Japan*, vol. 24, 2008). I thank Heinämaa for many helpful discussions on the relation between phenomenology and Kantian philosophy.

[9]Edmund Husserl, *The Crisis of European Sciences and Transcendental Philosophy*, trans. David Carr (Evanston: Northwestern University Press), p. 140, henceforth *CES*.

not vary culturally. For example, all humans identify shape and motion [*CES*, p. 139].

There are interesting parallels between Husserl's and von Wright/Stoutland's ways of tackling questions related to the limits of knowledge and the range of necessity. Most evident is the shared focus on description and clarification rather than justification. Further, Husserl and Stoutland both conceive the a priori as intertwined with experience, though it may be that the differences between their conceptions of *how* the priori depend on experience are more significant than the similarities. The main point with Husserl's discussion of the a priori in *Crisis* is to claim that we can understand the *meaning* of a priori necessity only because we experience necessity in the life-world. Stoutland does not so much question (or ground) the Kantian concept of a priori as claim that its range is limited. He gives empirical science the task of deciding which phenomena can be explained by natural laws. From a phenomenological point of view this limitation of the a priori in favour of the a posteriori is so drastic that it appears as naïve realism.

von Wright and the Logic of the Practical Syllogism

Krister Segerberg

Georg Henrik von Wright was a seminal philosopher: seeds he sowed now grow in many soils. Not least has his philosophy inspired a number of developments in philosophical logic. The most recent example, which he did not live to see, is the modal logic of *cæteris paribus* preference, a take-off from his prohairetic logic (see [1] and [4]).

von Wright was a logician as well as a philosopher. But he did not try to formalize his ideas about the practical syllogism. Indeed, to do so would not have been a simple matter. In this paper some reflexions on that topic are offerred.

The anatomy of the practical syllogism

The practical syllogism

A syllogism is an inference pattern with a number of premises and a conclusion. In the simplest case the premises are two:

$$\frac{A \quad B}{C}$$

In the well-known ordinary syllogisms, A, B (the *premises*) and C (the *conclusion*) are propositions (statements). The propositions have a certain formal structure, each proposition involving a quantifier (all, some, no) as well as a copula (is, isn't, are, aren't). In the less well known practical syllogisms, A is a *premise of the good*, B a *premise of the possible* (to use Aristotle's terminology), and C is an *action* (or—in the literature, almost always—a proposition describing an action). Here is one of Aristotle's own examples ([8] p. 40):

> I should make something good.
> A house is something good.
> At once I make a house.

And here is one of von Wright's:

> I want to make the hut inhabitable.
> Unless I heat the hut, it will not become inhabitable.
> Therefore I must heat the hut.

There are many variations on this theme.

A logician wishing to formalize these types of practical syllogism has several formal languages to choose between. One that seems congenial is that of modal logic.

The premise of the good

The premise of the good will be written on the form $\mathbf{W}\phi$, where ϕ stands for a proposition; $\mathbf{W}$ is to be read either as "the agent wants that" (the third-person perspective) or "I want that" (the first-person perspective).

Wants come in many forms, of course, from hard to soft. Without claiming to be in accord with ordinary language usage let us use "intention" for hard wants and "desire" or "mere desire" for soft wants. Accordingly we distinguish between *hard syllogisms* and *soft syllogisms*, depending on whether the premise of the good is hard (the want is an intention) or soft (the want is a mere desire).

The premise of the possible

The premise of the possible will be written on the form $\mathbf{B}\theta$, which may be read either as "the agent believes that θ" (the third-person perspective) or "I believe that θ" (the first-person perspective). Here θ is a proposition. The question is only, what proposition?

One striking difference between the two examples given above is the way the premise of the possible in formulated. Using ϕ and α to stand for propositions and actions, respectively, we see that in the first case the premise of the possible is of the logical form "ϕ if α", while in the second case it is of the logical form "ϕ only if α". The former example may be said to be of the *if-type*; all Aristotle's examples are of this type. The second should accordingly be said to be of the *only-if-type*; this is the only type with which von Wright is concerned.[1]

---

[1] The reason for this restriction is presumably the view that only syllogisms of the only-if-type could possibly be regarded as valid. Kenny regards

In the formal language we are building (or at least outlining) let us agree to write (ϕ/α) for "ϕ if α" and $(\phi\backslash\alpha)$ for "ϕ only if α". A tentative formalization of the two types of practical syllogism is then

$$\frac{\mathbf{W}\phi \quad \mathbf{B}(\phi/\alpha)}{\alpha} \qquad \frac{\mathbf{W}\phi \quad \mathbf{B}(\phi\backslash\alpha)}{\alpha}$$

The conclusion

As written here the conclusion is an action; for the purposes of this paper, this choice seems appropriate. But in the literature the conclusion is almost always rendered by some proposition to the effect that the agent performs or must perform or should perform the action in question. We could of course try to introduce a new agentive operator such as **does**, where **does** α means something like "the agent does α" or "the agent sets himself to do α" (the third-person perspective) or "I do α" or "I set myself to do α" (the first-person perspective). To do so would be to follow von Wright. However, from a formal point of view such an extension invites problems, technical as well as interpretational. (Cf. [**11**].)

Upshot

We have arrived at the following—simplest—form of the practical syllogism:

$$\frac{\mathbf{W}\phi \quad \mathbf{B}(\phi\cdots\alpha)}{\alpha}$$

where $\phi\cdots\alpha$ stands, ambiguously, for one of the alternatives listed above: either ϕ/α or $\phi\backslash\alpha$. (Thus "$\cdots$" is an auxiliary, not a formal, symbol.)

∗Towards a formal analysis

It is tempting to stop at this stage of the analysis of the syllogistic schema. However, to do so would be miss many distinctions. Unfortunately, a full formal analysis is fraught with difficulty and so far has eluded the ambitions of at least this author. Nevertheless, here are some musings.[2]

If I want to go from Stockholm to Uppsala, I can choose between several *ways of doing* this: by train, by bus, or by car.

---

this restriction as "an impoverishment of the scope of practical reasoning". ([**6**], p. 71)

[2]The asterisk in the section heading indicates that this section may be omitted by readers not interested in technical matters. (At least on a first reading!)

Going by bicycle or walking are theoretical, if unrealistic, possibilities, as are skating and skiing in cold winters. These possibilities illustrate the concept of *subaction* or *subevent*.[3] Going to Uppsala by car is a subaction of the more inclusive action of going to Uppsala. And going to Uppsala in a Volvo is a subaction of both.

The *execution* or *carrying out* of an action or the *occurrence* of an event is a different matter. Actually going to Uppsala by car on a certain day is a specific particular that can be described in boring detail: the time of day, the weather, the colour and condition of the car, the duration of the ride, etc. A particular execution of going to Uppsala by car would also be an execution of going to Uppsala; but not all executions of going to Uppsala are executions of going to Uppsala by car.

Thus the distinction between action and execution of an action, like the distinction between event and occurrence of the event, is a distinction between type and token. It is related to the distinction between event and outcome in probability theory, where an event is identified with a set of possible outcomes.

In the formal object language built here, we will use the symbol $\leqslant$ for the notion of subaction or subevent. We will not represent executions in the object language. But this does not mean that we cannot talk about them in the meta-language. For example, we consider that

> $\alpha \leqslant \beta$ is true on a certain occasion if and only if every execution of α, on that occasion, would count as an execution of β.

And we are happy to quantify over the set of executions that are available on a certain occasion.[4] Thus we consider that

> $\forall \xi \theta$ is true on a certain occasion if and only if, for every event letter γ, θ_ξ^γ is true on that occasion,

> $\exists \xi \theta$ is true on a certain occasion if and only if for some event letter γ, θ_ξ^γ is true on that occasion,[5]

---

[3]In this paper we are vague about the difference between the concepts 'action' and 'event'.

[4]This move raises theoretical problems. But, as von Wright sometimes says about a problem he has identified: "*It* will not be discussed in the present work." ([**15**], p. 118)

[5]We assume that every event is named by at least one event letter.

where θ_ξ^γ is the result of replacing every free occurrence of ξ in θ by an occurrence of γ. We also introduce new operators $[\alpha]$ and $\langle \alpha \rangle$ with the following understanding:

> $[\alpha]\theta$ is true on a certain occasion if and only if θ would be true upon the completion of every possible execution of α.
>
> $\langle \alpha \rangle \theta$ is true on a certain occasion if and only if θ would be true upon the completion of some execution of α.

With the help of these new concepts we can offer four different readings of "ϕ if α":

(i) $\forall \xi (\xi \leq \alpha \to [\xi]\phi)$ every way of doing α will achieve ϕ

(ii) $\forall \xi (\xi \leq \alpha \to \langle \xi \rangle \phi)$ every way of doing α may achieve ϕ

(iii) $\exists \xi (\xi \leq \alpha \wedge [\xi]\phi)$ some way of doing α will achieve ϕ

(iv) $\exists \xi (\xi \leq \alpha \wedge \langle \xi \rangle \phi)$ some way of doing α may achieve ϕ

It would not be difficult to offer examples of all of them.

For "ϕ only-if α" we only wish to suggest two readings:

$$\forall \xi (\neg (\xi \leq \alpha) \to \neg [\xi]\phi)$$
$$\forall \xi (\neg (\xi \leq \alpha) \to \neg \langle \xi \rangle \phi)$$

which of course are logically equivalent to

(v) $\forall \xi ([\xi]\phi \to \xi \leq \alpha)$ only subactions of α are sure to achieve ϕ

(vi) $\forall \xi (\langle \xi \rangle \phi \to \xi \leq \alpha)$ only subactions of α can achieve ϕ

But our formal language is still poor; we also need temporal operators:

> $[\mathsf{F}]\theta$ is true on a certain occasion, with regard to a certain development, if and only if θ is true for on every future occasion of that development,
>
> $\langle \mathsf{F} \rangle \theta$ is true on a certain occasion, with regard to a certain development, if and only if θ is true for on some future occasion of that development.

And "historical" operators:[6]

> $[H]\theta$ is true on a certain occasion if and only if
> θ is true for every possible future development,
>
> $\langle H\rangle\theta$ is true on a certain occasion if and only if
> θ is true for some possible future development.

If in Procrustean fashion we wish to try to fit Aristotle's practical syllogisms into this regimented format, there are evidently four possibilities:

$$\frac{\mathbf{W}\phi \quad \mathbf{B}[\alpha][H]\langle F\rangle\phi}{\alpha} \qquad \frac{\mathbf{W}\phi \quad \mathbf{B}[\alpha]\langle H\rangle\langle F\rangle\phi}{\alpha}$$

$$\frac{\mathbf{W}\phi \quad \mathbf{B}\langle\alpha\rangle[H]\langle F\rangle\phi}{\alpha} \qquad \frac{\mathbf{W}\phi \quad \mathbf{B}\langle\alpha\rangle\langle H\rangle\langle F\rangle\phi}{\alpha}$$

If we try to fit von Wright into this scheme of things, the best we can do is perhaps this pattern:

$$\frac{\mathbf{W}\phi \quad \mathbf{B}\forall\xi([\xi][H]\langle F\rangle\phi \to \xi \leqslant \alpha)}{\alpha}$$

It might be suggested that a better representation of von Wright's understanding of practical inference would be

$$\frac{\mathbf{W}\phi \quad \mathbf{B}\forall\xi([\xi][H]\langle F\rangle\phi \to \xi = \alpha)}{\alpha}$$

where $\xi = \alpha$ stands for the conjunction of $\xi \leqslant \alpha$ and $\alpha \leqslant \xi$. But that suggestion seems too demanding.

It would simplify matters if we were to limit ourselves to actions with respect to which the agent is in full control. The corresponding formal condition is that the schema $\langle\alpha\rangle\phi \leftrightarrow [\alpha]\phi$ be valid: ϕ might be true after an action has been performed if and only if ϕ would be true after that action has been performed. But for the purpose of analysing the general case, such simplification should be resisted.

There are still further possibilities of extending the object language. For example, we have said nothing about probability. But enough is enough, at least for now.

---

[6] "Historical", since a development may be thought of as a history.

The logic of jumping to a conclusion

Before continuing, let us contemplate an example of nonmonotonic logic, namely, Ray Reiter's default logic.[7] Theoretical computer scientists—who in interesting ways engage in many questions that have been the traditional concern of philosophers—have developped a new form a reasoning called *nonmonotonic logic*, a discipline that may be described as the theory of rational ways of jumping to a conclusion. The connexion with the topic of this paper is the idea that a logic of the practical syllogism may perhaps be treated as kind of a nonmonotonic logic.

Here is an example that goes back to the computer scientist John McCarthy. You are told that Tweety is a bird; and that is all you are told. You naturally infer that Tweety can fly. This conclusion may be correct—most birds can fly. But it may be wrong: Tweety may turn out to be a penguin.

A really thoughtful person, careful not to rush to judgment, would exercise caution and not draw an inference that did not apply to all species of birds. But even such caution is not be enough: Tweety is a particular bird, and in the absence of further information one doesn't know what she has been through and what her present condition is. Perhaps this particular Tweety (a swallow with a broken wing, say) will never fly again.

It may be suggested that there are really two moral lessons of this example, never mind that they are in conflict with one another. One moral lesson is that a really thoughtful person will not draw any conclusion from the information available that is not logically implied by it. Another moral lesson is that even a really thoughtful person will sometimes do well to jump to a conclusion, only it must be done sensibly. According to the latter moral, there is an art of rushing to judgment: the logic of jumping to a conclusion. The first moral lesson accords with classical logic, which is congenial to reasoning in mathematics and the exact sciences. The second moral lesson is that we often reason about complex matters in a simplified way. The question arises whether there is a logic describing how such reasoning can be carried out in a responsible manner. Nonmonotonic logic, is one answer. In a classic paper [9] the computer scientist Ray Reiter has proposed

---

[7]See [9]. For two relevant discussions of Reiter's logic, see [7] and [10]. In the latter work, Reiter's default logic is formulated as a dynamic doxastic logic.

his own kind of nonmonotonic logic, default logic, which will be of particular interest here.[8]

Unlike ordinary classical logic, Reiter's default logic allows the agent "to fill in some gaps in the knowledge base, i. e., to further complete the underlying [...] theory so as permit the inferences necessary to act." Jumping to the conclusion that Tweety can fly is typically correct and may be useful in the situation you are in. The fact that in untypical cases this kind of jumping to a conclusion can lead one astray may be a risk that is worth taking or even ought to be taken. As Reiter says, "there will arise situations in which it is necessary to act, to draw inferences, despite the incompleteness of the knowledge base."

In the simplest case a default rule in Reiter's logic is an inference rule of the type

$$\phi : \psi \ / \ \theta$$

Here ϕ is the *premise* and θ the *conclusion*, while ψ is called the *justification*; it is required that ϕ be logically consistent with ψ.[9] Rewriting this rule on the format used above would yield a result such as this:

1. I believe that ϕ.
2. I have no reason to believe that ψ is not true.
3. Therefore θ.

In the language of modal logic:[10]

$$\frac{\mathbf{B}\phi \qquad \neg \mathbf{B} \neg \psi}{\mathbf{B}\theta}$$

Or in a form closer to the rules considered above:

$$\frac{\mathbf{B}\phi \qquad \neg \mathbf{B} \neg \psi}{+\theta}$$

where $+\theta$ represents a *doxastic action*, "expansion by θ", which is well-known from the theory of belief revision. (Expansion by θ consists in adding to one's current set of beliefs the belief that θ and then closing under logical consequence.)

---

[8] A logic is said to be *monotonic* if it satisfies the following test: whenever Γ is a set of formulæ and ϕ is a formula, then Γ implies ϕ in the logic in question only if Γ' also implies ϕ in that logic, where Γ' is any formula set that includes Γ. Classical logic passes this test and hence is monotonic. But default logic does not: adding premises may destroy an implication.

[9] In the general case, a default rule in [9] is of the type $\phi : \psi_1, \cdots, \psi_n/\theta$. In this case it is required that the premise ϕ be logically consistent with each of the justifications $\psi_1, \cdots, \psi_n$.

[10] Here **B** represents defeasible belief. See [10] for further comments.

The idea is that, according to this particular rule, from ϕ ("Tweety is a bird") you may derive θ ("Tweety can fly") provided that ψ ("There is nothing to indicate that Tweety is not a typical bird"). In other words, the justification you need in order to apply this rule is that it is consistent with everything you know that Tweety is a normal specimen of a kind of creature for which flying is natural. This particular example has been flogged to near death, but it survives since it is so apposite. Jumping to conclusion is a necessity of real life. As Reiter says, sometimes we just have to act.

Jumping to an action

In Reiter's default logic, agents are allowed to jump to a conclusion. Jumping to a conclusion, jumping to an action—perhaps there is some connexion between the logic of the practical syllogism and nonmonotonic logic. In this section we will explore this idea.

What actions look like

There is a distinction in von Wright's philosophy between 'event' and 'action' (or "act", in von Wright's own terminology) that is fundamental.

> It would not be right, I think, to call acts a kind or species of events. An act *is* not a change in the world. But many acts may quite appropriately be described as the bringing about or *effecting* ('at will') of a change. To act is, in a sense, to *interfere* with the course of nature. ([**13**] p.35f.)

But events and actions are of course intimately connected. In fact, they may "look" the same:

> When we say that an individual event happens on a certain occasion we may regard this occasion for the happening of *the event as constituted by two successive occasions for the obtaining of certain states of affairs.* [...] Similarly, when we say that an individual act is done on a certain occasion we may regard this occasion for *the doing of the act as constituted by the two successive occasions for the corresponding individual event.* ([**13**] p. 37, emphasis added.)

In fact, not only may an action and the corresponding event "look" the same, also two different actions may "look" the same:

> The act of opening a window and that of cooling a room are *logically distinct*, because of the nature of their results. But there is a sense in which the two acts may be said to 'look' exactly alike. The sense in which they look alike is that the *activity* involved in performing the two acts may be identical. ([13] p. 41)

How can we express in our formalism the idea that an event and an action can "look" the same even though they are different kinds of things? And that two actions can "look" the same even though they are different actions? In order to do so we must extend our formal language.

Let $\mathcal{R}_\alpha^\phi$ be any practical syllogism of the kind considered in this paper:

$$\frac{\mathbf{W}\phi \quad \mathbf{B}(\phi \cdots \alpha)}{\alpha}$$

This syllogism can be seen as a rule that can be applied if ϕ represents something the agent wants and, furthermore, the agent has the relevant belief $\phi \cdots \alpha$. Furthermore, if it is applied, α will be performed. In fact, $\mathcal{R}_\alpha^\phi$ is applied by performing α. For each rule $\mathcal{R}_\alpha^\phi$, add propositional operators $[\mathcal{R}_\alpha^\phi]$ and $\langle \mathcal{R}_\alpha^\phi \rangle$ with the following suggested readings:

> $[\mathcal{R}_\alpha^\phi]\theta$ is true on a certain occasion if and only if
> after the application of $\mathcal{R}_\alpha^\phi$, it will be the case that θ,
> $\langle \mathcal{R}_\alpha^\phi \rangle \theta$ is true on a certain occasion if and only if
> after the application of $\mathcal{R}_\alpha^\phi$, it may be the case that θ.[11]

By "after the application", read "immediately after the completion of the application".

Among things to be considered is that many actions take time, and that actions taking time may be interrupted or interfered with. Suppose that the agent has a want represented by $\mathbf{W}\phi$

---

[11] Apologies for the ambiguity of ordinary language. What is meant is, in the former case, that no matter how the application of $\mathcal{R}_\alpha^\phi$ turns out, ϕ is true on completion, whereas in the latter case, there is at least one way things can turn out such that ϕ is true on completion.

and a belief represented by $\mathbf{B}(\phi \cdots \alpha)$. Then what is true of the environment after the application of $\mathcal{R}_\alpha^\phi$ is completed is the same as what is true after the execution of α. This is different from von Wright's notion of the agent setting himself to do α, a notion that would seem to correspond to the agent committing himself to applying $\mathcal{R}_\alpha^\phi$, a notion that in our current formalism perhaps can be rendered (in context) as **does** α, where **does** is the operator discussed in Section 1.[12]

One new valid schema is

$$\langle \mathcal{R}_\alpha^\phi \rangle \top \to (\mathbf{W}\phi \wedge \mathbf{B}(\phi \cdots \alpha)).[13]$$

This schema "says" that the rule $\mathcal{R}_\alpha^\phi$ is applicable only in a situation in which the agent wants ϕ to be the case and believes that (what is represented by the formula) $\phi \cdots \alpha$ is the case.

Another valid schema is

$$\langle \mathcal{R}_\alpha^\phi \rangle \top \to ([\mathcal{R}_\alpha^\phi]\rho \leftrightarrow [\alpha]\rho), \text{ if } \rho \text{ is a real formula.}$$

This schema "says" that when $\mathcal{R}_\alpha^\phi$ is applicable, then the effects of applying it are the same as the effects of the event α occurring. This is in agreement with one of the observations above. And the following valid schema is in agreement with the example involving the opening of a window and the cooling of the room, which "says" that two actions may "look" the same:

$$\langle \mathcal{R}_\alpha^\phi \rangle \top \wedge \langle \mathcal{R}_\alpha^\psi \rangle \top \to ([\mathcal{R}_\alpha^\phi]\rho \leftrightarrow [\mathcal{R}_\alpha^\psi]\rho), \text{ where } \rho$$
is a real formula.

Notice that our formalism is compatible with "over-determination".[14]

Validity

Validity is a semantic concept. Normally one would say of an argument schema that it is valid if, for every possible argument that is an instance of the argument schema, if the premises are true, then also the conclusion is true ("must be true"). If this view is generalized, the validity of a practical syllogism would consist

---

[12]The parenthetical remark "in context" hides a difficulty. Suppose we introduce an operator $\bigstar_\alpha^\phi$ to represent the agent's commitment to the application of $\mathcal{R}_\alpha^\phi$. Would the schema $\bigstar_\alpha^\phi \to$ **does** α or the schema $\bigstar_\alpha^\phi \to$ [H]⟨F⟩**does** α be valid? Or is there is gap between commitment and real action? We return to this question below.

[13]This conditional can be turned into a valid biconditional by expanding our terminology and adding a conjunct on the right to express that it is possible for the agent to do α.

[14]"Assume the door is shut but opens "of itself" at the very moment I am about to open it." ([**15**] pp.125ff.)

in the action "following" from the premises: if the premises are true, the action is done ("must be done").

Can practical syllogisms be valid in anything like this sense?[15] von Wright thought so:

> We must, I think, accept that practical syllogisms are logically valid pieces of argumentation in their own right. Accepting them means in fact an enlargement of the province of logic. We cannot reduce the practical syllogisms to other patterns of valid inference. ([**14**] p. 167f.)

For our discussion it will be helpful to consider the artificial agents one finds in theoretical computer science. In Michael Wooldridge's well-known textbook there is the following definition of a planner:

> A planner is a system that takes as input representations of the following.
>
> (1) A *goal, intention* or [...] a *task*. This is something that the agent wants to achieve [...] or a state of affairs that the agent wants to maintain or avoid [...].
> (2) The *current state of the environment*—the agent's *beliefs*.
> (3) The *actions* available to the agent.
>
> As output, a planning algorithm generates a *plan* [...]. This is a course of action—a 'recipe'. If the planning algorithm does its job correctly, then if the agent executes this plan ('follows the recipe') from a state in which the world is as described in (2), then once the plan has been completely executed, the goal/intention/task described in (1) will be carried out. ([**12**], p. 70)

The brief quotation outlines a theory, an outline that can be completed in several ways and thus give rise to different theories. To formalize one of those theories would be a task of the same kind as to formalize a theory of Euclidean geometry or Newtonian mechanics. In all those cases the concept of validity is theory dependent, going beyond pure logic. Logical validity is a stronger concept than validity in a theory.

---

[15]Kenny [**6**] outlines a theory of validity designed for practical reasoning. But his sense of validity is different.

For our discussion it will also be helpful to consider a slogan, coined by P. R. Cohen and H. Levesque in [**2**] but going back to the philosopher Michael Bratman: intention is choice plus commitment. Actually, a slogan we find even more helpful (for our purposes) is a variation:

$$intention = desire + commitment.$$

The next three sections are structured in accordance with this modified Bratman-Cohen-Levesque slogan.

Hard wants: intention

Intention is a demanding concept. In particular, intention demands action, if not immediately at least under conditions that von Wright himself has done his best to specify. If the agent has an intention to act now, we expect him to act now. So if $\mathbf{W}\phi$ is read as "it is the agent's intention that ϕ", we run into the problem of the man who intends to run to the train but does not, and the problem of the would-be-assassin who freezes and does not carry out his mission. In the former case (written several years before the latter) von Wright accepts that the man changed his intention: "He of course *wanted* to be at the station in time. He still *wishes* he could have been. [...] But he no longer wants this as an *end of his action*. Therefore he is not moved to act." ([**14**] p. 171, italics in the original.) The discussion of the other case is more difficult to assess. To insist that there must be a way to explain the non-action of the failed killer would be "to turn the validity of the practical syllogism into a standard for interpreting the situation" and amount to "dogmatism" ([**15**] p. 117). The main point here is that "the premises of a practical inference do *not* with logical necessity entail behavior".[16]

It is not clear (to this writer) what von Wright's difficulty really is. Is it not simply the usual problem concerning theory and application—that theory is one thing, application is another? Suppose that all the wants in a Wooldridge planner are hard and that the set of these hard wants (intentions) is consistent (in the sense that it is logically possible to realize all the wants). Then if the design is correct and a certain implementation of it is well made, the latter will in time carry out all the relevant actions. If in the real case no action is forth-coming, experts should be able to agree about what went wrong: either there is something

---

[16]I find the example of the would-be-assassin unconvincing, as have others (for example, Martha Nussbaum ([**8**] p.117)).

wrong with the design, or else something went wrong with the implementation.[17]

Underlying this whole discussion is the tension between the traditional understanding of a valid argument as producing true conclusions from true premises, and the fact that logic, even supplemented with intentions, plans, goals, desires, wants and beliefs, will not by itself produce real action. For real action a real agent will always be needed.

Soft wants

Let us now turn to the weaker reading of $\mathbf{W}\phi$ as "the agent desires that". Under this reading it is of course easy to imagine that the premises of a practical syllogism are true and nevertheless no action is forth-coming. But with this interpretation, how can one claim that a practical syllogism is valid if $\mathbf{W}\phi$ is the premise of the good?

The short answer is that one cannot.[18] But this case is interesting nevertheless. For the existence of a rule $\mathcal{R}_\alpha^\phi$ does not mean that if the agent desires ϕ to be the case and believes that α is a way to achieve it (in our jargon: believes that $\phi \cdots \alpha$), then that the action follows. It means that, if the rule is applied, then it is *this particular belief* and *this particular desire* that *move the agent* to *this particular action*. To apply the rule is to perform the action. The application of the rule, we may perhaps say, elevates a mere desire to an intention. This would fit von Wright's remark that it is only after the fact that the action is there on which to "hang" the syllogism. In the same spirit one might perhaps say that it is only after the fact that the intention can be "seen".

A formal theory of soft syllogisms would look different from a theory of hard syllogisms. In the latter case a fixed set of types of type $\mathcal{R}_\alpha^\phi$ would be available and always permissible to use. But in the former case it would be up to the agent to decide whether to apply a certain rule and then take responsibility for having applied it. An existing desire and an existing belief may indicate a certain action according to a certain rule $\mathcal{R}_\alpha^\phi$. But what actually happens—whether α is performed or not—depends on the agent. Thus another (more dynamic) theory would be needed.

---

[17]Yes, there is a third possibility: that there is not enough information to decide whether there is something wrong with the design or there is something wrong with the implementation. But in this connexion that possibility is not important: given enough information, surely the experts would be able to fault either the design or the implementation.

[18]In Kenny's logic, referred to above, the situation is of course different.

No doubt such a theory could be developped. One might begin by considering the planner described by Wooldridge, allowing that the wants of the agent may not be consistent with one another. This means that they can no longer all be realized; which actions are realized will depend on the order in which the planner executes its instructions. Here again there is a connexion with nonmonotonic logic (cf. the deliberation walks in [**10**]).

Commitment

Perhaps it is the commitment part of the modified Bratman-Cohen-Levesque slogan that causes such difficulty for von Wright. How can one preclude that a human agent, as distinct from an artificial agent, may fail to maintain a commitment to the end? von Wright goes to great lengths in trying to stave off action failure, and yet is not satisfied. In Wooldridge's example (which works in theory but might fail in practice), commitment is built into the agent. But in a human this cannot be done.[19] Even if we were to introduce some kind of higher-order agent, the problem would recur. This problem is related to—or is the same as?—the problem of weakness of will. (Cf. [**3**].)

The philosopher's craving for clarity

The gist of von Wright's position is expressed in this last quote:

> To regard practical syllogisms as logically conclusive arguments is, I would say, to knit or tie together in a peculiar way the concepts of wanting an end, understanding a necessity, and setting oneself to act. It is a contribution to the molding or shaping of these concepts. The justification of this molding procedure is partly its conformity with actual usage and partly that which it does to meet the philosopher's craving for clarity in these matters. ([**14**] p. 171.)

"The philosopher's craving for clarity." I like that phrase. I like that concept. The philosopher's craving for clarity!

Yes, it is our craving for clarity that drives us on. von Wright himself is a prime example, till the end driven by his craving for clarity. And, in a modest way, it is this craving that has made

---

[19]Remember the problem in Kavka's paper [**5**]. An agent may of course delegate his power, as Ulysses was careful to do before approaching the sirens. But delegation does not solve von Wright's problem.

me go back to this part of von Wright's philosophy that I first encountered thirty-five years ago and found so interesting.

But craving for something is no guarantee for getting it. I did not then understand von Wright's theory of the practical syllogism. I still don't understand it.

I still find it interesting.

Bibliography

[1] van Benthem, Johan, Patrick Girard & Olivier Roy. To Appear. "Everything else being equal: a modal approach to ceteris paribus preferences." *Journal of philosophical logic.*

[2] Cohen, P. R. & Levesque, Hector. 1990. "Intention is choice with commitment." *Artificial intelligence,* vol. 42, pp. 213-261.

[3] Frankfurt, Harry. 1971. "Freedom of the will and the concept of a person," *Journal of philosophy,* vol. 68, pp. 5-20.

[4] Girard, Patrick. 2008. "Modal logic for belief and preference change." Dissertation. Department of Philosophy, Stanford University.

[5] Kavka, Gregory. 1983. "The toxin puzzle." *Analysis,* vol. 43, pp. 33-36.

[6] Kenny, Anthony. 1975. *Will, freedom and power.* Oxford: Blackwell.

[7] Lukaszewicz, Witold. 1988. "Considerations on default logic: an alternative approach." *Computational intelligence,* vol. 4, pp. 1-18.

[8] Nussbaum, Martha Craven. 1978. *Aristotle's* De Motu Animalium. Princeton, N.J.: Princeton University Press.

[9] Reiter, Ray. 1980. "A logic for default reasoning." *Artificial intelligence,* vol. 13, pp. 81-132.

[10] Segerberg, Krister. 1999. "Default logic as dynamic doxastic logic." *Erkenntnis,* vol. 50 (1999), pp. 333-352. Reprinted in *Dynamics and management of reasoning processes,* edited by J.-J. Ch. Meyer & J. Treur, pp. 159-176. *Handbook of defeasible reasoning and uncertainty management systems,* vol. 6, edited by Dov M. Gabbay & Philippe Smets. Dordrecht: Kluwer, 2001.

[11] Segerberg, Krister. 2002. "Outline of a logic of action." In *Advances in modal logic,* vol. 3, edited by F. Wolter, H. Wansing, M. de Rijke & M. Zakharyaschev, pp. 365-387. River Edge, N.J. & London: World Scientific.

[12] Wooldridge, Michael. 2001. *An introduction to multiagent systems.* Chichester, England: John Wiley & Sons.

[13] von Wright, Georg Henrik. 1963. *Norm and action: a logical inquiry.* London: Routledge & Kegan Paul.

[14] von Wright, Georg Henrik. 1963. *The varieties of goodness.* London: Routledge & Kegan Paul

[15] von Wright, Georg Henrik. 1971. *Explanation and understanding.* Ithaca, N.Y.: Cornell University Press

Logical Determination and the Principle of Bivalence

Dag Prawitz

In the volume of *The Library of Living Philosophers* dedicated to the philosophy of Georg Henrik von Wright[1], there is, as usual in these volumes, an autobiography of the philosopher in question. To it Georg Henrik has added a postscript dated 1980, where he says that after having finished his autobiography several years earlier, he has written two papers that "started two new lines along which my thoughts have been moving ever since." One of them he labels "Time, Truth, and Necessity." The three concepts – time, truth, and necessity – were certainly prominent already in his earlier works, and several contributors to the Schilpp volume commented upon his writings on them.[2] However, the very constellation "Time, Truth and Necessity" was now approached in a new way in von Wright's work that could not reasonably be dealt with in the Schilpp volume, planned already at the beginning of the 1970's. It may, therefore, be appropriate that I pay attention to that theme in this book in memory of Georg Henrik von Wright.

"Time Truth, and Necessity" also occurs as the title of a paper by von Wright,[3] one of his first works on this new theme, which is concerned with problems dealt with by Aristotle in chapter 9 of *De Interpretatione*, connected with what is often referred

---

[1]P. A. Schilpp and L. E. Hahn, eds., *The Philosophy of Georg Henrik von Wright* (Open Court, 1989), to be referred to as the *Schilpp volume*.

[2]For instance, Krister Segerberg contributed a paper "Von Wright's Tense Logic," and Dagfinn Føllesdal a paper "Von Wright's Modal Logic."

[3]Georg Henrik von Wright, "Time Truth, and Necessity," in Cora Diamond and Jenny Teichman, eds., *Intention and Intentionality: Essays in Honour of G. E. M. Anscombe* (Cornell University Press 1979), pp 237-250.

to as the *Sea Battle Argument*. The great attention that has been devoted to this text, he writes, "is due, no doubt, partly to the intrinsic interest of the problems and partly to difficulties in understanding the text." I shall here limit myself to problems around determinism, necessity, and the principle of bivalence (the principle saying that every declarative sentence is true or false) that appear in this text by Aristotle and are dealt with by von Wright in his paper.

My own interest in these problems has several origins. Like von Wright, I am intrigued by what Aristotle says[4] and by the problems themselves; problems around determinism and causality constitute an old interest of mine (I wrote about causality in the Schilpp volume on von Wright), and questions about the validity of the principle of bivalence have engaged me in connection with intuitionism and the metaphysical discussions on realism versus anti-realism in the form that originated with Michel Dummett. My orientation is here quite different from Georg Henrik's. However, it turns out that our evaluations of the problems raised by Aristotle's Sea Battle Argument, although different at many points, nevertheless converge in some respects.

I. The Sea Battle Argument

In the greater part of chapter 9 of *De Interpretatione*, Aristotle presents an argument for determinism that concludes that everything is predetermined or, as Aristotle puts it: "everything is or happens of necessity."[5] The premise of the argument is the principle of bivalence, saying that every affirmation is true or false, which is applied to statements about the future. The argument first derives the conclusion that for every affirmation, either it is necessarily true or its negation is necessarily true. The part of the argument that ends here, I shall call the *determinist argument*. It is taken to mean or imply that everything is predetermined, which

---

[4]This interest has been stimulated by long-term seminars on Aristotle's *Organon* led by Per-Martin Löf at Stockholm University and by an ongoing research project on Aristotle's work led by Per-Erik Malmnäs, in which philosophers and scholars in ancient Greek at Stockholm University collaborate. I thank members of these groups for helpful comments on a draft of this paper.

[5]I am following Ackrill's translation in *Aristotle's Categories and De Interpretatione* (Oxford: Clarendon Press, 1963 – reprinted several times). Von Wright is following Elisabeth Anscombe's translation (his paper appearing in a Festschrift to her), which was published with comments in Elisabeth Anscombe, "Aristotle and the Sea Battle," *Mind* 1965, pp 1-15.

I. THE SEA BATTLE ARGUMENT   113

is elaborated by Aristotle by saying: "It follows that nothing either is or is happening, or will be or will not be, by chance or as chance has it, but everything by necessity."

Aristotle connects this predetermination with fatalism: "there would be no need to deliberate or to take trouble (thinking that if we do this, this will happen, but if we do not, it will not)." It is to a large extent because of this connection that the determinist argument was so much debated in antiquity, some parties accepting it while others rejecting it. There is, however, a more direct argument for fatalism that has attracted many people of a logical bent and not only philosophers. It starts, almost as in the determinist argument, with the innocent remark that for any event it is true that it either will happen or not happen. The fatalist then considers the two alternatives separately, in other words applying what logicians call a dilemma, and reasons as follows: Assume that it is true that the event will occur. Then I cannot prevent it from happening, because if I succeeded in doing that, it would not be true that the event will occur, contrary to the assumption made. Assume instead that it is true that the event will not occur. Then, similarly, I cannot make it happen, because if I succeeded in doing that, it would not be true that the event will not occur, contrary to the assumption now made. Thus in either case, I cannot change the course of events.

In Aristotle's text the connection with fatalism is only made in a passing remark. The focus is on the determinist argument and the absurdity of the determinism that it is taken to imply. In the Modern Era, determinism is usually discussed in terms of the notion of causality. Here we are presented with what seems to be a truly logical argument for a kind of determinism, commonly called *logical determinism*. Instead of saying that everything has a cause and is therefore predetermined, it is argued that if something *is* the case, then it *must* be so. The principle that is essentially used in the determinist argument can be formulated as saying that if something is true, it is necessarily true.

The nature of the necessity here invoked is not discussed by Aristotle, and we shall soon return to the question how it is to be understood. Let it now just be noted that to be necessary is here something like being 'fixed and settled,' as von Wright suggests, or 'ineluctably settled,' as Ackrill puts it. The idea of such a necessity seems to go well with Aristotle's correspondence theory of truth: A sentence is true only if there is a corresponding fact, and given such a fact, the sentence cannot be anything but true;

it *must* be true. The kind of necessity figuring in the principle that truth implies necessity, I shall call *factual necessity*.

Applying this principle, the surface structure of the determinist argument may be exhibited as a dilemma like the one used in the fatalist's reasoning above, or we may simply summarize the argument as follows, where A stands for any sentence:

(1) A is true or A is false. (Assumption; principle of bivalence)
(2) If is A is true, then A is necessarily true. (Truth implies necessity)
(3) If A is false, then not-A is true.
(4) If not-A is true, then not-A is necessarily true. (Truth implies necessity)
(5) A is necessarily true or not-A is necessarily true. (From (1), (2), (3), and (4))

In view of (3) and the converse, which Aristotle also affirms, the principle of bivalence and the law of excluded middle, saying that for every sentence A, either A is true or not-A is true, can be obtained from each other. Both the principle of bivalence and the law of excluded middle are taken in the determinist argument to hold necessarily, and they can be used interchangeably. The main move in the argument may therefore be described as resulting in a distribution of necessity over disjunction, that is, as going from

(1′) it is necessary that either A is true or not-A is true

to (5), or to what is simply another wording of (5):

(5′) either it is necessary that A is true or it is necessary that not-A is true.

It would be an oversimplification to say that the argument discussed by Aristotle is simply the one from (1) to (5). The argument is much more involved and serves among other things to establish that truth implies necessity as stated in (2) and (4). But there is a fair degree of consensus that (1) is the premiss, (5) is the outcome, and (2), (3), and (4) are ingredients in the argument, and since (1)-(5) are sufficient for a valid argument (given that the premiss holds), we may confine ourselves to these elements. Having reached the conclusion (5), and after having connected it with determinism and fatalism, Aristotle rejects the conclusion of the determinist argument. He argues that "what will be has an origin both in deliberations and in action" and that "not everything is or happens of necessity: some things happen as chance has it."

Then Aristotle gives his diagnosis of what has gone wrong in the above argument. The key passages are as follows:

(a) What is, necessarily is, when it is; and what is not, necessarily is not, when it is not. But not everything that is, necessarily is; and not everything that is not, necessarily is not. For to say that everything that is, is of necessity, when it is, is not the same as saying unconditionally that it is of necessity.

(b) Everything necessarily is or is not; but one cannot divide and say that one or the other is necessary. I mean for example: it is necessary for there to be or not to be a sea battle tomorrow; but it is not necessary for a sea battle to take place tomorrow, nor for one not to take place tomorrow - though it is necessary for one to take place or not to take place. ... the same necessarily holds for contradictories also. ... With these it is necessary for one or the other to be true or false - not, however, this one or that one.

Many commentators agree concerning what has been said so far about Aristotle's argument, but the opinions diverge when it comes to saying what precisely Aristotle takes to be the error of the determinist argument and how his final conclusion is to be understood.

II. Some interpretations of the Sea Battle Argument

There have been numerous commentators on Aristotle's *De Interpretatione*, in antiquity as well as in modern times. It is common to speak of two radically different lines of interpreting the ninth chapter, which I shall refer to as the *realist* and *anti-realist* interpretations.[6] The anti-realist interpretation takes Aristotle's conclusion to be that the law of bivalence does not hold for sentences about the future. According to this interpretation, often

---

[6]In comments on his translation, J. L. Ackrill (op. cit., pp 132-142) instructively discusses Aristotle's text by describing two such different lines of interpretation. The terms "realist" and "anti-realist" interpretation I have taken from Börje Bydén, who uses them in comments on his own translation of Aristotle's text into Swedish: *Aristoteles, De interpretatione. Om sofistiska vederläggninga* (Thales 2000). The term stands there for essentially the same two main lines of interpretation that Ackrill speaks of.

referred to as the *traditional interpretation*[7], Aristotle finds nothing wrong with the determinist argument except for its initial assumption, namely the principle of bivalence. In support of this interpretation, one can point to the fact that at the beginning of the chapter Aristotle makes a distinction between sentences that speak of "what is and what has been" and of "particulars that are going to be": for the first kind of sentences "it is necessary for the affirmation or the negation to be true or false" but for second "it is different". In the last sentences of the chapter, Aristotle seems to come back to the idea that sentences about the future constitute an exception from what otherwise holds, saying: "it is not necessary that of every affirmation and opposite negation one should be true and the other false. For what holds for things that are does not hold for things that are not but may possibly be or not be; with these it is as we have said."

Aristotle's wording in the very beginning and the very end of the chapter certainly seems to indicate that he takes the principle of bivalence (or a slightly more wordy principle that comes to the same) to fail for sentences about the future. "With these it as we have said," he writes as conclusion of the chapter. But what is it that has been said? According to the anti-realistic interpretation the answer is that a sentence referring to a point of time in the future normally lacks truth-value as long as the point of time belongs to the future but gets a truth-value when it becomes actual. To support this claim one has to make the passages (a) and (b) quoted above fit with it. The problem is that they do not explicitly say anything that backs up this claim. On the contrary, it seems that in passage (b), Aristotle states that the law of excluded middle holds for everything, including there being a sea-battle tomorrow.

---

[7]This is a misnomer according to Sorabji and Kretzmann in *Ammonius, On Aristotle On Interpretation 9* (tr. by Black), *with Boethius On Aristotle On Interpretation 9* (tr. by Kretzmann), (Duckworth, 1998). They agree that the anti-realist interpretation is the oldest one on record, being the one that the Stoics charge Aristotle with, accusing him of tampering with the laws of logic in order to save indeterminism; the Stoics' own standpoint being that the determinist argument (including its premiss) is valid. But Sorabji and Kretzmann are of the opinion that there are rival interpretations endorsed by Ammonius and Boethius, which are almost equally old and which defend Aristotle, claiming that he rightly rejected the determinist argument without giving up the universal validity of the principle of bivalence. This opinion is in turn rejected by Wiedemann (in *Aristoteles, Peri Hermeneias*, Übersetzt und erläutert von Herman Weidemann (Akademie Verlag 1994)), who claims it to be built on a misunderstanding of Ammonius and Boethius.

II. SOME INTERPRETATIONS OF THE SEA BATTLE ARGUMENT 117

According to the other main line of interpretation, the realist one, Aristotle never gives up the principle of bivalence or the law of excluded third for sentences about the future. Instead he rejects the reasoning in the determinist argument, specifically steps 2 and 4 in the argument formulated above, that is, the principle that if something is true then it is necessarily true. This principle holds for sentences about the past and the present but not for all sentences about the future.[8] More precisely, a true sentence like "a sea battle takes place" is necessarily true *at the time at which the event takes place* – "what is, necessarily is, *when it is*" – but that does not mean that all true sentences are necessarily true; for instance, "a sea battle takes place tomorrow" may be true, but it does not need to be necessarily true already today – "not everything that is, necessarily is."

Some sentences about the future may however be necessarily true already today. For instance, it is already now necessarily true that a sea-battle will occur or will not occur tomorrow, and similarly all instances of the principle of bivalence hold of necessity even when being about the future.

Having rejected the universal validity of the principle that truth implies necessity, the determinist argument is blocked. Although "everything necessarily is or is not, and will be or will not be," there are some things that "happen as chance has it," and as far as they are concerned "one cannot divide and say that one or the other is necessary," that is, one cannot say that it is necessary that the thing will happen or that it is necessary that the thing will not happen. The passages (a) and (b) seem to fit with this

---

[8]There is another interpretation that is also realistic in the sense of preserving the principle of bivalence for sentences about the future, but which takes Aristotle to reject altogether the principle that truth implies necessity. It interprets the distinction that Aristotle makes in (a) as concerning the scope of the necessity, in other words as a distinction between on the one hand
 (i) Necessary (if p, then p)
and, on the other hand,
 (ii) If p, then necessary p.
It presupposes another reading of the Greek sentences that have become passage (a) in Ackrill's translation: in particular, the first sentence in that passage is instead rendered in such a way that necessity governs the whole sentence. For a criticism of such a translation see e.g. Wiedemann (f.n. 7).

Although this interpretation is not uncommon (it is followed e.g. by Anders Wedberg, *A History of Philosophy*, vol. I (Oxford University Press, 1982)), it presupposes another interpretation of the determinist argument, which makes it much less interesting, reducing it to a trivial confusion between principles (i) and (ii).

interpretation, which is, however, difficult to reconcile with what Aristotle says at the beginning and end of the chapter.

Some interpretations that have been suggested do not fall in any of these two groups. This is the case with Jaakko Hintikka's[9], which I shall say something about because of its own interest and because it has influenced von Wright in various ways. Hintikka claims that Aristotle's main problem is not whether application of the law of the excluded middle to future events gives rise to an argument for determinism but is caused by Aristotle's view of necessity, which compels him to consider a sentence as necessarily true if it has always been true. Since a sentence that predicts the occurrence of a future event at a specific time has always been true, if it is true at all, this has the embarrassing consequence that all such sentences are necessarily true, even when they predict events that more reasonably are taken as contingent. There is textual evidence for saying that Aristotle reasons this way in the part of the determinist argument meant to establish the principle that truth implies necessary truth.

Hintikka observes that Aristotelian examples of sentences describing events are almost always token-reflexive, and hence their truth-values vary with the time and situation in which they are uttered, typical examples being sentences like "Socrates is sitting." If we fix the time reference of such a sentence to a specific chronological time, then we get a sentence "Socrates is sitting at time t_0," which, if true, has always been true and is therefore necessarily true. For such sentences, the principle that truth implies necessary truth holds, according to Aristotelian views, and although this gives rise to the embarrassing derivation (1)-(5) above, Aristotle does not give up the principle of bivalence, Hintikka claims.

Aristotle's "solution" is instead, according to Hintikka, to disregard such sentences whose time reference is fixed to a specific chronological time and concentrate on the token-reflexive ones like "Socrates is sitting." The latter kind of sentences may be true without having been always true, and they can therefore be used to state a non-deterministic thesis. What Aristotle observes in passage (a) is interpreted by Hintikka to be that for sentences of the latter kind truth does not imply necessary truth, although such an implication holds for sentences like "Socrates is sitting at time t_0." By sticking to token-reflexive sentences, Aristotle is thus

---

[9]Jaakko Hintikka, "The Once and Future Sea Fight: Aristotle's Discussion of Future Contingents in *De Interpretatione* IX", *The Philosophical Review* 73, 1964, pp 461-492.

able to express that "some things happen as chance has it." This move does not block the deterministic argument for all sentences, but it does so for sentences of the kind preferred by Aristotle. However, "Aristotle's main problem was not a metaphysician's vague worry about whether present truth about the future prejudges future events," Hintikka says, "it was the difficulty of a systematist who has defined his notions for too narrow range of cases and was then forced to accommodate awkward new cases in his framework."

Hintikka repudiates the traditional anti-realistic interpretation and argues that Aristotle accepts the law of excluded middle and the principle of bivalence for both kinds of sentences – for instance, that Socrates is sitting or not sitting, and that he is sitting or not sitting at any *specific* time in the future. Not only does Aristotle state this explicitly in (b), but when he seemingly denies it at the beginning and the end of the chapter, what he is really denying is a principle saying that any one of the contraries is necessarily true.

Hintikka's interpretation differs also from the realist ones as described above, since he does not think that Aristotle rejects the principle that truth implies necessity for sentences about a *specific* time in the future. As we saw, according to Hintikka, the sentences for which Aristotle rejects the principle that truth implies necessity are of the token-reflexive kind like "Socrates is sitting:" even if it is true that Socrates is sitting, it is not necessarily true (because, in the past, it has not always been true that he was sitting).

III. Von Wright on the Sea Battle Argument

Von Wright's paper (see footnote 3) is in many respects a response to the paper by Hintikka. After having referred to that paper, von Wright first takes an opposite stand on what Aristotle's problem was, saying that it seems to him that the problem was exactly the puzzlement aroused by seemingly being able to derive from the law of excluded middle the determinist conclusion that the future is predetermined and unavoidable. However, shortly afterwards, he declares himself to be in definite agreement with Anscombe and Hintikka on another issue, saying "I think that they are absolutely right" as regards their contesting the traditional view that Aristotle's way out from this puzzlement was to deny the principle of bivalence for sentences about the future.

The main part of von Wright's paper is concerned with certain relations between time and the concepts of truth and necessity. As to time and truth, his standpoint is that *plain* truth is timeless, *atemporal*, and that the tensed use of truth is spurious and otiose. Saying "it will be true tomorrow that a sea battle occurs" is the same as saying "a sea battle will occur tomorrow", but the first form may be misleading in giving rise to the wrong identification of *a*temporality with *omni*temporality. Von Wright thus dissociates himself from the idea that if for some x (a sea battle, for instance) it is true that x occurs at a specific time t_0, then it is *now and always* true that x occurs (or has occurred, or will occur) at t_0. He thus rejects the kind of reasoning that, according to Hintikka, gave rise to Aristotle's problem and although he admits that Aristotle was struggling with these thoughts, he thinks that Aristotle never accepted them.

Concerning time and necessity, von Wright suggests that there are at least two kinds of necessity in the ninth chapter of *De Interpretatione* – one he refers to as *the necessary character of truth as facts* and the other as *necessity simpliciter* – and that both are related to time in particular ways. Something is necessary in the first sense when it is 'fixed' or 'settled'. When an event has occurred, it is a fact that it has occurred, which cannot be changed – it is *fait accompli* – and, in this sense, that the event has occurred is true necessarily. This is obviously the same kind of necessity that I called *factual necessity*, and I shall continue to refer to it under that name.

While plain truth is atemporal, necessity in the factual sense is temporal. A true sentence that speaks about an event occurring at time t becomes necessary at time t, at the latest, and then remains necessary for ever. But it may have become necessarily true already at some time t' before t, if something made it settled already at t' that the event would occur. It is also possible that a sentence has always been necessary. The last is the case for a sentence like "A sea battle will occur at time t or it will not occur at time t".

The other kind of necessity, *necessity simpliciter*, is something that can be applied to what von Wright calls open sentences, i.e. sentences that are open with respect to time in the sense that they do not express any proposition before one or several time parameters have been assigned values. Token reflexive sentences like "Socrates is sitting" but also formulas like "Socrates is sitting at time x" with an explicit parameter x, are examples of such open sentences. An open sentence is necessary simpliciter if it is true for all values of the time parameter.

Von Wright refers to passage (a) as the place where Aristotle makes this distinction between two kinds of necessity. "What is, necessarily is, when it is" is taken to refer to factual necessity, and is taken to say that something is (factually) necessary at the time at which it occurs or is the case. When Aristotle continues, saying, "But not everything that is, necessarily is," he is taken to refer to necessity simpliciter, and to imply that there are sentences like "A sea battle occurs" that may be true for some but not for every value of its time parameter, and which therefore may be true without being true necessarily in this second sense. As we can see, the reason that von Wright ascribes to Aristotle for rejecting some instances of the principle that truth implies necessity (simpliciter) is the same as the one that Hintikka ascribes to him for making this rejection. But the reasons that they ascribe to him for saying that a truth is necessarily true when it is true, are quite different; here von Wright is following the realist interpretation as described above.

At the end of his paper, von Wright discusses Aristotle's proposed "solution" in a way that is close to Hintikka's position (although he does not refer in this connection to Hintikka). Hintikka's idea was that Aristotle's crucial step is the distinction between sentences that speak of future events occurring at specific times and sentences that speak of future events just occurring. Von Wright suspects that Aristotle may have thought that to refute determinism it is sufficient to make a related distinction between the two kinds of necessities that von Wright identifies and to observe that there are things which are not always, but only sometimes, true and which therefore are not necessary *simpliciter*. If this is how he thought, he was mistaken, von Wright says, and he goes on explaining why this was a mistake by making a distinction between something being *contingent* and being *predetermined*. An open sentence $A(x)$ with a time parameter x may be said to be contingent, if neither not-$A(x)$ nor $A(x)$ is necessary *simpliciter*, that is, if for some time t, $A(t)$ is true, and for some other t, $A(t)$ is false (which is to say that $A(x)$ is true for some values of x and false for some other values). $A(t)$ is a predetermined truth or falsehood if there is some time s before t such that $A(t)$ is true necessarily at s or false necessarily at s, where necessity is taken as factual necessity. Von Wright then observes that the existence of a contingent $A(x)$ is fully compatible with $A(x)$

being predetermined for any value t of x. Hence, he concludes, to save contingencies, as one may say that Aristotle did in his way, is not to show that things are not predetermined, and therefore, does not amount to a refutation of determinism.

IV. Further comments

Von Wright's interpretation mixes as we have seen a realist interpretation with elements from Hintikka's interpretation by introducing two kinds of necessities. I shall argue that when the first sentence of passage (a) is understood in terms of factual necessity, it is more reasonable to interpret the second sentence in the same terms, and that therefore there is no need to introduce two kinds of necessities. When modified in this way, von Wright's interpretation (in which his understanding of factual necessity is a crucial element) becomes a well articulated and possible reconstruction of a rejection of the determinist argument (section IV.1).

Although I think, unlike what seems to be von Wright position, that available evidence is not just on one side in the debate between the realist and anti-realist interpreters of Aristotle, and that the best interpretation may be a combination the two lines of interpretation, I share von Wright's conviction that to refute the determinist argument, there is no need to think of truth as temporal and to give up the principle of bivalence (section IV.2).

Apart from how Aristotle is best interpreted, there is a need to compare and further articulate the realist and anti-realist pictures of the future and their ontological views of factual necessity and possibility (section IV.3). It is also of interest to investigate an epistemic notion of necessity with respect to the future and the past, and I shall therefore sketch epistemic and objective notions of truth and necessity that behave like the realist's notions of truth and factual necessity with respect to observable events (section IV.4).

IV.1. Staying with factual necessity

As has already been noted, when von Wright speaks of the necessary character of truth as facts, he is elaborating the realist interpretation I described briefly in section II. It seems very reasonable to understand Aristotle's phrase "what is, necessarily is, when it is" as referring to the time at which something is necessary, so that one could rephrase him as saying "what is, is necessary *at the time at which it is*", and therefore to reconstrue this kind of necessity as a temporal notion. Formulating this idea for sentences in a

IV. FURTHER COMMENTS

more perspicuous way, we may let A_t stand for a sentence that says of something that it occurs or is the case at time t. The valid principle of truth implying necessity can then be formulated by saying that the following implication holds:

(I_1) if A_t is true, then it is necessary *at t* that A_t is true.

In comparison, Hintikka interprets Aristotle's phrase "what is, necessarily is, when it is" as saying

(IH_1) if A_t is true, then it is necessary that A_t is true,

or as he puts it, letting A be a sentence open with respect to time, like "a sea battle occurs,"

(IH_1') if A at time t is true, then it is necessary that A at time t is true.

In other words, in Hintikka's interpretation it is not the necessity of an atemporal truth that is tensed but it is a generic state or event that is made specific with respect to time and is then necessitated – the necessity is not tensed independently. One may say that Hintikka's position is that one could rephrase Aristotle as saying something like "for what is at a specific time, it holds necessarily that it is at that time". The reasons that Aristotle could have had for affirming (I_1) and (IH_1') as developed by von Wright and Hintikka, respectively, must of course be quite different. Without taking any stand on the question of whose reconstruction of Aristotle's reasoning at this point comes closest to how Aristotle was reasoning – perhaps it can be argued that Aristotle subscribed to both principles – I find (I_1) a more reasonable and interesting principle in itself, and I shall stick to it in this discussion.

While Aristotle affirms that what is, is necessary, *when it is*, which we are now interpreting as an affirmation of (I_1), he immediately afterwards denies that everything that is, is necessary. Instead of interpreting him as then speaking about another kind of necessity, as von Wright does, I propose to understand him as using the terms in the same sense as immediately before. What Aristotle is saying can then be read as denying that the implication

(I_2) if A_t is true, then it is necessary that A_t is true

always holds. The truth of the latter implication (I_2), which lacks explicit time reference as to when it is necessary that A_t is true, and which therefore has to be taken as implicitly referring to the time at which it is uttered, depends among other things on the relation between the time t and the time of utterance. If the implication is uttered at t, it is valid according to what is said by the implication (I_1), and if uttered at a later time, it would also be valid according to what has been said before (what becomes necessary, remains necessary, a principle that Aristotle does not state but would probably agree to). But if it is uttered before t, then the implication need not be valid because of these other principles, and that it may actually fail is a possible reason for Aristotle rejecting "what is, necessarily is". We may still allow that for some specific A_t, (I_2) is valid even when uttered before t, namely if it would be already fixed at the time of utterance that A_t is true.

I am thus proposing that we do not need to introduce two kinds of necessity, factual necessity and necessity simpliciter, but can interpret passage (a) as being about factual necessity all the way through. It is undoubtedly simpler to understand Aristotle saying, "But not everything that is, necessarily is," as saying something in opposition to what he has just said, more precisely, as denying that we can leave out the time specification "when it is" from "What is, necessarily is, when it is" and still have a valid principle. If the first affirmed principle is rendered as (I_1), then what is denied as always holding should be rendered as (I_2), obtained from (I_1) by leaving out the specification "at t". (To use von Wright's notion of necessity simpliciter, one could say that (I_2) is not necessary simpliciter, but such an iterated use of necessities is an unneeded complication; it is sufficient to say simply that (I_2) is sometimes false, having already introduced the idea that factual necessity is relative to time.)

When formulating the implication (I_2) that Aristotle rejected as not always holding, I considered only sentences with a specific time reference (indicated by a subscript: A_t), but we could have considered more generally all kind of sentences, including open and token-reflexive ones, thus getting the implication

(I_2^*) if A is true, then it is necessary that A is true.

There are token-reflexive sentences which when put for A in (I_2^*) give implications that do not hold. An obvious example already suggested in section II is "a sea battle will take place tomorrow." Since for any time t of its utterance, the sentence speaks of an event that is said to occur at a time after t, and since furthermore it is rarely settled at time t that a sea battle will take place the next day, we have here a counter-example to (I_2^*) of the same kind as above. But for von Wright, who takes Aristotle to deny (I_2^*), interpreted as speaking of necessity simpliciter, "a sea battle will take place tomorrow" is a counter-example for the different reason that a sea battle does not always take place tomorrow.

When A is a sentence like "Socrates is sitting," which has no explicit time reference at all, the outcome is different. We find that then (I_2^*) always holds when the necessity is taken as factual: since both the necessity and the verb in A now have to be understood as referring to the time of utterance, we have a case where something is asserted to be necessary at the time at which it is, in other words a case where the implication (I_1) applies. But when interpreted in von Wright's way, we have again a counter-example to (I_2^*): Sentences like "Socrates is sitting" are prime examples of sentences that are true for some points of time and yet are not necessarily true simpliciter, due to the fact Socrates is not always sitting. Factual necessity thus behaves quite differently from von Wright's necessity simpliciter.

In other words, when Aristotle's "not everything that is, necessarily is" is understood as speaking about factual necessity, it gets a quite different function from the one that von Wright assigns to it when interpreting Aristotle's words in terms of necessity simpliciter. The point is no longer to remind us of the existence of contingencies but to tell us what has gone wrong in the determinist argument. The principle that truth implies necessity, which was used in that argument, is valid when time is introduced in the appropriate way as stated in (I_1). But, Aristotle says, the principle in question does not hold unconditionally as would be needed if the determinist argument were to go through.

The result is thus that passage (a), when interpreted in this way, can be understood as blocking the determinist argument, unlike the situation in von Wright's interpretation. This is to return to the realist interpretation, briefly described in section II, now developed in a little more detail. Aristotle read in this way does not give "a refutation of determinism," which would be to require too much, but he does refute the determinist argument.

IV.2. The realist and antirealist interpretation, pro and con

When weighing the pros and cons for the two main lines of interpretation, the realist and anti-realist ones, I have noted that passages (a) and (b) fit well with the realist interpretation but not with the beginning and end of the chapter, and that it is the reverse for the anti-realist interpretation.

Bringing in other passages of the chapter, one may turn to an interlude between the development of the determinist argument and Aristotle's remark about the absurdity of its conclusions where Aristotle says: "Nor, however can we say that neither is true" – for instance, that neither "there will be a sea battle tomorrow" nor "there will not be a sea battle tomorrow" is true. It has been suggested that this is an explicit rejection of the anti-realist idea that singular statements about the future lack truth-values, but Aristotle may be understood instead as denying here that both can be false.[10] Furthermore, it is difficult to say whether the passage, which is followed by an argument for what has been said, is to be taken as a part of the determinist's reasoning that is rejected by Aristotle or should be understood as an investigation of whether a reasonable way out from the determinist argument would be to assume that none of the two sentences is true.

We may also try to take into account Aristotelian doctrines in other texts. One is the correspondence principle of truth, which, as suggested in section II, is naturally invoked in order to explain the principle that truth implies necessity: to say that a sentence is true is to say that there is a corresponding fact, and if there is a corresponding fact then the sentence *must* be true, i.e. is necessarily true. Referring to this principle, one may say on behalf of the anti-realist interpretation that before the occurrence or the non-occurrence of a sea battle tomorrow, there is no fact that can make the sentence "there will be a sea battle tomorrow" true or false, and that therefore the sentence must lack truth-value today. It may be replied that this is to beg the question, since the issue is whether already today there is either an existing fact as to the occurrence of a sea battle tomorrow or an existing fact as to the non-occurrence of such an event. However, one may then ask what the motivation is behind the restriction of the principle that truth implies necessity to sentences about the present and the past. The natural thing to say is that for a sentence about the past or present, there is a fact in view of which the sentence is either necessarily true or necessarily false, but for a sentence about the future there may not yet be any such fact. But if so, there is no fact that makes the sentence true or false. In other words, lacking facts that prompt necessary truth or necessary falsity, the facts that, according to the correspondence theory, could prompt truth or

---

[10]Wiedemann makes this point against Anscombe and Hintikka, who have invoked the passage against the anti-realist interpretation (see the works cited above).

falsity are also lacking, and therefore a prediction of a future event may not yet have any truth-value. From this perspective the anti-realist interpretation appears more coherent than the realist one. I shall soon return to the issue by considering more sophisticated correspondence theories of truth.

There is of course much more to say in favour and disfavour of the two interpretations, but it seems hard to bring up enough evidence to say that one side in this debate is "absolutely right." The best thing to say is perhaps that there are tensions in Aristotle's text that do not allow a coherent interpretation. It should be noted, however, that the two interpretations might be modified so as to bring them into line with each other.[11] One might agree that given the considerations formulated in passage (a), the determinist argument is blocked as suggested by the realist, but that this does not exclude Aristotle's also rejecting the premiss of the determinist argument (perhaps because such a rejections yields a more coherent position, although not formally needed in order to avoid the determinist conclusion). Abandoning the position that plain truth is atemporal, one may then say that sentences about the future sometimes lack truth values now, but that nevertheless any sentence of the form "A or not-A" is now true even when the sentence A is about the future. This has the remarkable consequence that a disjunction may be true at a time t although neither of the disjuncts is true at t. An interpretation of this kind seems to accord with the beginning and end of the chapter as well as with the passages (a) and (b) and may come close to what Aristotle had in mind.[12]

The debate between the realist and the anti-realist interpretations has anyway the merit of drawing attention to the fact that there are two independent ways of escaping the determinist conclusion. The best interpretation of Aristotle's text may be to combine elements from both interpretations, but to solve the problems raised by the Sea Battle Argument it is sufficient to take up one of the suggested lines of interpretation. This brings up the question of the most reasonable solution of these problems, quite apart from the question how Aristotle wanted to solve them. In the rest of the paper I shall make some further remarks on that.

IV.3. The nature of factual necessity

---

[11] I owe this idea to suggestions from Per-Erik Malmnäs and Per Martin-Löf.

[12] It seems that Wiedemann supports such an interpretation.

A key question is, of course, how factual necessity should really be explained. Many people have remarked that the notion in question is not the notion of necessity now mostly studied in modal logic. Indeed, factual necessity seems to have little to do with truth in all *possible* worlds; the point seems rather to be that certain propositions are factually necessary in view of how the facts are in the *actual* world. But how is this to be understood more precisely?

Anscombe remarks in her paper (footnote 5) that the concept of necessity referred to when it is said that sentences about present or past events are necessarily true, if true, and necessarily false, if false, is unfamiliar to us, and suggests that "A modern gloss that can be used here, ... and without which it is it is not possible for a modern person to understand his [Aristotle's] argument, is: and cannot be shown to be otherwise." Her point seems to be that necessity in this context is to be understood as an epistemological notion and that to be necessary means something like: is certainly true, there is nothing that could tell against it. Her paper is, however, cryptic and there is no hint of a systematic account.

Von Wright makes anyway clear in his paper that he disagrees with Anscombe on this point and emphasizes that the necessity of that which is or has been should not be understood primarily in epistemic terms. He remarks that *epistemically* the past is just as open to alternatives as the future. Although von Wright does not here (as he has done in other works) explicitly use the picture of states of the world as nodes in a branching tree, his position is best understood in such terms. He suggests that "the past is a closed linear order of successive states," while the future lies "open," having "room for alternative developments," which is to say that from the node representing the present state of the world, the tree branches out towards the future, while in the other direction there is just one branch or trunk. This is to be understood as representing how things really are ontologically; it is in the nature of things that the future is not yet completely settled. Von Wright seems here to state his own position, but he thinks that Aristotle shares it.

Both the realist and the anti-realist may use trees of this kind as models of how the world has developed and may develop in the future. The states of the world up to the present time may be thought of as determined by the facts that prevailed or prevail at the respective points of time. The branches that fork towards the future are to represent different possible ways in which the world may develop, their nodes representing possible future states of the world. Let us say that these states are determined by the *potential* or *possible* facts that may prevail at the points of time in question. The facts or potential facts belonging to a state of the world first of all determine what sentences are true at that state of the world.

For sentences about the future, one may think of at least two possible semantics with reference to such models of the world. One possibility is to say that a sentence A about a specific time t in the future is *true now*, if every branch that goes from the present state towards the future contains a state at which A is true. It follows that a sentence of the form "A or not-A" formed from such a sentence A is true now, since we may suppose that for whatever branch one chooses, when one reaches the time t, one will come either to a state with a potential fact corresponding to A, in which case A and hence "A or not-A" are true, or to a state with a potential fact corresponding to not-A, in which case not-A and hence again "A or not- A" are true. But since different alternatives may hold for different branches, neither A nor not-A need to be true now. This is a semantics that suits the anti-realist standpoint: the principle of bivalence does not hold universally, the future is indeterminate, genuinely open, but all instances of the law of excluded third hold true when put in the form used just now, where truth is ascribed to the whole disjunction and is not distributed over the disjuncts.

A semantics adapted to the realist standpoint, where truth is atemporal as von Wright emphasizes, must of course be different. Necessary truth (in the factual sense) now takes the place of truth in the anti-realist semantics, so to say: A sentence A about the future is *necessarily true now* if every branch that goes from the present state towards the future contains a state at which A is true. In this way, factual necessity for sentences about the future after all resembles truth in all possible worlds. But how is truth to be explained? A realist about the future has to say that, although there are several possible ways in which the world may develop, represented by the branches going towards the future, there is one branch that represents how the world will *actually* develop, and a sentence A speaking about what happens at a certain time t in the future is true if the state at time t in *that* branch contains a potential fact corresponding to A; from this perspective one may as well drop the attribute "potential." Every sentence, even those about the future, has therefore a truth-value, and since truth explained in this way does not vary with the nodes in the actual history of the world, we should speak just about truth and not about truth at a certain node. But possible and necessary truths always hold only with respect to nodes.

Both the anti-realist and the realist assert that the future is open, in other words, that the world could develop in different ways as represented by the different paths that one can follow in the tree starting from the present state of the world. As anyone must admit, the world will develop along exactly one of these paths, but no one will say that this path exists *already now*. For the realist this path exists – but in a timeless sense. For the anti-realist there is no such timeless existence, but he must admit potential facts that will successively come into existence as the world develops along one of its possible routes. One may wonder how best to speak of these things that do not exist but will come into existence. Since the anti-realist holds that for any sentence A about the future, either A will come true or not-A will come true, he should be willing to say that for each time, one of the possible states of the world will come into existence, and hence also that there is one path along which the world will develop. The anti-realist could say that the path along which the world will develop exists *indeterminately*, to apply an expression used in antiquity to designate this kind of quasi-existence. In contrast, for the realist, the future must be said to be *determinate*. Or, more precisely, any sentence about the future is determined as true or false by the existing future states. But again, although the states that the world assumes at different points of time are so to say indexed by time, their existence is outside of time; they do not exist already. The realist may therefore maintain that the future, although determinate, is not *predetermined*, the meaning of which is explained in terms of the temporal notion of factual necessity.

In this sketch, the realist notion of truth is explained in terms of correspondence with existing facts, while the anti-realist notion of truth is explained in terms of correspondence with potential facts. The sketches must of course be developed much further to say whether both standpoints are really coherent, and if they are, what their comparative advantages and disadvantages are. For instance, the anti-realist must allow for disjunctions that are true while none of the disjuncts is and for conjunctions that are false without any of the conjuncts being false, which is quite a departure from what we are used to. The anti-realist must also find a way to evaluate predictions A made at s about an event at a future point of time t, not only by saying that A is true or false, as the case may be, at t, but also by assessing A at s from the point of view of t without falling into contradictions. For instance, from the point of view of tomorrow, when, say, today's prediction of the occurrence of a sea battle the following day has turned out to be "correct" (as one says in ordinary language), we want to say of this prediction that it was the case already when it was made, that it *would become* true, although it is not the case today from the point of view of today that the prediction *will be* true.[13]

Both the realist as represented by von Wright and the antirealist emphasize as already noted that the future is open in an ontological sense: the openness is not just a matter of our ignorance, the future *is* really open. The intriguing questions are what the ontological openness of the future really amounts to, whether there is any deeper difference between the two views in this respect, and if so what that consists in. Having no answers to these questions, I find it of interest to investigate whether it is not possible, after all, to understand the necessity that has figured in these discussions in an epistemic way with less ontological presuppositions.

IV.4. Epistemic necessity from a constructivist perspective

In order to avoid explaining truth in terms of "facts" in future states of the world or "potential facts" in all "possible" future states of the world, one does better not to explain it in terms of facts at all. This is the leading idea of an epistemic notion of truth that explains truth in terms of what establishes a sentence as true, which in turn is taken to depend on the meaning of the sentence. Given such a semantics, the facts of the world may be seen as determined by which sentences are true, rather than the other way around. In the terminology of Michael Dummett, such an approach will lead to a *realist* or an *anti-realist* conception of a subject matter, if, in the sector of language in which we speak

---

[13] A double relativisation of truth with respect to time in order to allow exactly this kind of speech is suggested in Michael Dummett, "Truth from the Constructive Standpoint", *Theoria* LXIV, 1998, pp 122-138. Another way to achieve the same thing is discussed by Crispin Wright ("Trumping Assessments and the Aristotelian Future", *forthcoming*), who considers this as an example of relativism and points out problems when seen in that perspective. Von Wright has also discussed various ways of speaking about the past future by adding temporal operators and evaluating them with respect to models of the world in form of trees. For discussion and further references, see e.g. Dag Prawitz, "Von Wright on the Concept of Cause", in *The Philosophy of Georg Henrik von Wright*, pp 417-444.

about that subject matter, the principle of bivalence holds or fails, respectively.

If we equate *true* with *established to be true*, truth will be tensed in a way that contradicts fundamental pre-theoretical ideas of truth, but if we equate *true* with *being possible in principle to be established as true*, it is different. Mathematics affords the clearest example of a domain in which applying such an epistemic notion of truth has been tried: the truth of a sentence is equated with the existence of a proof (which does not need to be known by us) instead of with the existence of a corresponding mathematical fact, and since there is no guarantee that, for every sentence involving quantification over infinite domains, there either is a proof of it or of its negation, we have no guarantee for the validity of the law of excluded middle or the principle of bivalence when applied to such sentences. The result is an anti-realist conception of some subject matters involving mathematical infinity.

This approach is compatible with different views of time. If we say that sentences about the past or future are true depending on whether there is *now* available evidence for their truth, the result is an anti-realist view of both the past and the future. Michael Dummett has in some periods been inclined to such a view. For my part, I have always thought that this way of construing the truth of the past and the future distorts our meaning of tensed sentences, and that we should rather say that a sentence concerning a certain time that has passed is true, if *at that time* in the past it was possible in principle to establish the sentence as true, and similarly that a sentence concerning a certain time in the future is true, if *at that time* in the future it will be possible in principle to establish the sentence as true. If we take that view, which Michael Dummett nowadays agrees with, we get a notion of truth that can be taken as atemporal and for which we find that the principle of bivalence and the law of excluded third hold for all sentences about observable events, regardless of whether they are in the past, present, or future. In these respects the results obtained accords with von Wright's way of thinking in spite of the very different starting points.

The question is whether from such a basis one can define an epistemic notion of necessity that with respect to tensed sentences behaves like factual necessity as described above. When we are in possession of compelling evidence for the truth of A, then we often say naturally that A *must* be true. We have here a kind of epistemic necessity, which may be understood as signifying that confronted with compelling evidence, we have no choice but to hold the sentence true. However, for such a notion of necessity, the principle that truth implies necessity does not hold in the way it does for factual necessity, because a sentence may be true, while we are not in possession of the evidence for the truth; truth now meaning that evidence could in principle be found (or could in principle have been found, or will in principle be possible to find).

We may try to introduce a more objective notion of epistemic necessity that is not tied to our actual possession of evidence. One proposal is to say that a sentence A is necessary at time t, if (compelling) evidence could in principle be available at time t for the truth of A, in other words, provided that certain possible precautions are taken, evidence can be had at time t for the truth of A. To see how such a notion of necessity behaves, let A_t be a sentence stating that a certain observable event takes place at time t and suppose that A_t is true. Then evidence for the truth of A_t is available in principle at time t (can be had simply by observing the event in question), and hence A_t is true necessarily at time t in this epistemic sense. This conforms with Aristotle's statement that "what is, necessarily is, when it is" in the same way as factual necessity does as developed above, i.e. the implication (I_1) holds for this notion of necessity.

Furthermore, we get the same kind of exceptions to the principle that truth implies necessity. More precisely, the implication (I_2) does not always hold for this kind of epistemic necessity: If t is a point of time that comes after the time of utterance, then A_t may true without A being necessarily valid (i.e. at the time of utterance), since it may not be the case that the evidence for the truth of A_t could in principle be available at the time of the utterance. More generally, if s is a point of time coming before t, then, lacking a proof for determinism, there need not be any evidence for the truth of A_t that could in principle be available already at s.

This conformity with factual necessity is a result of the obvious epistemic openness of the future. What about the past? As von Wright points out, the past is also open in an epistemic sense: as far as we know, there may be several different previous states of the world from which the present state could have developed. But we are now speaking, not of what is known, but of evidence that could be available in principle. Still, as time passes, evidence may get lost forever, and therefore evidence that was available in principle may not be so any longer. However, we may argue that any specific evidence that is available at some time could in principle be saved for the future. In other words, any specific evidence available in principle at time t could in principle be available at any later time u. Therefore, if we accept this, and if u is a point of time coming after t, then there is evidence for the truth of A_t that could in principle be available at time u, and hence A_t is true necessarily at time u.

We can summarize what holds for this notion of epistemic necessity by considering the following examples:

i) It is necessary (now) for there to be or not to be a sea-battle tomorrow.

The disjunction refers to tomorrow and is true if it can be established tomorrow as true. We can prove now that this is the case, because by making the appropriate observations tomorrow, we will find that there is a sea battle or that there is not. In either case, we will have established tomorrow that one of the disjuncts is true and hence that the disjunction is true. The disjunction can thus be established tomorrow as true. We have thus a proof now that the disjunction is true, and hence we can conclude that it is necessarily true.

ii) Either it is necessary that there is a sea battle now or it is necessary that there is not.

By making the appropriate observations now we will have evidence now for there being a sea battle now or for there not being one now. In either case, one of the disjuncts is true and thereby also the disjunction is true. Hence, the disjunction is true.

iii) There is in general no guarantee that either it is necessary that a sea battle takes place tomorrow or that it is necessary that it does not.

We showed the disjunction appearing as a subsentence in i) to be true by arguing that tomorrow one of its disjuncts could be established as true. Thereby we had *now* a proof for that disjunction and concluded that it is necessarily true. However, from the fact that tomorrow we shall be able to establish one of these disjuncts as true, it follows only that *tomorrow* one of them will turn out to be necessarily true. To show that the disjunction that we are now considering is true, we have to show that one of the disjuncts is true, which in turn requires that we could in principle have evidence *now* for one of the disjuncts, but for that there is no guarantee.

iv) Either it is necessary that there was yesterday a sea battle or it is necessary that there was not.

One could have made appropriate observations yesterday that would have given us evidence for that there was a sea battle yesterday or for that there was not. In the first case, this evidence could in principle have been preserved to today, i.e. evidence could in principle be available today for there having been a sea battle yesterday, which means that the first disjunct is true; the disjunction is thereby true. Similarly, in the second case, the second disjunct is true and the disjunction is thereby again true. In both cases the disjunction is thus true.

Part 2

Logic and Philosophy, Then and Now

Logic and Philosophy
in the Twentieth Century

Georg Henrik von Wright[1]

---

1. In what follows I try to evaluate the place of logic in the philosophy of our century. The attempt is necessarily subjective. Its outcome may be different depending upon whether the evaluator is primarily a logician or primarily a philosopher. I think of myself as a philosopher who, over a period of almost sixty years, has at close quarters been watching and also, to some extent, participating in the development of logic.

As I see things, the most distinctive feature of 20th century philosophy has been the revival of logic and the fermenting role which this has played in the overall development of the subject. The revival dates from the turn of the century. Its entrance on the philosophical stage was heralded by movements which had their original centers at Cambridge and in Vienna, and which later fused and broadened to the multibranched current of thought known as analytical philosophy. As the century is approaching its end we can notice, I think, signs of decline in the influence of logic on developments in philosophy.

Our era was not the first in history which saw logic rise to prominence in philosophy. In the orbit of Western civilization this has happened at least twice before. First it happened in Ancient Greece, in the 4th and 3rd centuries B.C. The second great epoch of logical culture was in the Christian Middle Ages. This was connected with the rediscovery of Aristotle mediated by

---

[1] Originally given at the 11th Congress of Logic, Methodology, and Philosophy of Science in Uppsala in 1991, the lecture is here reprinted from *Logic, Methodology, and Philosophy of Science IX*, ed by D. Prawitz, B Skyrms, and D. Westerståhl (Elsevier Science, 1994), pp. 9-25, with kind permission of Springer Science and Business Media.

the Arabs, and it lasted, roughly, from the middle of the 12th to the middle of the 14th century.

In between the peaks logic 'hibernated.' Its latest winter sleep lasted nearly half a millennium – from the mid-fourteenth to the mid-nineteenth century. In this period, there were also logicians of great ability and power. The greatest of them was Leibniz. But his influence *as a logician* on the philosophic climate of the time was small. It was not until the beginning of our century, when Louis Couturat published his *La logique de Leibniz* and a number of unedited fragments that Leibniz the logician was discovered.

Logic in the state of hibernation was respected for its past achievements, but not thought capable of significant further development. This attitude is epitomized in Kant's well known *dictum* that logic after Aristotle "keinen Schritt vorwarts hat tun können, und also allem Ansehen nach geschlossen und vollendet zu sein scheint."[2]

2. What we nowadays commonly understand by 'logic' was not always referred to with that name.

Although the word derives from a Greek root, Aristotle did not use it for what we think of as his works in logic. Initially, they had no common label at all. The name for them, *Organon* ('instrument') dates from the first century B.C.. The Stoics used, with some consistency, the term *dialectics* for what we would call logical study. This term was transmitted to the Middle Ages through the Latin tradition of late Antiquity. One of the earliest works which signalizes the revival of logic is Abelard's *Dialectics*. The same author, however, also used the name 'logics' which then became current during the Golden Age of Scholasticism – only to yield ground once more to the rival 'dialectics' in the period of the Renaissance. Later, also the name 'Organon' was revived.[3] In German writings of the 18th and 19th centuries the terms 'Vernunfts-' and 'Wissenschaftslehre' were largely used.[4]

For the rehabilitation of the name 'logic' the once influential *Logique ou l'art de penser* (1662), also known as the Logic of Port Royal, appears to have been of decisive importance. This revival,

---

[2]Kant, *Kritik der reinen Vernunft*, p. 7. (Pagination of the second edition, 1787.)

[3]Most notably with Francis Bacon's *Novum Organum* (1620); later also with Lambert's *Neues Organon (1764);* and once again with William Whewell's *Novum Organon Renovatum (1858)*.

[4]Thus, for example, by Bolzano whose *Wissenschaftslehre (1837) is* one of the early precursors of logic in its modern form.

however, was concurrent with a deprecation of the medieval tradition and with efforts to create something more in tune with the emerging new science of nature. The logic of Port Royal is not 'logic' in our sense. It is more like what we would call 'methodology,' an 'aid to thinking' as the title says.

Kant, who thought Aristotelian logic incapable of development, wanted to renew the subject by creating what he called a *transcendental* logic. This was to deal with 'the origin, scope, and objective validity' of *a priori* or 'purely rational' knowledge.[5] And Hegel who, it is said,[6] more than anybody else is responsible for the final establishment of the term 'logic,' says in so many words that the time has come when the conceptions previously associated with the subject "should completely vanish and the position of this science (sc. logic) be utterly changed."[7]

Hegel was not entirely unsuccessful in his reformist zeal. What has since been known as Hegelian or dialectical logic has had a foothold in philosophy up to the present day. But it is not *this* which I had in mind when extolling the role of logic in contemporary philosophic culture. Far from it!

It is characteristic of the terminological vacillations that when the true *logics rediviva* entered the philosophic stage in the early decades of our century, it too wanted to appear under a name of its own. Couturat proposed for it the neologism *logistique*;[8] in German it became *Logistik*. The idea was to emphasize, not only its novelty, but also its difference both from the corrupted logic of the immediately preceding centuries and from the Aristotelian and the Scholastic traditions thought obsolete.[9] It was in this 'spirit of modernity' that I, for example, was trained in logic as a young

---

[5] Kant, op. cit., p. 78.

[6] Heinrich Scholz, *Geschichte der Logik, p. 12*. Junker und Dünnhaupt, Berlin 1931.

[7] Hegel, *Wissenschaft der Logik,* Teil I, p. 36: "'Allein - sind überhaupt die Vorstellungen auf denen der Begriff der Logik bisher beruhte, teils bereits untergegangen, teils ist es Zeit, dass sie vollends verschwinden, class der Standpunkt dieser Wissenschaft höher gefasst werde und dass sie eine völlig verdnderte Gestalt gewinne." (Quoted from *Werkausgabe*, Suhrkamp Verlag, Frankfurt am Main 1969.)

[8] See the article "Logistique" in Lalande's *Vocabulaire technique et critique de la philosophie*.

[9] Whitehead, in his Foreword to Quine's early work *A System of Logistic* (1934), wrote: "In the modern development of Logic, the traditional Aristotelian Logic takes its place as a simplification of the problem presented by the subject. In this there is an analogy to arithmetic of primitive tribes compared to modern mathematics."

student. That the term 'logistic' never acquired wide currency in English is probably due to the fact that the plural form of the word already had an established use with a different connotation in this language.[10] Instead, the attributes 'mathematical' and 'symbolic' were long used to distinguish the new logic from its ancestral forms.

3. In view of the confusion in terminology and multiplicity of traditions, it is necessary to say a few words about what I – and I believe most of us moderns – understand by logic.

Kant appears to have been the first to use the term 'formal' for logic in the tradition of Aristotle and the School.[11] Logic studies the *structural* aspects of the ratiocinative processes we call argument, inference, or proof. It lays down rules for judging the correctness of the transition from premises to conclusions – not rules for judging the truth of the premises and conclusions themselves. This gives to logic its *formal* character – and it was with a view to it that both Kant and Hegel complained of the subject's 'barrenness' and lack of *content*.

The 'content' of formal logical study are *concepts*, one could say. Logic studies them, not in their external relation to the world, but in their internal relationships of coherence or its opposite. This is what we call 'conceptual analysis.' In the simplest cases it takes the form of Aristotelian definitions through specific differences within proximate genera. In more complex and interesting cases it consists of the construction of conceptual networks or 'fields,' the structural properties of which give meaning to the entities involved. Formalized axiomatic systems are examples of such constructs. Hilbert aptly called them 'implicit definitions.'

The study of inference and of meaning relations between concepts are the two main pursuits of the discipline of logic. Some would perhaps wish to separate the two aspects more sharply from one another and distinguish them as 'formal logic' and 'conceptual analysis' respectively. Both attitudes can be justified. The fact remains that it is the close alliance of the two aspects which has given to philosophy in our century its strong 'logical coloring.'

4. When one of the many subdivisions of philosophy – be it metaphysics or ethics or logic – assumes distinctive prominence, this is usually connected with some *other* characteristic features

---

[10]Cf. comments on the term 'logistic' in C.I. Lewis, A *Survey of Symbolic Logic* (1918), p. 3ff. Dover Publications, New York 1960.

[11]Scholz, op. cit., p. 14. Kant, op.cit., p. 76ff.

of the cultural physiognomy of the time. This holds also for the three epochs in Western culture when the study of logic excelled.

In the history of philosophy, the 4th and 3rd centuries B.C. succeeded the period usually named after the Sophists. This had been an era of childish delight in the newly discovered power of *words* (the λγοι) in the uses and misuses of *arguments* for settling disputes in courts or in the market. The challenge to reflect critically on these early eruptions of untamed rationality gave rise to the tradition in philosophy known as Socratic and, within it, to the more specialized study of the forms of thought we call logic. This was also the time of the first attempts to systematize knowledge of mathematics – as witness Eudoxos' doctrine of proportions and the pre-Euclidean efforts to axiomatize the elements of geometry.

The cultural setting in which medieval Scholasticism flourished was very different. Mathematics and the study of nature were in low waters. The rational efforts of the time were turned toward elucidating and interpreting the *logos* of the Christian scriptures. In its deteriorated forms this activity acquired a reputation for hairsplitting. But it should be remembered that the 'hairs' split were *concepts* and that their 'splitting,' when skillfully done, was conceptual analysis of an acuteness which rivals the best achievements of our century.

With the calamities which befell Europe in the 14th century, the intellectual culture of the Christian Middle Ages also declined. Gradually, a new picture of the world and of man's place in it took shape. It was based on the study of natural phenomena and the use of mathematical tools for theorizing about them. Scholasticism fell in disrepute, and on logic dawned the half-millennial slumber to which we have already alluded.

What was the cause for the revival of logic in the late 19th century? One might see it in the fact that Western science had by then reached a maturity which made it ripe to reflect critically on its own rational foundations. The organ of the new scientific world-picture being mathematics, it was but natural that the reflexion should start with people who were themselves primarily mathematicians like the two founding fathers of modern logic: Boole and Frege.

Their respective approaches to the subject, however, were rather different.[12] Boole, like his contemporary Augustus de Morgan, was concerned with the application of mathematical tools to traditional logic. Their trend was continued, among others, by Peirce and Schröder. Frege's objective was different. He wanted to secure for mathematics a foundation in pure logic. To this end he had not only to revive but also to reshape it.

5. The revitalization of logic thus took its origin from foundation research in mathematics.

The line first taken by Frege and then continued by Russell was, however, but one of a number. In the light of later developments, Frege's and Russell's approach is perhaps better characterized as an attempt to give to mathematics a set-theoretic foundation rather than to derive mathematics from a basis in pure logic. Cantor's figure looms heavily in the background of the logicists' efforts.

Another approach to the foundation problems was Hilbert's conception of mathematics as a family of axiomatized formal calculi to be investigated for consistency, completeness, independence, and other 'perfection properties' in a *meta-mathematics*. Hilbert's program is in certain ways a revival of Leibniz's conception of a *calculus ratiocinator*, operating within a *characteristics universalis*.

A third venture into the foundations of mathematics, finally, was Brouwer's intuitionism. It had forerunners in Kronecker's constructivism and the 'semi-intuitionism' of Borel and Poincaré. Brouwer's view of the role of logic was very different both from that of Frege and Russell and from that of Hilbert.[13] The bitter polemics between 'intuitionists' and 'formalists' bear witness to this. By raising doubts about one of the cornerstones of traditional logic, viz. the Law of Excluded Third (or Middle), Brouwer and his followers were also pioneers of what is nowadays known as Deviant or Non-Standard or Non-Classical Logic(s).

---

[12] The difference is interestingly reflected in the titles of the works with which they embarked on their respective tasks. Boole's was called *The Mathematical Analysis of Logic, Being an Essay towards a Calculus of Deductive Reasoning*. Frege's pioneering work had the title *Begriffsschrift, eine der arithmetischen nachgebildete Formelsprache des reinen Denkens*.

[13] A contemporary account of the state of foundation research in mathematics, still very worth reading is A. Heyting's *Mathematische Grundlagenforschung, Intuitionismus, Beweistheorie*, Julius Springer, Berlin 1934.

Logicism, formalism, and intuitionism were the three main schools which, rivals among themselves, dominated the stage during what I propose to call 'the heroic age' in the reborn study of logic. It lasted about half a century, from Frege's *Begriffsschrift* (1879) and *Grundlagen der Arithmetik (1884)* to the appearance of the first volume of Hilbert's and Bernay's monumental *Grundlagen der Mathematik* in *1934*. As one who was brought up in the aftermath of this era, I cannot but look back on it with a certain amount of nostalgia. It came to an end in a dramatic climax. I shall shortly return to this. But first, we must take a look at the more immediate repercussions on philosophy which the new logic had had.

6. In earlier days it used to be said that logic studies 'the laws of thought.' This had been the title of Boole's *magnum opus*. But it was also said that logic was not concerned with (the laws of) psychological thought processes. So what aspect of thought did logic study then? One could answer: *the articulation of thought in language*. Language is, so to speak, the raw material with which logic works. (The Greek *logos* means, ambiguously, both speech and ratiocination.) A time when logic holds a place in the foreground of philosophy is also one in whose intellectual culture language is bound to be prominent.

This is eminently true of the Golden Age of logic in antiquity. The Sophist movement had been an outburst of exuberant delight in the discovery of language as *logos*, i.e. as an instrument of argument, persuasion, and proof. The disciplines of logic and of grammar were the twin offsprings of this attitude.

The logic of the School, too, has been described as a *Sprachlogik* or logic of language.[14] An excessive interest in the linguistic leg-pulling known as 'sophismata' seems to have been a contributory cause of the disrepute into which Scholasticism fell in its later days.

The 'linguistic turn,'[15] which philosophy has taken in our century, has become commonplace. So much so that one may feel tempted to view logic as one offshoot among many of the study of language, other branches being theoretical linguistics, computer science, and the study of artificial intelligence and information

---

[14]The term presumably first used by Martin Grabmann in his renowned work *Geschichte der scholastischen Methode I-II*, Freiburg i B. 1909-1911.

[15]The phrase borrowed from the title of Richard Rorty's book *The Linguistic Turn*, Chicago 1967. Rorty attributes the invention of the phrase to Gustav Bergmann.

processing. But this would be a distortion of the historical perspective. Unlike what was the case with the Ancients, with whom logic grew out of an interest in language, it was the revival of logic which, with us, made language central to philosophy. Here Frege's work became a seminal influence. But it is noteworthy that Frege the philosopher of language was 'discovered' very much later than Frege the philosopher of logic. This renaissance of Frege's influence and of Fregean studies took place only with 'the turn to semantics' in logic in the mid-century.

Hilbert's concern with the language fragments we call calculi did not much influence developments in the philosophy of language.[16] Nor did Brouwer's work do this directly. But Brouwer's attack on formalism is, interestingly, also a critique of language as an articulation of the intuitions underlying mathematical thinking. With his thoughts on the limits of language as well as with some other ideas of his, Brouwer is a precursor of the philosopher who, more than anybody else, has contributed to making language a major concern of contemporary thinking.

7. Even though Wittgenstein never adhered to the logicist position in the philosophy of mathematics, he stands in the *Tractatus* firmly on the shoulders of Frege and Russell. The place of this book in the picture we are here drawing is peculiar.

It would be quite wrong to think of Wittgenstein's contribution to logic as limited to the discovery of the truth-table method for propositional logic and the conception of logical truths as truth-functional tautologies. (The truth-table idea has a long tradition going back way before Wittgenstein.)

Foremostly, *Tractatus* is an inquiry into the possibility of language. How can signs mean? The answer Wittgenstein gave was his picture theory about the isomorphic reflection of the configurations of things in the world, in the configurations of names (words) in the sentence. The essence of language is the essence of the world – their common logical form. This, however, is veiled by the grammatical surface structure of actual speech. The logical

---

[16]I would conjecture, however, that Wittgenstein's notion of 'language game' and his ideas from the early 1930's of language as calculus have a remote source of inspiration in the influence of Hilbertian formalism on the discussions about logic and the philosophy of mathematics among members of the Vienna Circle. Cf. *Ludwig Wittgenstein and der Wiener Kreis. Gespniche, aufgezeichnet von Friedrich Waismann*. Aus dem Nachlass herausgegeben von B.F. McGuinness. In: *Ludwig Wittgenstein, Schriften* 3, Suhrkamp Verlag, Frankfurt am Main 1967.

deep structure of language is a postulated ideal which shows itself in meaningful discourse but which, since presupposed, cannot be itself described in language.

If we abstract from the peculiarities, not to say eccentricities, of the picture theory and the mysticism of the saying-showing distinction, the *Tractatus* view of logic reflects what I think are common and deep-rooted conceptions of the nature of logical form, necessity, and truth. Indirect confirmation of this may be seen in the coolness, and even hostility, with which logicians and mathematicians, until recently, have received the partly devastating criticism to which Wittgenstein later submitted, not only his own earlier views of logic, but foundation research in general.

The 'metaphysics of logic' – as I would like to call it – of the *Tractatus* has survived and, moreover, experienced revivals in more recent times. I am thinking of developments in linguistic theory and in the partly computer-inspired philosophy of mind represented by cognitive science and the study of artificial intelligence.

The 'never-never language'[17] which Wittgenstein had postulated in order to explain how language, as we have it, is possible, has been resurrected in equally speculative ideas about innate grammatical structures or about an ineffable language of thought ('mentalese'), deemed necessary for explaining the child's ability to assimilate with the language community where it belongs. Chomsky's revived *grammaire universelle* or 'Cartesian linguistics' is another 'crystalline structure' of the kind Wittgenstein in the *Tractatus* had postulated for logic.[18]

For these reasons alone, I think that Wittgenstein's criticism has a message worthy of attention also for contemporary philosophy of language and philosophy of mind. The similarity between

---

[17]The phrase was invented by the late Professor Max Black. See his *A Companion to Wittgenstein's Tractatus*, p. 11. Cambridge University Press, Cambridge 1964.

[18]Wittgenstein, *Philosophische Untersuchungen* (1953), § 107: "Die Kristallenreinheit de Logik hatte sick mir ja nicht *ergeben,* sondern sie war eine *Forderung.*"

the *Tractatus* views and these latter day phenomena has not escaped notice.[19] But it has, so far, hardly been deservedly evaluated from a critical point of view.[20] The present situation in cognitive and linguistic research offers interesting parallels to the search for 'foundations' which earlier in the century made logic central to the philosophy of mathematics, and which reached what I would call its self-defeating climax in Wittgenstein's *Tractatus*.

8. "Every philosophical problem," Russell wrote on the eve of the First World War, "when it is subjected to the necessary analysis and purification, is found either to be not really philosophical at all, or else to be – logical."[21] But he also said that the type of philosophy he was advocating and which had "crept into philosophy through the critical scrutiny of mathematics" had "not as yet many wholehearted adherents."[22] In this respect a great change was brought about in the post-war decades by the movement known as logical positivism, stemming from the activities of the Wiener Kreis and some kindred groups of science-oriented philosophers and philosophy-oriented scientists in Central Europe. One saw a new era dawning in the intellectual history of man when philosophy too, at long last, had attained *den sicheren Gang einer Wissenschaft*.

According to an influential formulation by Carnap, philosophy was to become the logical syntax of the language of science. This was an extreme position and was in origin associated with views, inherited from earlier positivist and sensualist philosophy, of how a logical constitution of reality, a *logischer Aufbau der Welt*, was to be accomplished.

It is nowadays commonplace to declare logical positivism dead and gone. It should be remembered, however, that the movement was conquered and superseded largely thanks to self-criticism generated in its own circle. This combination of self-destruction with self-development is perhaps unique in the history of thought. At

---

[19] See R.M. McDonough, *The Argument of the 'Tractatus'. Its Relevance to Contemporary Theories of Logic, Language, Mind, and Philosophical Truth*. State University of New York Press, Albany, N.Y. 1986. Particularly pp. 172-183.

[20] The best attempt known to me of such critical evaluation is that of Norman Malcolm. See in particular his book *Nothing is Hidden, Wittgenstein's Criticism of His Early Thought*, Basil Blackwell, Oxford 1986.

[21] Russell, *Our Knowledge of the External World, As a Field for Scientific Method in Philosophy* (1914), p. 42. Quoted from the edition by Allen & Unwin, London, 1949.

[22] Russell, op. cit., p. 14.

least I know no comparable case. As a result, a narrow conception of philosophy as the logic of science gradually gave place to a conception of it as logical analysis of all forms of discourse. For a just assessment of logical positivism, it is necessary to see the movement as the fountain-head which eventually grew into the broad current of analytic philosophy with its multifarious bifurcations. No one would deny that *this* has been a mainstream – I should even say *the* mainstream – of philosophy in our century. It is in these facts about its origins: first with foundation research in mathematics, and then with the extension of the use of logical tools to the conceptual analysis of scientific and, eventually, also everyday language, that I found my claim that logic has been the distinctive hallmark of philosophy in our era.

9. What I called the heroic age in the history of modern logic came to an end in the 1930's. The turn to a new era[23] was marked by two events, themselves of 'heroic' magnitude. The one was Gödel's discovery of the incompleteness properties of formalized calculi; the second Tarski's semantic theory of truth. There is, moreover, an intrinsic connection between the two achievements.[24]

Gödel's incompleteness theorem had serious repercussions on the formalist program of axiomatization, consistency proof, and decidability. It set limits to the idea, ultimately of Leibnizian origin, of the formalization of all ratiocinative thought in syntactic structures and of reasoning as *a jeu de charactires,* a game of signs ignoring their meaning. The related achievement of Tarski meant a transcendence of the syntactic point of view and its supplementation by a semantic one. Therewith it made the relation of language *structure* to language *meaning* amenable to exact treatment. The immensely fertile field of model theory is an outgrowth of this opening up of the semantic dimension of logic. For its further investigation, Tarski's later work was also of decisive, seminal importance. His pioneering rôle is in no way minimized by the fact that, seen in the perspective of history, basic ideas in model theory go back to the earlier work of Skolem and Löwenheim.

---

[23]On this turn and its repercussions on foundation research in mathematics, see the excellent account by Andrzej Mostowski, *Thirty Years of Foundation Studies, Lectures on the Development of Mathematical Logic and the Study of the Foundations of Mathematics* in 1930-1964. Basil Blackwell, Oxford 1966.

[24]23 Tarski, '*Der Wahrheitsbegriff in den formalisierten Sprachen.*' *Studio Philosophica I*, 1935. Postscript (Nachwort), p. 404f.

Gödel's impact on the formalist program, although devastating for the more ambitious, philosophic aspirations of the Hilbert school, also greatly furthered its less ambitious aims. Proof-theory crystallized in the arithmetization of metamathematics and in the theory of computable and recursive functions.

Something similar happened to the line in logic stemming from Frege and Russell and continued through the 1930's, most conspicuously in the work of the young Quine. The antinomies turned out to be a more serious stumbling block than it had seemed after the early efforts of Russell's to conquer the difficulties which had threatened to wreck Frege's system. The semantic antinomies, like the Liar, required extensions beyond type-theory which in none of their suggested forms can be said to have gained universal recognition. The sought for basis of mathematics in pure logic gradually took the shape of a foundation in set-theory. Set-theory, being itself a controversial branch of mathematics, gave prominence to another challenge, viz. that of clarifying the axiomatic and conceptual foundations of Cantor's paradise. Even though the difficulties which the logicist approach encountered can be said to have ruined the original aspirations of its initiators, this heir to their program remains, in my opinion, the philosophically most challenging aspect of foundation research in mathematics today. Not surprisingly Gödel, the perhaps most philosophic-minded mathematical logician of the century, devoted his later efforts mainly to work in this area.

The third mainstream in the early foundation research, intuitionism, also changed its course. In 1930 Heyting codified, in a formal system, the logical rules which were thought acceptable from the intuitionist point of view. Thereby he created an instrument which has turned out to be very useful in the mathematical study of proof, and thus for vindicating that part of Hilbert's program which remained unaffected by Gödel's discoveries. In view of the acrimony which once embittered the fight between formalists and intuitionists and not least the relations between the founders of the two schools[25] their reconciliation in the later developments of proof-theoretic study may even appear a little ironic.

Brouwer himself was of the opinion that no system of formal rules can encompass the entire range of mathematically sound intuitions. He could therefore not attach great importance to

---

[25] Cf. Heyting, op. cit., p. 53f. Also D. van Dalen, 'The War of the Frogs and the Mice, or the Crisis of the *Mathematische Annalen*,' *The Mathematical Intelligence 12*, 1990.

Heyting's achievement. Of Gödel's results he is reported to have said that their gist had been obvious to him long before Gödel presented his proofs.[26]

In his rebuttal of the idea that logic could provide a foundation for mathematics, Brouwer can be said to anticipate the attitude of the later Wittgenstein. Wittgenstein also shared the constructivist leanings of the intuitionists and their critical reflection on some basic principles of classical logic.

The change of climate in logic after the 1930's I would describe as a 'disenchantment' *(Entzauberung)* in Max Weber's sense. When the grand dreams and visions of the formalist, intuitionist, and logicist schools had lost their philosophic fascination, what remained and grew out of them was sober, solid science. The discipline which had been the mother of the new logic, viz. mathematics, took back its offspring to its sheltered home.

The homecoming did not fail to raise suspicions among the settled members of the family, however. Early in the century, Poincare had objected to the *logisticiens,* that they pretended to give 'wings' *(ailes)* to mathematics but had in fact provided it only with a 'hand-rail' *(lisiere)* and, moreover, not a very reliable one.[27] On my first encounter with Tarski a few years after the war, Tarski told me of the difficulties and frustrations he had experienced trying to make mathematical logic respected in the mathematics department at Berkeley. I recall something similar from the mathematical establishment in my own country in the form of complaints that some of the most promising students had left the subject and migrated to philosophy. Now, forty years or more later, this attitude no longer prevails in the mathematical profession, except maybe in corners of the world not yet much touched by modern developments.

10. When viewing the history of modern logic as a process of 'rational disenchantment' in areas of conceptual crisis or confusion, one is entitled to the judgment that the most exciting development in logical theory after the second world war has been the rebirth of modal logic. The study of modal concepts had flourished in the Aristotelian tradition—not only with its founder, but also with its medieval continuation. In the renaissance starting with Boole and

---

[26]Hao Wang, *Reflections on Kurt Gödel,* p. 57 and p. 88. The MIT Press; Cambridge, Mass. 1987.

[27]Poincare, *Science et Métode (1909),* p. *193f.* The references are to the Edition Flamarion, Paris 1924, *Cf.* also Russell, op. cit., p. 68.

Frege, this study, however, long remained neglected. When eventually it was revived in the work of Lukasiewicz and C.I. Lewis, its rebirth was something of a miscarriage. This was so because it took the form of a critique of Russellian logic. Modal logic was thought of as a 'non-classical' alternative or even rival to it.

It was only with the conception of modal logic, not as an alternative to Russell's but rather as a 'superstructure' standing on its basis, that the logical study of modalities got a good start in modern times. This conception did not gain ground until after the second world war, although it had had precursors in the 1930's with Gödel and Feys.

A result of the new start was something that could be called a General Theory of Modality. Instead of 'General Theory' one could also speak of a *family* of related 'logics' of a similar formal structure. These offshoots of an old stem of traditional modal logic have become known as epistemic, doxastic, prohairetic, deontic, and interrogative logic. Historical research has revealed ancestors of many of them either in ancient and medieval logic or with Leibniz, this prodigious logical genius, whose seeds mainly fell in the barren soil of his own time.

One thing which has made the study of modal concepts controversial is that it problematized one of the basic principles of logic—it too of Leibnizian ancestry—known as the law of intersubstitutivity *salva veritate* of identities. Such substitutivity in sentential contexts is the hallmark of what is known as *extensionality* in logic. A system of logic which disputes or limits the validity of Leibniz's principle is called *intensional*. Modal logic may therefore be regarded as a province within the broader study of *intensional logic*.

Already Frege had drawn attention to limits of extensionality in doxastic and epistemic contexts. Formal operations in intensional contexts, particularly the use in them of quantifiers, have seemed doubtful and unsound to many logicians of a conservative bent of mind. Above all, Quine has been an acute and staunch critic of modal and other forms of intensional logic. But his criticism has also been a challenge and source of inspiration for a younger generation of logicians, partly following in Quine's footsteps, to clear the jungle of modal and intensional concepts and make their study respectable. To this has contributed the invention of the very powerful techniques known as possible worlds semantics. The Leibnizian echo in the name is not mere accident.

With these later developments the study of modal and intensional logic has become progressively less 'philosophical' and technically more refined. Another process of 'disenchantment' is taking place, an initially controversial subject being handed over by philosophically-minded logicians to logically-minded mathematicians.

11. Modal logic, also intensional logic in general, is still in some quarters called 'non- classical.' There is no received view of what should count as 'classical,' or not, in logic. As long as modal logic was regarded as an *alternative* to some already canonized structure, the name might have been justified. But modal logic is *not* an 'alternative' to the logic systematized by Frege and Russell – at least not to that part of it which is known as first order logic and which consists of the two layers of the propositional and the predicate calculus.

A way of distinguishing classical from non-classical logic, which cuts deeper both historically and systematically, is the following: Classical logic accepts as unrestrictedly valid the two basic principles, first stated by Aristotle and subsequently known as the Law of (Excluded) Contradiction and Law of Excluded Middle (or Third). Both are also fundamental in the logic of Frege and Russell. To question the one or the other is tantamount to doubting the division of what is sometimes called *logical space* in two jointly exhaustive and mutually exclusive parts.

Doubts about the exhaustive nature of the partition were already entertained by the founding father of logic himself. (Yet I do not think it right to interpret Aristotle's discussion of the 'Sea-Battle Problem' in the ninth chapter of *Peri Hermeneias* as a denial of the universal validity of the *tertium non datur.*) The same doubts reappeared in the Middle Ages – together with groping attempts to construct a many-valued logic for coping with them. Within modern logic these efforts were renewed by Lukasiewicz. His grand vision of polyvalent logic as a generalization of classical logic did not turn out as fertile as its originator had imagined it to be. The idea of polyvalence has useful technical applications. But the conception of it as a grating of logical space finer than the true-false dichotomy encounters interpretational difficulties. It is therefore doubtful whether many-valued logic should even count as nonclassical in the sense which I have in mind here.

A more consequential onslaught on the Law of Excluded Third and some other 'classical' ideas associated with it, such as the

Principle of Double Negation, came from Brouwer and the intuitionists. As already noted, formalized intuitionist logic has turned out to be a useful conceptual tool for proof-theoretic study. It provides the logical backbone for a constructivist approach to the notion of existence in mathematics and is also helpful for efforts to clarify the concept of the actual infinite. To count with truth-value 'gaps' has become standard in many fields of formal study where one deals with concepts of restricted definability or of an open texture. The Law of Excluded Middle can hardly any longer be regarded as a controversial topic in the philosophy of logic.

More firm and less assailed, until recently, has been the second pillar of classical logic, the Law of Contradiction, which prohibits truth-value 'overlaps.' Therefore, doubts about it, once they are raised, cut much deeper into the foundations of logic than doubts relating to the *tertium non datur*.

In fact, already Aristotle realized that there might be problems here. First among the moderns to see the possibility of a non-classical opening were Lukasiewicz and the Russian Vasiliev.[28]

Throughout the history of thought, antinomies have been a headache of philosophers—and since the origin of set-theory also of mathematicians. Antinomies exemplify seemingly impeccable logical inference terminating in conclusions contradicting each other. If this is thought unacceptable, one has to look for some error in the reasoning—and lay down rules for how to avoid the calamity. This was what Russell did with his Type-Theory and Vicious Circle Principle.

Moreover, the appearance of a contradiction in a context of reasoning, such as for example an axiomatic system, seems to have the vitiating consequence of making everything derivable within the system, thus trivializing or, as one also says, 'exploding' it. Hilbert's efforts were partly aimed at proving that sound systems are immune to such disasters. This presupposed that the logic of the meta-proofs has the required immunity. Hilbert saw a warrant of this in what he called the *finite Einstellung* ('finitist stand'), allowing only *finite Schlussweisen*.

Another way of meeting the challenge presented by contradictions is to scrutinize the idea of logical consequence itself. Contradictions may have to be rejected as false, but must they have

---

[28] N.A. Vasiliev, *Voobrezaemaja Logika, Izbrannye Trudy*, Ed. by V.A. Smirnov. Nauka, Moscow 1989.

the catastrophic consequences which 'classical' logic seems to allow by virtue of what is sometimes referred to as Duns Scotus' Law after the *doctor subtilis* of the School? Efforts to modify the classical view of logical consequence or entailment have been the motivating force behind the venture called Relevance Logic. A more recent and more radical step in the same direction is known as Paraconsistent Logic. One of its aims is to show how contradictions can be 'accommodated' within contexts of reasoning without fear of trivialization or collapse.

These non-classical developments in logic, of the past decades, have found an unexpected, but I think not very trustworthy, ally in Dialectical Logic, ultimately of Hegelian inspiration. The best one can hope for is that the treatment of dialectics with the formal tools of paraconsistent and related 'deviant' logics will contribute to a demystification of those features of it which have made it little palatable to rational understanding. A similar service which these new tools may render is that of reducing to its right proportions what Wittgenstein called "the superstitious dread and veneration by mathematicians in face of contradiction."[29]

Just as classical logic, i.e. the logic of Frege and Russell, can be called the sub-structure on which stand the several branches of modal and intensional logic—in a similar way the two main varieties of non-classical logic: the intuitionist-like ones which admit truth-value gaps and the paraconsistent-like ones which admit truth-value overlaps, will serve as sub-structures from which a variety of alternative epistemic, deontic and other logics will grow out and be further cultivated. But these developments are still in early infancy.

12. I have tried to review the development of logic in this century as a gradual progress *from* the philosophic fascination of a foundation crisis in mathematics and the confusions excited by the rediscovery of fields of study long lying fallow *to* increased clarity, exactness, and conceptual sobriety. But logic thus transformed ceases to be philosophy and becomes science. It either melts into one of the old sciences or contributes to the formation of a new one. What happened to logic was that it fused with the multifarious study of mathematics, but also with newcomers on the scientific stage such as computer science and cognitive study,

---

[29]Wittgenstein, *Remarks on the Foundations of Mathematics*, Third Edition, Basil Blackwell, Oxford 1978, p. 122. In German: 'Die aberglaubige Angst and Verehrung der Mathematiker vor dem Widerspruch.'

cybernetics and information theory, general linguistics – all being fields with a strong mathematical slant.

Transformations of parts of philosophy into independent branches of scientific study are well known from history. The phenomenon has gained for philosophy the name 'mother of the sciences.' Physics was born of natural philosophy; in some English and Scottish universities it still bears that name. The second half of the 19th century witnessed the birth of psychology and sociology through a transformation of predominantly speculative thinking into experimental and empirical research. In our century something similar happened with logic.[30]

Already in the early days of the developments which we have here been following, Russell wrote: "Mathematical logic – is not *directly of* philosophical importance except in its beginnings. After the beginnings, it belongs rather to mathematics than to philosophy."[31] And in an unpublished typescript of Wittgenstein's we read: "Die formale Logik – ein Teil der Mathematik."[32]

Philosophy, I would say, thrives in the twilight of unclarity, confusion and crisis in fields which in their 'normal' state do not bewilder those who cultivate them or cause excitement in their intellectual surroundings. From time to time, however, philosophic storms will occur even in the seemingly calmest of waters. We can be certain that there will always remain obscure corners in logic too, thus assuring for it a permanent place among the concerns of ,philosophers. And I can well imagine that individual thinkers will find in logic the raw material for bold metaphysical constructions. As an example might be cited Gödel's conceptual realism with echoes of Plato and Leibniz. But it seems to me unlikely that logic will continue to play the prominent role in the overall picture of an epoch's philosophy which it has held in the century now approaching its end. This will be so partly because of logic's own success in integrating itself into the neighboring sciences just

---

[30]In a well-known simile, John Langshaw Austin compared this process to philosophy perpetually being 'kicked upstairs' – and he envisaged that his own endeavors would result in the birth of an independent descriptive study of conceptual features of linguistic uses, in a 'linguistic phenomenology'. J.L. Austin, 'Ifs and Cans,' *Proceedings of the British Academy, Vol.* XLII, Oxford University Press, Oxford 1956.

[31]Russell, op. cit., p. 50.

[32]Wittgenstein, TS 219. Wittgenstein's relegation of formal logic to mathematics is not in conflict with the fact that he calls his own investigations n philosophy 'logical.' The adjective then means roughly the same as *conceptual* or, in Wittgenstein's somewhat eccentric terminology, *grammatical*.

mentioned. But it will also be due to the rise on the philosophical horizon of new clouds calling for the philosophers' attention and craving for clarification.

Big shifts in the centre of philosophy signalize changes in the general cultural atmosphere which in their turn reflect changes in political, economic and social conditions. The optimistic mood and belief in progress, fostered by scientific and technological developments, which has been our inheritance from the time of the Enlightenment, is giving way to a somber mood of self-critical scrutiny of the achievements and foundation of our civilization. No attempt to survey the overall situation in contemporary philosophy can fail to notice this and to ponder over its significance.

I shall not try to predict what will be the leading trends in the philosophy of the first century of the 2000's. But I think they will be markedly different from what they have been in this century, and that logic will *not* be one of them. If I am right, the twentieth century will even clearer than now stand out as another Golden Age of Logic in the history of those protean forms of human spirituality we call Philosophy.

A note on von Wright's Lecture on Logic and Philosophy in the Twentieth Century

Nuel Belnap

Though time has fudged the edges of my memory, according to my recollection, it was sometime in the later nineteen sixties that von Wright visited, for a term, the University of Pittsburgh Department of Philosophy, where he was warmly received. I was groping for a kind of "modal logic of action," and well aware of von Wright's seminal ideas on structuring our thinking about both modal logic and action, I visited him in his office where he was kind enough to spend half an afternoon watching me blackboard some half-baked ideas that, by hindsight, could plausibly count as unsatisfactory precursors to the logic of "sees to it that" (*stit logic*) that only emerged as a worked-out theory decades later in *Facing the Future: Agents and Choices in our Indeterminist World*.[1] Whereas I was excited by the direction indicated by those insufficiently baked ideas, von Wright, though attentive, was clearly not bowled over. Indeed, later that same afternoon, von Wright, reversing the situation, came into *my* office, where he blackboarded for me some of his ideas on the logic of change and the logic of action. Although at the time I failed to be bowled over by those particular thoughts, I was certainly boulversée by von Wright himself as a an unfailing source of philosophical-logical ideas and inspiration, especially in connection with modalities and action. He has been for me, through conversations, lectures, and writings, an estimable model.

von Wright was an avowed pessimist regarding the future of logic, putting forward the negative view that logic will *not* play as

---

[1]Belnap, N., Perloff, M., and Xu, M. (Oxford University Press, 2001).

prominent a role in the philosophy of the current century as it did in the twentieth century, which von Wright called a "Golden Age of Logic." That sounds all too right, and is not to be gainsaid. It seems to me equally right to endorse von Wright's view that logic as we know it has left behind the "green and tender" salad days of great questions posed by Frege and Russell and Brouwer, and the excitement of the unparalleled discoveries of Gödel and Tarski. Logic is no longer an organizing concern of philosophers. Its transformation into parts of computer science, of formal linguistics, of mathematics, and of cognitive science, as well as of other allied formal disciplines, some yet to be imagined, can in some sense be seen as a kind of demotion of logic to the status of the not-very-philosophical.

On the other hand, this very transformation means that logic is not about to wither, even if it survives as more "science" than "philosophy." It still needs to be said that in addition to standing as underlaborer in various formal fields, logic as a separate discipline, rightly taken as part of philosophy, is *the* part of the Academy that stands as guardian of the ideal of rigorous thinking as such. It is all the more important that it should serve this function in these times during which rational discourse is being disvalued in many ways. Not the least of these is the stranglehold on our intellectual and artistic pursuits that mindless television seems to have. "If I were king," my first act would be to outlaw all television of any description.

Putting aside such hopeless fancies, however, there is a thread or two in the complex tapestry of von Wright's essay on which I should like to give a gentle tug.

As an aspect of his discussion of non-classical logic, von Wright offers two perspectives on the antinomies or paradoxes that have haunted logic. I take as a simple example the Liar Paradox in the theory of truth. The two strategies that von Wright mentions are these: (1) We may accept some philosopher's account of the outright errors or blunders in reasoning that caused us to deduce contradictory conclusions regarding the Liar Paradox. In this fashion, by sticking to some philosopher's notion of blunder-free reasoning, we may avoid contradictions that at first seemed inescapable. (2) We may put the troublesome reasoning in the context of a non-classical logic that embraces, or at least "accommodates," contradictions by keeping them sufficiently isolated so as not to be fatally poisonous.[2]

---

[2]The quotes are von Wright's.

There is a third approach, due to Anil Gupta.[3] It depends on making a distinction between *descriptive* and *normative* accounts of the reasoning leading to the various paradoxes. Descriptively, Gupta argues that our concept of truth is a *circular concept*, a fact that explains both its normal features and its paradoxical features.[4] Users of such a concept *inevitably* risk contradiction; but to risk disaster is not itself to court disaster. One safe way to avoid the contradictions that are enshrined in our circular concept of truth is described in the following normative advice: Avoid the circular concept in certain limited situations, using instead a non-circular concept that is obtained by truncating the full power of the original concept in a fashion that appears to be "good enough" for a particular application. For example, one may enforce the levels-of-language policy to the modest extent needed for a *particular* application that one has in mind. To carry out this advice, one by no means needs a "one size fits all" so-called "solution" to (or diagnosis of) the Liar and other paradoxes. For example, we may be interested in contrasting the concepts of *proof* and *truth* as they apply to elementary arithmetic. One does not, in that endeavor, need the full, circular concept of truth. Nor does one need a once-for-all "solution" to the Liar Paradox. It suffices to invoke a local version of the levels-of-language approach and a *partial* concept of truth, thus carrying out an explanation of *proof* vs. *truth* with becoming modesty.

---

[3]Gupta, A. 1982, "Truth and paradox," *Journal of philosophical logic* 11, 1-60. Reprinted in R. L. Martin (ed.) *Recent Essays on Truth and the Liar Paradox* (Oxford University Press, 1984), pp. 175-235. For a full discussion, see Gupta, A. and Belnap, N. 1993, *The revision theory of truth* (MIT Press, 1993).

[4]This description is not itself contradictory.

Logic and Philosophy in the Century That Was

Johan van Benthem

It is a great pleasure to write in honour of Georg Henrik von Wright. We met around 1980, when he came as a distinguished visitor to the philosophical institute in Groningen, where a Dutch student defended a dissertation on von Wright's intellectual *Werdegang*. The student had carried his enthusiasm to what some might consider extremes, by also learning Finnish and marrying a Finnish lady. But our visitor turned out to be a modest and highly accessible person. I recall that, when praised for starting the famous Finnish school of logic, he merely said: "Oh no, I did very little. I just taught Jaakko Hintikka."

Von Wright's address makes many points which I would consider 'received history', but of course, lucidly and intelligently. He describes how modern logic came to influence modern philosophy in stages, through the foundations of mathematics, the widening of this methodology in the Vienna Circle, and finally the flowering of analytical philosophy, backed up by developments in philosophical logic. He also notices how this is the third time that logic entered philosophy concomitantly with a linguistic turn that stresses the role of language in thinking – which fits the logical junction of 'structure' and 'language.' These are the still melodious strains of the great classical symphony of our golden age.

But then dissonance appears in the score, and von Wright starts questioning the lasting value of all this. One is that successful logical theories move away into other disciplines: mathematics, computer science, cognitive science, or linguistics, leaving philosophy behind. As Austin once said: "Philosophy gets kicked upstairs." Or, in the words of my colleague Theo de Boer in Amsterdam around 1970 when ideological disputes reigned supreme:

this is the 'left-overs view' of philosophy as studying the scrapings after the meal has gone. And even if this parting does not happen, it might just be that logic has played its role in clearing up the philosophical issues that were important in the past - or maybe these issues have just gone out of fashion. But there is absolutely no reason to think that it will be called on again to play the same role in the philosophical agenda of the future. Indeed, von Wright thinks that it will not in the 21st century.

Many academics see red at once when their utility and historical role is called into question. People collapse with anger over John Horgan's "The End of Science" – of course without having read his intelligent analysis and the facts he cites for his thesis. But I myself have no problem with devastating self-criticism and feelings of gloom. I find a lot of claims I hear about the Long March of philosophy and the sciences very naïve, and driven by the same sort of unthinking historical optimism that leads people to believe that things will just get better all the time. Old Europe and America will (of course) remain rich and influential, other cultures just join in, and the family gets ever larger and happier. To be sure, I have nothing against such scenarios; they just do not seem very likely to me.

But *will* logic go down? Can substantial intellectual disciplines disappear? In the past, some have indeed come close to extinction. Steven Toulmin pointed out the fragility of mathematics in Antiquity, carried by just a few hundred people at the best of times. One century of darkness and the continuity is broken. A witty Dutch historian of logic even said: "One good old-fashioned winter and philosophy in The Netherlands is over." Yes, all this is possible, but it is not likely. Many social mechanisms are operative today that did not exist before: a web of funding processes, Ph.D. programs, tenured appointments. Appoint one young logician, and a university is stuck with the field for 40 more years. Also the organizational power structure of academia is conservative: it is hard for new disciplines to get in and even harder for insiders to be kicked out. Please note, I am not saying that all this is good! In this organisational setting, academic fields can be active and powerful long after they are brain-dead. I sometimes long for some Darwinism.

These are generalities which do not yet point in any particular direction for our main theme. Now for my more concrete views about logic and philosophy. Let me start with some 'negatives' in von Wright's account that I agree with, perhaps even more so than he himself would have wished, being the cautious and considerate gentleman that he was. I will speak apodictically in what follows, but these are critical points I have made on various occasions, so my bridges are burnt anyway.

Yes, the grand foundational inspiration for logic and philosophy is largely over. Yes, one often does not notice this because old agendas are being rehashed for decades, piling comments on comments in the way of Antiquity, in boring inward-looking manners. What is even worse is the historicizing remnant, in some circles, of foundational research that I call 'fundamentalism'. Instead of thinking about new agendas, people preach a return to the past. As against this I say, if logic is to survive, we need something new.

More bad news! Yes, logic is under pressure, and that in many fields simultaneously. In philosophy, the heyday of philosophical logic is clearly over; in computer science, the momentum is with algorithmics rather than semantics; in cognitive science, the old logical-computational paradigm seems largely irrelevant to brain-centered neuroscience; in linguistics, corpus-based computational and statistical methods have dethroned formal semantics, and so on. Of course, this does not mean that logic plays no significant role in these fields today, but it is a diminished role. Even formal philosophers who work with mathematical tools will often turn to statistics, decision theory and game theory, rather than logic for their conceptual analysis. The Queen is now a Concubine.

And to complete this litany of woes, yes, a lot of logic work done and published today is mathematical industry at best, devoid of larger intellectual significance.

But so what? Most of what I have said so far holds for many disciplines, which develop inevitable bouts of agenda inertia and periodically find themselves in tight spots because of academic competition. But tight spots are not necessarily lost wars. Indeed, I think that when we face the facts in the above frank manner without the self-serving 'Horgan Reflex', we will see more encouraging signs than those to which von Wright pointed.

First, I feel that von Wright's 'philosophical history of ideas', familiar as it sounds to those of us who were brought up on this line, gets the facts wrong, while also using the wrong literary metaphor for the relationship between logic and philosophy. In his story, abandonment is for good: the prodigal son leaves, never to return. But the historical realities are much more dynamic and interesting than that. My chapter in the recent *Handbook of the Philosophy of Logic* (Elsevier, Amsterdam, 2007, Dale Jacquette, ed.) shows this for seven key themes at the interface, including conditionals, compositional semantics, and epistemology. Crucial insights often arise within philosophy, perhaps with the help of logical tools, then they migrate into other academic fields, then they return to philosophy, and so on. For instance, the study of conditionals from the 1940s until now runs from the philosophy of science to philosophical logic, then into artificial intelligence, computer science, and cognitive science, and then back into philosophy. Epistemic logic started around 1960 in philosophy, then made its way into computer science and economics, and it is now returning to philosophy in various innovative manners. I see all this as befitting the position of philosophy at a cross-roads of academic disciplines: one leaves, and one returns. I do not have the space here to back up the above points, but I will just say this. The true history of the relationship between logic and philosophy in the 20th century remains to be written. And it is not von Wright's.

My second point concerns the 'new agendas' and competitors that would threaten the role of logic in philosophy. Shudders have run through the community from time to time, say, when Kuhn and others started introducing historical and social accounts of the actual functioning of science. When ephemeral beliefs, power, 'social construction' and gossip come through the front door, it is time for logic to leave. But is it? In reality, many of these challenges have turned into substantial and successful agenda items for logical study. Belief revision is now an established area of logical research, and multi-agent interaction is even at the heart of logic, according to some. In other words, the challenge provided a much-needed push to the logical agenda, upsetting old internal equilibria, and creating room for new topics. And the same points can be made for other 'challenges': brain function and neural nets lead to default logics and conditionals, and the success of probabilistic methods leads to new mergers of logical and quantitative methods that may add a whole new dimension to our current understanding of logical systems. If these challenges did not exist, we would have to invent them!

Of course, the preceding two phenomena, trans-disciplinary migrations and responses to challenges, do change our conception of what Logic is. *Which discipline* is it that survives this whirlpool of events? Surely, there is no contemporary consensus on that. Von Wright states the traditional view of logic as the study of reasoning, though he adds the analysis of language, meaning and concepts as a second, not necessarily reasoning-centered item. In my own view, modern logic will only come into its own if we view it as a general study of informational processes and intelligent interaction, moving on beyond, though still building on the earlier foundational phase. But that is just to put my cards on the table. The only point here is that I would not hold such views of what logic should be if our history were over.

My final point of disagreement with von Wright is the way he presents the partnership between logic and philosophy. To me, 'clearing up of confusions' is an uninspiring and, when used by others, condescending image of a field. Moreover, letting logic help in only that way echoes the role of a logician as a lawyer (Arthur Prior's famous analogy) or maybe, in more unsettled times, a CIA advisor. They come, clear up something at best, then leave. In my view, the true relationship is *symmetric*. There are natural conceptual questions in philosophy, and logical tools are one useful way of approaching these – in addition to mathematical tools, linguistic analysis, and just plain common sense. Also, logical systems provide a sort of conceptual laboratory where one can play with philosophical ideas in some isolation from the true complexities of life, find new notions, input these into the philosophical discussion, and so on. Moreover, when logicians start doing research on 'automatic pilot', merely producing formal systems and meta-theorems, it is often philosophers who ask the conceptual questions that breathe some life into the machine again. Thus, philosophers and logicians are partners!

My optimistic conclusion. Peel off the crust of fossilized research agendas, give up the 'standard grooves' of interpreting the field of logic, look at what really happened between logic and philosophy in the 20th century, and there is much more light at the end of the tunnel than you would think. There may not even be a *tunnel*.

The Demise of Modern Logic?

Sven Ove Hansson

von Wright's overview of modern logic is fascinating and full of valuable insights, not least the connections he points out between the development of logic in the 20th century and other intellectual developments in the same period. He is certainly right in asserting that the expansion of logic was the most important and distinctive feature of 20th century philosophy. This was the century of Russell, Gödel, and Turing. It was also the century of semantics and completeness proofs, formalized modal logic, intuitionistic, inductive and non-monotonic logic, and the implementation of logic in electronic circuits, to make just a short selection from a long series of remarkable achievements.

To anyone who doubts that there can be "progress in philosophy," 20th century logic should put doubts to rest. Gödel's incompleteness theorems are perhaps the best examples of innovative results whose philosophical importance cannot be questioned.

However, although von Wright's narration of the achievements of 20th century logic is unavoidably a success story, its upshot is pessimistic. "As the century is approaching its end", he said, "we can notice... signs of decline in the influence of logic on developments in philosophy." [p. 139] He predicts that whatever the leading trends will be in 21st century philosophy, "logic will *not* be one of them". [p. 157] He seems to regard modern symbolic logic in almost the same way that Kant regarded Aristotelian logic.

The realm of logic

How justified is this pessimism? In order to evaluate its foundations we need to have a close look at what logic is. Clearly, logic is concerned with reasoning, but not all types of reasoning are included in the subject matter of logic. When discussing the pros and cons of different cars, we use arguments couched in terms such as "safe," "comfortable," "easy to drive," etc. These terms and their interrelations are not part of logic. Similarly, the terms used in wine tasting, such as "earthy" and "fruity" have not been subject to logical analysis. The same applies, of course, to the vast majority of terms that we use in different types of arguments. Logic is only concerned with a small fraction of the concepts and patterns used in argumentation and reasoning.

In any discussion of the role of logic, its delimitation among the many types of terms and concepts that are used in argumentation is a crucial issue. von Wright is right in delineating logic as concerned with the structural aspects of ratiocination, not its substance. He is also right in pointing out that logic lays down "rules for judging the correctness of the transition from premises to conclusions – not rules for judging the truth of the premises and conclusions themselves." [p. 142] Logic is characterized by its emphasis on the structure of argumentation, and in particular on structural features that have a role in inference.

However, the distinction between structural and non-structural aspects of an argumentation is not given in the order of things. To the contrary, the isolation of structural aspects from an argumentation or discourse is a creative process that can be done in more than one way. We can call this a process of *structuralizing*. It is a form of idealization, i.e. it means to perform a "deliberate simplifying of something complicated (a situation, a concept, etc.) with a view to achieving at least a partial understanding of that thing. It may involve a distortion of the original or it can simply mean a leaving aside of some components in a complex in order to focus the better on the remaining ones." [McMullin 1985, p. 248]

More precisely, structuralizing is an idealization of patterns of argumentation that retains certain aspects of these patterns that are generalizable across a wide range of contexts, but removes the more context-specific aspects. Hence, from a discussion about good and bad actions we can isolate general notions of good and bad. The resulting logic of good and bad should presumably be the same as if we had isolated it from a discourse on good and bad apples, or good and bad clarinets. Its inference rules should be the same for these different application areas. [Hansson 1990]

The subject-matter of logic is, simply put, all those concepts that we have structuralized in this way and their interrelations, in particular in inferential contexts. This means that the delimitation of logic is not given once and for all, but depends on what concepts have been structuralized, and in particular on how general across contexts a concept has to be in order to be amenable to structuralization.

The most restrictive view on this matter is that only logical constants such as "not," "and," and "for all" are parts of the logical language. However, the definition of a logical constant is controversial. [MacFarlane 2005] In the 20th century, a large number of concepts have been structuralized (although the term "logical constant" seems to have been used only about some of them). In this way we have obtained logics of necessity and possibility, preference, goodness, moral obligatoriness, action, knowledge, belief, and many others. von Wright was himself a major contributor to this development [von Wright 1951, 1963], and in this lecture he mentioned "the extension of the use of logical tools to the conceptual analysis of scientific and, eventually, also everyday language." [p. 149] Unfortunately, he does not comment on its implications for the future of logic. Of course, it is not possible to predict if the demands of generality across contexts will continue to decrease so that additional concepts will be structuralized, leading to an extension of the scope of logic. However, it is easy to see that further structuralizations are possible. There are a large number of concepts that are used in many different contexts but have not yet been introduced into the realm of logic. This applies for instance to concepts used in scientific and technological reasoning, such as "hypothesis," "reliable," and "simulation." (von Wright was right in pointing out that the Port Royal Logic was mostly concerned with topics that do not belong to logic in our sense. In today's terminology this was a treatise on scientific methodology and rational thinking. However, much of it is concerned with concepts that could very well become structuralized through future developments.)

As can be seen from the problems involved in delimiting the notion of a logical constant, logic generates new philosophical issues. The philosophy of logic is a subdiscipline of philosophy that is interesting both in its own right and through its connections for instance with the philosophy of language.

Symbolic language

It is important to distinguish structuralizing from mathematizing or formalizing (into symbolic language).[1] Symbolic treatments of philosophical topics typically result from an idealization in two steps, first from common language to a regimented philosophical language (structuralization) and then from regimented into symbolic language (formalization). [Hansson 2000] Consider the derivation of a preference relation ($>$) from the non-regimented concept of preferring. The following is a comparison of three restaurants:

(1) Alice's Café is better than the Barking Dog,
but the Caravan Grill is worse than the Barking Dog.

In the process of structuralizing comparative value concepts, "worse" is usually taken to be the converse of "better", so that C is worse than B if and only if B is better than C. This is of course a simplification of ordinary language. We tend to use "better" when focusing on the goodness of the higher-ranked of the two alternatives, and "worse" when emphasizing the badness of the lower-ranked one. [von Wright 1963, p. 10] However, that distinction can only be made at the price of a much more complex philosophical terminology. If we give up that distinction, we can structuralize the above as follows:

(2) Alice's Café is-better-than$_{phil}$ the Barking Dog.
The Barking Dog is-better-than$_{phil}$ the Caravan Grill.

where "$_{phil}$" signifies a philosophical idealization. The second step of idealization takes us from "is-better-than$_{phil}$" to the preference relation "$>$"; hence we go from (2) to

(3) $$(A > B) \,\&\, (B > C)$$

where A, B, and C represent the three restaurants. There are major differences in meaning between "is better than" and "is-better-than$_{phil}$". In terms of most of the more philosophically significant differences, "is-better-than$_{phil}$" is closer to "$>$" than

---

[1] In accordance with common usage, the term "formalization" denotes translation into symbolic language.

to "is better than". Hence, intuitively speaking, most of the idealization took place in the first of the two steps of idealization (structuralization) rather than in the second (formalization).

Why logic?

The rise of modern symbolic logic is part of a more general development that has affected a large number of scientific and scholarly disciplines in the 20th century, namely, mathematization. Economics is probably the best example of a discipline that has gone from almost no use of mathematics to being dominated by the use of formal models. Formal models, perhaps in particular game theory, have a strong and increasing influence throughout the social sciences. Meteorology, climatology, and theoretical chemistry have become thoroughly mathematical, and the same applies to some branches of biology such as ecology and population genetics. The reason why mathematical tools were adopted in these and many other areas is of course that they have proven efficient; they have improved the predictive and explanatory capacity of the disciplines in question.

In my view, the increased role of logic in several areas of philosophy has a similar explanation. Hence, the reason why we increasingly use logical (and mathematical) tools in value theory is that we can do a better job as philosophers if we use these tools. In this matter, however, von Wright has a different opinion. In his view, "the cause for the revival of logic in the late 19th century" seems to have been that Western science had "reached a maturity which made it ripe to reflect critically on its own rational foundations." [p. 143] If the increased use of logic is seen as a fashion trend, then it makes sense to believe that it will soon recede. However, if philosophers use logical tools because of their usefulness, then we have no more reason to believe that they will stop doing so than that biologists will give up the use of microscopes or archaeologists the use of radiometric dating.

But is it philosophy?

Against all this it may be said that although logic will survive, it may not continue to be part of philosophy. Towards the end of his essay von Wright discusses that possibility. He recognizes that logic has developed into a tool for increasing clarity and exactness. "But", he says, "logic thus transformed ceases to be philosophy and becomes science." [p. 155]

This argument presupposes that philosophy is a non-science and must continue to be so. However, the division of intellectual subjects into science and non-science is convention-laden, and it is also of much younger date than is philosophy.

Originally, the word "science" denoted any form of systematic knowledge, practical or theoretical. In the 19th century, the meaning of the term was restricted to certain forms of academic knowledge, mainly those studying nature. [Layton 1976] Today, "science" refers primarily to studies of natural phenomena and individual human behaviour. Some of the disciplines that study human societies are called scientific whereas others are not. In some languages other than English, the demarcation is different. Hence, in German and several other Germanic languages the corresponding term ("Wissenschaft") covers both the sciences and the humanities. Since categories such as "science" and "Wissenschaft" are demarcated by a combination of epistemological and contingent criteria, the question whether philosophy belongs to them is largely a matter of conventions rather than principles. However, there is a much more important question underlying these debates, namely that of philosophy's role in the unified corpus of systematic human knowledge that is formed by an interdependent community of disciplines including both the sciences and the humanities. [Hansson 2008]

The unity of the corpus is most clearly seen from the mutual respect that widely divergent disciplines pay to each other's results and methodologies. An historian will have to accept the chemist's analysis of an archaeological artefact. In the same way, a zoologist will have to accept the historian's judgment on the reliability of an ancient text describing extinct animals. The important issue is, therefore, not whether or not philosophy is a science (or a Wissenschaft) but whether or not it is part of this community of interdependent disciplines. Historical evidence gives us strong reason to answer this question in the affirmative. Philosophy cannot be successful in issues related to natural or social phenomena without making use of the systematic knowledge about these phenomena obtained in other disciplines. The philosophy of time and space was revolutionized by relativity theory, the philosophy of sense perception by modern cognitive science, etc. (Admittedly, philosophy's adjustment to new empirical information is often irritatingly slow, but it is nevertheless unavoidable.) In this perspective, if logic "becomes science," this does not make it less philosophical.

The tasks of philosophy

In the end, all this boils down to the issue what the task of philosophy is. von Wright says: "Philosophy... thrives in the twilight of unclarity, confusion and crises in fields which in their 'normal' state do not bewilder those who cultivate them or cause excitement in their intellectual surroundings." [p. 156] When logic becomes scientific, the remaining tasks in logic that he sees fit for philosophers consist in taking care of the surviving "obscure corners in logic" [p. 156].

In my view, this is a misleading description of philosophy's relationship to (un)clarity. If philosophy thrives in the "twilight of unclarity," that is in the same sense as physicians thrive in epidemics, mediators in conflicts, and rescue workers in disasters. Philosophy is particularly needed in contexts of unclarity and confusion, but that is precisely because its task is to resolve unclarity and dispel confusion. Logic is one of the most efficient tools that philosophy uses for this purpose. I see no reason why it should not remain so.[2]

References

Hansson, Sven Ove. 1990. "Defining 'good' and 'bad' in terms of 'better'," *Notre Dame Journal of Formal Logic* 31:136-149.

Hansson, Sven Ove. 2000. "Formalization in philosophy," *Bulletin of Symbolic Logic* 6:162-175.

Hansson, Sven Ove. 2008. "Philosophy and other disciplines," *Metaphilosophy*, in press.

Layton, Edwin. 1976. "American Ideologies of Science and Engineering," *Technology and Culture* 17:688-701.

MacFarlane, John. 2005. "Logical constants," *Stanford Encyclopedia of Philosophy* (http://plato.stanford.edu/entries/logical-constants).

McMullin, Ernan. 1985. "Galilean Idealization," *Studies in History and Philosophy of Science* 16:247-273.

von Wright, Georg Henrik. 1951. "Deontic Logic," *Mind* 60:1-15.

von Wright, Georg Henrik. 1963. *The Logic of Preference* (Edinburgh University Press).

---

[2] I would like to thank Tor Sandqvist for valuable comments on an earlier version of this essay.

von Wright, Georg Henrik. 1993. "Logic and Philosophy in the Twentieth Century," (this volume).

The Place of Logic in Philosophy

Eva Picardi

Georg Henrik von Wright closed his lecture on the place of logic in philosophy with the surmise that general changes in the cultural atmosphere mean that logic will cease to play the leading role that the path-breaking discoveries enshrined in Frege's *Begriffsschrift* enabled it to play during the twentieth century. That century will be described by future generations as "the Golden Age" of logic, not only for its very substantial achievements as regards, for example, meta-mathematical results concerning the power and limitations of formalised languages, the development of proof-theory, and Tarski's work on the concept of truth and the foundation of model-theory, but above all for the fascination that the new conception of logic exerted on the philosophical imagination of generations of philosophers. It is this fascination, or spell, that von Wright deems unlikely to linger on: a "sombre mood of self-critical scrutiny of the achievements and foundation of our civilization" will set in, and as a result the great expectations of the pioneers that logic will enable us to address metaphysical, epistemological and ontological issues in a radically new way will strike future generations as a belated offspring of the philosophy of the Enlightenment.

1. That logic has played a major role in fostering the schism between various traditions of European philosophy is something that von Wright does not reflect on in his essay. The last twenty years have, however, witnessed the growth of a vast literature devoted to a reassessment of our recent philosophical past, with a special emphasis on the history of the Vienna Circle, of American Pragmatism, and of the Analytic Tradition. An example of what I mean can be found in the minutes of a conversation that took place around 1953 between Martin Heidegger and Professor Tezuka.[1] To Tezuka's question of what stands in the way of a proper understanding of the essence of language, Heidegger replied that the most serious threat comes from the development of logic into "Logistik" ("in der Ausbildung der Logik zur Logistik"). Strange as it may seem, it is *Logistik* that gives shelter to the claims of traditional metaphysics: "Und der Angriff gegen das Wesen der Sprache, der sich darin verbirgt, vielleicht der letzte von dieser Seite, bleibt unbeachtet."[2]

That *Logistik* should pose a threat to understanding the essence of language is a claim that nowadays would strike most readers as bizarre, for it entails a vast overestimation of the influence that a branch of specialized knowledge can exert on anything, let alone something as momentous as language. In any case, if language is hospitable to logical techniques, this is due to its systematic and compositional structure. Frege, of whom the young Heidegger had been appreciative,[3] was perhaps the first in the history of philosophy to underline this central aspect of natural languages. If wonder is what set philosophy in motion, this is the proper place for it to set in. Frege's third "Logical Investigation," *Gedankengefüge*, opens with this remark:

> It is astonishing what language can do. With a few syllables it can express an incalculable multitude of thoughts, so that even if a thought has been grasped by an inhabitant of the Earth for the very first time, a form of words can be found in which it will be understood by someone else to whom it is entirely new. This would be impossible, if we could not distinguish parts in the thought corresponding to the parts of a sentence, so that the structure (Aufbau) of the sentence can serve as a picture of the structure of the thought.[4]

It is through Frege's path-breaking insights that logic found its way into the philosophy of language, and Frege's philosophical agenda is still with us. His context principle, his principles of

---

[1] Published in M. Heidegger, *Unterwegs zur Sprache* (Tübingen: Neske, 1965).

[2] *Unterwegs zur Sprache*, 116.

[3] Cf. M. Heidegger, *Neuere Forschungen über Logik* (1912), in Heidegger's *Gesamtausgabe*, vol. 1 (Frankfurt:, Kostermann, 1976), pp. 17-43.

[4] G. Frege, "Logische Untersuchungen, Dritter Teil: Gedankengefüge," in *Beiträge zur Philosophie des Deutschen Idealismus* III (1923), 36-51.

functionality and compositionality, his account of sense and reference, of truth and assertion, still provide food for thought to philosophers of language. What Heidegger probably disliked about what he and others called *Logistik* was the algorithmic, almost mechanical character, that the formalization of logic reads into the flow of discourse, and one can see some justice in this complaint. In *Philosophy and the Mirror of Nature* Richard Rorty saw some justice in Heidegger's anti-representationalist conception of language and made him an honorary member of the Pragmatist Club, along with James, Dewey, and Wittgenstein.[5] We do need to understand better how it came about that the distinctive role that logic played in the making of analytic philosophy also contributed to deepen the unfortunate divide between the analytic tradition and the phenomenological and hermeneutic traditions. Transcendental logic has come to be seen not as a complement but as an alternative to *Logistik*, much as in *Sein und Zeit* the "natural conception of the world" was opposed to the "naturalistic" conception of the world fostered by the empirical and mathematical sciences.[6]

As von Wright pointed out, it is partly due to the fact that the "new" logic of Frege, Peano and Russell became entrenched in the philosophical practice of analytic philosophers that the sense of excitement has withered. The mastery of elementary logic (first-order logic with identity) has become part of the curriculum in most departments of philosophy, at the same time that logical research has returned to its mathematical home, its technical results often being as impervious to philosophers as any of the results in particular branches of mathematics. A question naturally arises: might it not be that it is because the "great expectations" of the pioneers were too grand, if not utterly misplaced, that it is unlikely that logic will keep future generations of philosophers spell-bound? I could find no clear answer to this question in von Wright's lecture.

2. Wittgenstein's *Tractatus* provides the best example of a philosophical work pervaded by the excitement alluded to by von Wright. In spite of recent attempts at a post-modernist interpretation, the *Tractatus* still strikes me as a metaphysical poem or, at any

---

[5] R. Rorty, *Philosophy and the Mirror of Nature* (Princeton University Press, 1979). Cf. also R. Brandom, "The Pragmatist Enlightenment (and Its Problematic Semantics)" in *European Journal of Philosophy* (2004), 1-16.

[6] See e.g. H. Philipse, "What is a Natural Conception of the World?" in *International Journal of Philosophical Studies* (2001), pp. 385- 400.

rate, a sustained ode to all-pervading logic. Logic, as a "Spiegelbild der Welt," must take care of itself, for it needs no theory of knowledge for its justification or metaphysics for a foundation. Wittgenstein famously stated that while he is confident that his work provides an answer (possibly THE answer) to certain fundamental questions concerning the connection between logic, world and language, he also stated that our most pressing concerns are not even touched by such insights – indeed, that the clarity thus obtained makes us painfully aware of how little is achieved when these problems are solved. Thus "the sombre mood" that von Wright thinks will prevail in future generations of philosophers is already foreshadowed in a work that fostered like few others belief in progress and in the "scientific conception of the world" announced in the manifesto of the Vienna Circle.

In Wittgenstein's *Philosophical Investigations,* "the sombre mood" became more prominent: the motto, taken from a play of Nestroy, *Der Schützling,* reminds us of a characteristic feature of progress, namely that it looks much greater than it really is. There is no denying that in his mature work, while still holding that philosophy must strive to achieve absolute clarity, Wittgenstein explicitly called into question his former conception of logic. Logic was no longer seen as casting light on the workings of our language. As von Wright pointed out, Wittgenstein came to relegate the later developments of formal logic to mathematics: "When he uses the word 'logical' in connection with his investigations, what he means is roughly the same as *conceptual* or, in Wittgenstein's somewhat eccentric terminology, *grammatical.*"

It is no wonder that logicians and formal semanticists, while still devoting considerable attention to the *Tractatus,* hardly take notice of Wittgenstein's later writings. Indeed, if we survey the recent philosophical literature, there is no doubt that the towering figure is Frege, in spite of the severe criticism Wittgenstein made of his work on logic and language. I will return to the Frege Renaissance that started around 1970, for it provides prima facie evidence against von Wright's surmise.

It would be wrong, however, to believe that the philosophical insights of the later Wittgenstein are directly responsible for the less prominent role that von Wright thinks logic will play in the cultural atmosphere of the new millennium, nor does he suggest that in his lecture. A likelier explanation why logic will no longer appeal to the philosophical imagination is that the linguistic turn has been replaced by the cognitive turn. To this one might retort that artificial intelligence, computer science, and cognitive studies have supplemented, rather than replaced, the role of logic in philosophy. But we must not forget that it is from these new quarters that telling criticisms have come of the failure of standard mathematical logic to come to grips with the actual features of human cognition and reasoning. The basic tenets of Quine's naturalized epistemology seem to be the accepted background for much of the work now done in philosophy of mind and the philosophy of science. As a result, there is a tendency to brush aside many philosophical questions connected with traditional logical issues as mere residues of old-fashioned debates characteristic of logic's Golden Age. It would be disastrous if this tendency were to prevail, for notwithstanding the wealth of logical and mathematical results at our disposal, many of the philosophical questions that the pioneers bequeathed on us remain wide open. Let me consider how this is so in some contemporary work.

3. It is well known that there is no consensus concerning ontological, epistemological, or semantical issues in the philosophy of mathematics. Roughly speaking, under "ontology" fall questions about the status of the entities that mathematics unfolds in such profusion, and under "epistemological" fall questions about the kind of knowledge that justifies our accepting mathematical statements. Semantic questions concern the truth-conditions appropriate to sentences as they occur in the context of formalized languages and everyday discourse.

The latter provide an excellent example of how logic can be relevant to philosophical questions, namely, the realism/antirealism dispute that was inspired by Michael Dummett's influential paper of 1959 on truth.[7] Dummett took this dispute to be fundamentally a semantic issue. What he called "semantic realism" was not Platonism, for the latter took the existence of abstract objects and structures as its *Urtatsache*. Semantic realism, on the contrary, emphasized the role of the Principle of Bivalence in construing the statements of a mathematical theory or other kinds of discourse. As Kreisel put it, what matters is the objectivity of mathematics, not the objects it allegedly deals with, for there may be no such objects. Dummett thus brought intuitionistic logic to bear on the theory of meaning and thereby forged new links between non-classical logic and semantics. He addressed the issue of the

---

[7] Reprinted in M. Dummett. *Truth and Other Enigmas* (London: Duckworth, 1978).

justification of logical laws, among them the controversial Law of Excluded Middle, in a new and very sophisticated way.[8] This makes me dubious about von Wright's claim that intuitionistic logic is still in early infancy.

4. A cursory glance at recent handbooks, such as *The Oxford Handbook of the Philosophy of Logic and Mathematics*,[9] may suggest to the naïve reader that the Golden Age of foundational programmes is having a revival. But the naïve reader would be wrong: the goal of finding a secure foundation for mathematics is no longer pursued. The issues concerning the semantics, ontology and epistemology of mathematics that were addressed in the foundational programmes are nevertheless still with us. *Foundations without Foundationalism* is not only the title of a book by Stuart Shapiro,[10] but the slogan that informs the *Handbook* he edited, where there are extensive discussions of the time-honoured issues of *a priori* knowledge, the concept of logical consequence, and the application of mathematics, and so on.

The central part of the *Handbook* is devoted to the new interpretation of Frege's logicism put forward by Crispin Wright in *Frege's Conception of Numbers as Objects*,[11] where the study of abstraction principles and second order logic plays a major role. Wright's work by and large follows Frege's lead, though it owes much to the technical results of George Boolos about the role of Hume's Principle as a standard for the equality of numbers in the derivation of Peano's axioms within the framework of second-order logic.[12] To be sure, not all is well: abstraction principles may lead us astray, and an investigation is needed to sort out sound applications of abstraction principles from illegitimate ones. If we could sort out well-behaved applications of abstraction principles from illegitimate ones, we could consider whether they can be used to support Frege's claim that numbers are logical objects. They

---

[8]M. Dummett, *The Logical Basis of Metaphysics* (London: Duckworth, 1991).

[9]S. Shapiro (ed.), *The Oxford Handbook of the Philosophy of Logic and Mathematics*, (Oxford University Press, 2004).

[10]S. Shapiro, *Foundations without Foundationalism: A Case for Second-Order Logic*, (Oxford: The Clarendon Press, 1991).

[11]C.Wright, *Frege's Conception of Numbers as Objects* (Aberdeen University Press, 1983).

[12]I am thinking here of Boolos' papers, "Saving Frege from Contradiction," "The Standard of Equality of Numbers," and many others, now reprinted in G. Boolos, *Logic, Logic and Logic* (Harvard University Press,1988).

lend themselves to various construals, however, including *structuralist* ones, which do not claim for natural numbers the status of individual objects, but only that of places in a structure.[13]

In sum, it is clear that the recent literature on abstraction principles and definitions by abstraction, on the one hand, and on the relationship between principles of abstraction and the context principle, on the other, constitutes an industry of its own, quite independently of the chances of a revival of the Logicist Programme.

Not everybody is impressed by the claims of neo-logicism. Nominalists such as Hartry Field help themselves to the advantages of Tarski's semantics, but reject its suggestion of a realist interpretation of the predicates and singular expressions in mathematical statements. Hence their deflationary construal of the notions of reference and truth, which exploits the technology and shakes off the ideology (the ontological commitments to abstract objects named by numerals). In *Science without Numbers*[14], Field argued that the parts of mathematics involved in present-day physics can be reconstructed within his nominalistic system. He maintained that arithmetical statements, taken at face value, i.e. with numerals in the role of proper names of numbers, are literally false. He does not want to tamper with the linguistic structure of arithmetical statements, as Russell thought we should, and he granted that numerical terms occur also in mixed statements, such as "There are three black-birds on the lawn." We certainly think that this sentence is true if and only if there are three black-birds on the lawn, and Field agreed. Returning to Frege's ingenious rendering of the adjectival occurrence of number-words in statement in terms of numerically definite quantifiers, Field argued that such statements do not commit us to the existence of abstract objects, for we remain within the province of first-order logic.

If implemented in practice, Field's variety of Nominalism would appear to involve a large scale revolution in our way of thinking and speaking about numbers. But perhaps he is better interpreted as a "hermeneutic" rather than a revolutionary Nominalist.[15] Rather than urging a reform of our ways of thinking, he is

---

[13]Cf. M. Resnik, *Mathematics as a Science of Patterns* (Oxford University Press, 1997) and the essay of J. Hellmann in the *Handbook* edited by Shapiro.

[14]H. Field, *Science without Numbers: A Defence of Nominalism* (Oxford: Blackwell, 1980).

[15]Cf., G. Rosen, J. Burgess, *A Subject with No Object* (Oxford: The Clarendon Press, 1997).

asking us to reflect on what we should *mean* if we did not lose sight of the fact that physical objects are the only objects there are. We competently employ number-words in the context of mathematical statements, but we lack a correct grasp of the content of our own thoughts; in fact, we are positively mistaken about them.

Field once described his Nominalism as a variety of Fictionalism: mathematical statements are false if taken at face value, but they have come to be believed to be "true in the story" – in the popular narrative handed down to us by generations of mathematicians and mathematical text-books.[16] Fictionalism is a very popular doctrine these days: among its adepts are Stephen Yablo, David Papineau, and Gideon Rosen.[17] According to Yablo, mathematicians go through the moves of a game of make-believe. They indulge in metaphorical language, knowing full well that there is no way of spelling out in literal terms the gist of what they mean.[18] Whereas uncompromising Nominalists see themselves as announcing a revolutionary reform of the theory and practice of classical mathematics, Fictionalists engage in hermeneutic clarification, in a therapeutic spirit, of our ways of talking and thinking.

5. This is not the place to tackle such complex issues in detail. I have intended only to offer a sample of current debates in order to suggest that von Wright's surmise about the place that logic will occupy in philosophy is exceedingly pessimistic. Technical results do not bear their philosophical significance on their sleeves, and the pace at which philosophy progresses – if that is the right word – is much slower than the pace at which science progresses. We are in only the first decade of the new millennium, and I am in no position even to guess whether the works I mentioned above are the harbinger of new trends or rearguard actions of the Golden Age. Who am I to dispute the depth of Georg Henrik von Wright's philosophical vision? It was a great privilege to be personally acquainted with him, and I treasure the memory of our conversations and his generosity.

---

[16]H. Field, *Realism, Mathematics and Modality* (Oxford: Blackwell, 1989).

[17]D. Papineau, "Mathematical Fictionalism", *International Studies in the Philosophy of Science*, 2 (1988), 151-74; G. Rosen "Modal Fictionalism", *Mind*, 99 (1990), 327-54.

[18]See, e.g. S. Yablo, "Go Figure: a Path Through Fictionalism", *Midwest Studies in Philosophy*, XXV (2001), pp. 72-102 and "Abstract Objects: A Case Study", in S. Sosa, E. Villanueva (eds.), *Philosophical Issues 12: Realism and Relativism*, pp. 220-40.

von Wright on the Future of Logic and Philosophy

Soren Stenlund

1. Von Wright's "Logic and Philosophy in the Twentieth Century" was clearly a lecture given by a philosopher whose faith in formal logic as a philosophical discipline had been seriously damaged. To the disappointment of many philosophical logicians in the audience he declared that it is unlikely that logic will continue to play the prominent role in philosophy it has held in the 20th century. His doubts were connected with an increased awareness of how the logic-oriented mainstream of analytic philosophy, within which von Wright himself had been active and done original work, was inspired and fuelled by "the optimistic mood and belief in progress, fostered by scientific and technological development" [14]. With the increased awareness in the 1960's and 1970's of the negative environmental effects of technology and of the intimate connection between science, military industry and global politics, von Wright experienced certain features of our present situation as deeply problematic and even as threats to human life.

In his lecture, he prefers to state his doubts in the form of a prophesy about the future, a prophesy expressed from an external perspective in which he reflects on the situation of his times, but he nonetheless stays quite close to the received story about the successful development of logic and its prominent role in philosophy in the past decades. This could give the impression that his message is merely a political one, as though he was simply making the (politically incorrect) claim that the popularity and seductive powers of formal logic as a philosophical discipline will fade away in the next century. But the claims regarding the success and usefulness of formal logic in philosophy expressed by the most prominent analytic philosophers around the middle of the

20th century (including von Wright himself) were no doubt seriously meant as *philosophical* claims about the nature of philosophy, and not merely as political attempts to promote logic as a trend or fashion. The gist of the message was that philosophy, through modern formal logic, "at long last, had attained *den sicheren Gang einer Wissenschaft*" (in von Wright's words, [7]). I think that von Wright's misgivings about the role of logic in philosophy in the future were rooted in his doubts about these philosophical claims.

If that is true, how did the "belief in progress, fostered by scientific and technological development" manifest itself in these philosophical claims about the nature of philosophy? How did this "belief in progress" sustain the (allegedly value-neutral) formal methods and scientific ways of working within analytic philosophy around the middle of the 20th century?

In trying to answer this question, it is helpful to reflect on the following remark by Wittgenstein:

> Our civilization is characterized by the word progress. Progress is its form, it is not one of its properties that it makes progress. Typically it constructs. Its activity is to construct a more and more complicated structure. And even clarity is only a means to this end and not an end in itself.[1]

What is typical of what von Wright calls 'the mainstream of philosophy in our century,' and in particular of the logically-oriented branch of analytical philosophy, is precisely that *one constructs*. The spirit of progress is manifest in the endeavour towards theory-construction and the ideal of scientific rigour. One constructs new theories. One reconstructs existing theories and notions. And *rigour is assured by the notions and methods of formal logic* (propositional calculus, quantification theory, set theory). One would expect that a philosophy that calls itself 'analytic philosophy' and claims that 'logical analysis' is the true method of philosophy would be concerned mainly with analysis, i.e. with dividing complex structures into their parts or components, rather than with the construction of new complex structures. But analysis is

---

[1] Wittgenstein, L., 1998, *Culture and Value*, ed. G.H. von Wright, translated by Peter Winch (Oxford: Blackwell, 1998), p. 9.

only a preparatory stage in a 'logical analysis.' It is completed through a 'rational reconstruction.'[2]

This does not simply mean that the notions and methods of formal logic had the function of tools or instruments in theory-construction. What is more important to realize is that formal logic was assigned the role of a *paradigm of clarification*, a paradigm with an absolute and universal scope. With the work of Gödel and others in the early thirties as *exemplary* work, formal logic in the form of quantification theory was accepted as a universal framework for clarification, for what the result of a successful clarification in philosophy must look like, what *form* it must have.

There is, of course, nothing wrong with laying down a paradigm for clarification in a *scientific* context, to delineate a scientific approach or discipline by prescribing a paradigm for clarification or a model for explaining certain phenomena. Classical mechanics, for instance, is such an approach for clarifying and explaining natural phenomena. But problems arise when a paradigm for clarification is totalized, when the scientific notion is given a philosophical status that makes it absolute and universal. The model of clarification is then turned into dogma, a dogma on the basis which a proposed clarification may count as a good clarification although it clarifies nothing (i.e. it does not clarify anything for anyone). Such a proposed clarification only tends to rearticulate the dogma about what form a clarification must have. The totalizing attitude of what von Wright calls 'scientific rationalism' was taken to be justified by the spirit of the times; it merged into the blind faith in science and technology.

That the logical framework had been given the function of an absolute norm manifests itself in the jargon of analytic philosophy, for instance, in the frequent use of words such as 'exact', 'precise', 'satisfactory' as *absolute* notions. Someone may state that his aim is to give a satisfactory theory about some subject matter, which may simply mean that the theory will have a certain external form which almost by itself makes it satisfactory. Paraphrasing a notion expressed in ordinary English into logical symbolism is often seen as a necessary condition for turning a 'vague' notion into a 'precise' one. Note the similarity of this attitude to a common attitude in the use of new technology, for instance, information technology: if a certain human practice can be made more automatic using

---

[2]My teacher, Stig Kanger, who made significant contributions to logic, used to deny that he was an analytic philosopher. He preferred to think of himself as concerned with what he called 'constructive philosophy.'

computers, then making it more automatic by means of computers is *in itself* considered as progress and is therefore considered as something that must be done.

I believe that during the 1970's von Wright became uncomfortable with this dogmatism about clarification. As is clear from his autobiographical writings, he could no longer endorse it in an unreserved way. He seems to have felt that it was part of a philosophical attitude that had little or no place for the various manifestations of human life in the world more generally and that it had become part of the blind faith in "progress, fostered by scientific and technological development."

Of course, there is nothing wrong with analysis and theory-construction when carried out as a limited scientific enterprise within the framework of formal logic. Thus, von Wright could speak of the *success* of logic in integrating itself into the neighbouring sciences as the way in which formal logic can and will survive, and as one reason why formal logic will have a less important role in philosophy in the future. On this point I find myself in complete agreement with von Wright, and it seems to me that the development of formal logic and its applications during the last decades has confirmed von Wright's prediction. But there is, it seems to me, an unresolved tension, or even conflict, in von Wright's message. He has serious doubts about the philosophical status of formal logic and about the scientific rationalism connected with it, but his account is none the less in accord with the received story about the prominent place of logic in philosophy in the 20th century, which is a story about great philosophical achievements. I think, on the contrary, that the dominance of formal logic since the 1930's has resulted in several respects in a philosophical decline – not in all, but in too many respects.

2. The dogmatism about clarification emerges in the 1930's and marks the end of what von Wright calls 'the heroic age' in the study of logic. The search for clarity about logical concepts during 'the heroic age' was a more genuine, less dogmatic search. Conflicting ways of thinking were in the air. Philosophers as well as mathematicians were involved in the discussion, and some of the leading figures, such as Hilbert and Weyl, changed their minds on fundamental issues several times during the period. With the exception of the scientism of Russell and the logical positivists, ideas and attitudes with roots in Kant's critical philosophy were still alive in the views discussed, and in particular the attitude that philosophical issues are on a different level than scientific problems. Hilbert, for instance, thought about his *finite Einstellung*, not as a scientific or formal method, but as an *apriori* condition of the possibility even of mathematical knowledge.

Already in the 1910's, Russell had proclaimed *logical construction* as the true method of the new 'scientific philosophy' he was advocating. But there were problems with the very conception of logic in Frege's and Russell's Logicism. There was no precise notion of the difference between first- and second-order logic in the logicist framework, and therefore the difference between logic and set theory was not clear. There were problems with the logicist treatment of the quantifiers and, due to the logicist conception of the generality of logic, there was no place for metalogical considerations in the logicist framework. These difficulties were removed in Hilbert's approach to logic through his 'axiomatic method,' which he had used successfully in geometry and theoretical physics. An explicit conception of first-order logic occurs for the first time in 1928 in Hilbert and Ackermann's *Grundzüge der Theoretischen Logic*. Building upon Hilbert's approach to logic, Gödel's work in the early 1930's was decisive for creating the attitude to first-order logic as a universal clarificatory framework that has dominated the stage in analytical philosophy since then. Warren Goldfarb has given an apt description of Gödel's early work from the point of view of this change. Referring to the discussion about logic in the 1920's, he writes:

> What is new [with Gödel's early work] is the *absolute clarity* that Gödel brings to the discussion.... Gödel delineates explicitly the realm of quantification theory, separates syntactic from semantic notions, and elucidates the notion of satisfiability. He further defends this notion, nonconstructive as it is, against claims that mathematical existence should be explicated in terms of syntactic consistency. (The implicit claim that satisfiability *is* an appropriate explication of existence also emphasizes the role of quantification theory *as an underlying logic for all of mathematics*.) Thus Gödel establishes the appropriate framework for the study of first-order logic, in this sense his work represents the culmination of the period, *not so much in what he proves, but more in setting straight how we should think about the subject*....[3]

---

[3]Goldfarb, W. "Logic in the Twenties: The Nature of the Quantifier," *The Journal of Symbolic Logic*, vol. 44, 3, 1979, p. 351. (my emphasis).

Gödel's ideas of how "we should think about the subject" of logic – ideas that were further developed by Tarski, Carnap and others – became generally accepted, and in the following decades, the philosophy of mathematics was dominated by mathematical logic and set theory. With satisfiability as the appropriate explication of existence and quantification theory as the underlying logic for all of mathematics, Gödel had also prepared the way for metaphysical realism or Platonism, which became the accepted view in the philosophy of mathematics around the middle of the 20th century, and it inspired a general paradigm for how to conceive of 'ontological and metaphysical issues' within analytic philosophy.

It is difficult to see this change as a sign of *philosophical* progress, which received wisdom takes it to be. I doubt that the participants in the discussion about logic and the foundations of mathematics in the 1920's were happy with Gödel's way of thinking about logic and its role in mathematics. It is a mistake to think that the conceptual problems that concerned Hilbert, Poincaré, Brouwer, Weyl, Skolem, Ramsey, and others (engaged in clarifying the infinite in mathematics) were solved and settled by Gödel's work. The truth is rather that many of the philosophical issues discussed in the 1920's were simply ignored and forgotten, and that is true in particular of every trace of Kant's philosophy in them. The philosophical issues were pushed into oblivion by the new paradigm of clarity that Gödel inspired. I am almost inclined to say that even if Gödel's work resulted in great scientific, technical-mathematical results by opening the way to a *mathematical* study of logic, they represent, from a philosophical point of view, a decline compared to the situation in the 1920's. In the early 20th century, the attitude in the foundational discussion was often (if not always) more open and self-critical, and there was a greater awareness of philosophical thinking as an activity that is distinct from scientific work. The problems of formal logic and its role in mathematics were dealt with and discussed in more direct contact with the philosophical issues that were felt to be important and decisive among many mathematicians.

Hilbert's epistemological motive for using, for instance, the distinction between real and ideal objects (and statements), which is important in his proof theory, would have been quite pointless if he had endorsed the philosophical view that Gödel expressed as follows:

> Classes and concepts may... also be conceived as real objects, namely classes as 'pluralities of

things' and... concepts as properties and relations of things existing independently of our definitions and constructions. It seems to me that the assumption of such objects is quite as legitimate as the assumption of physical bodies....[4]

I do not think that the philosophical view expressed here has clarified anything, but has rather caused confusion (for instance, in the suggestion that the existence of physical bodies is an 'assumption' of ours). If it was 'absolute clarity' that Gödel brought to the discussion about logic, why wasn't that clarity reached earlier in the Hilbert school? They certainly had all the technical resources needed; the difficulty was philosophical, the impediment being Hilbert's epistemological ambitions.[5] Even if Hilbert's program as a technical-mathematical research-project did not fulfil these ambitions, it was designed to reach a deeper level of clarity that is completely absent in the paradigm for clarity that Gödel was promoting. But it is Gödel's paradigm that dominates the stage in the following decades. When I read a classical textbook in mathematical logic such as Kleene's *Introduction to Metamathematics* (first published in 1952), in which he presents the philosophical views that were alive in the discussion in the 1920's, including Hilbert's epistemological motives for central features of his proof theoretical program, what strikes me is that the philosophical content is completely dead for the author. What excites Kleene is the technical machinery of mathematical logic. The book is a textbook in mathematical logic and proof theory as a new branch of mathematics.

3. That formal logic since the 1930's has the status not only as a method or instrument for the construction of new concepts and theories, but also as a norm for philosophical clarification, manifests itself in various ways within philosophy in the twentieth century, and within the received picture we have of it. In the philosophy of mathematics, it manifests itself, for instance, in the fact – pointed out by Kitcher and Aspray – that "the distance between

---

[4]Benacerraf, P. and Putnam, H. (eds.) *Philosophy of Mathematics*, 2nd ed (Cambridge University Press, 1983), p. 454.

[5]It is a mistake to think of Hilbert's meta-mathematical program (as a technical-mathematical research project for proving consistency results) as *defining* Hilbert's epistemological ambitions. The technical research project was an *instrument* for realizing the epistemological ambitions. That Hilbert never abandoned the epistemological ambition is clear from his preface to the first volume of Hilbert's and Bernay's *Grundlagen der Mathematik*.

the philosophical mainstream and the practice of mathematics seems to grow throughout the twentieth century."[6] The situation was different in the 1920's. Many, perhaps most, participants in the philosophical discussions of the 1920's were mathematicians. But as a result of the acceptance in the 1930's of quantification theory as the universal norm for clarification, mainstream philosophy of mathematics became less relevant to the concerns of most mathematicians.[7] There were surely mathematicians with philosophical interests and concerns in the 1930's and later on, but a mathematician that was not educated in mathematical logic and captive to it as a universal norm for clarification could not always recognize what the philosophers had to say as relevant to *her* philosophical concerns. If a problem about the nature of arithmetic were the mathematician's concern, the philosopher-logician would immediately start to talk about first-order arithmetic as though the passage from ordinary arithmetic to the formal system of first-order arithmetic were a philosophically innocent and legitimate step. The conceptual framework that mathematical logic had created has no room for certain philosophical issues, and in particular for the ones that call this framework itself into question, (which is why it is appropriate to call it 'a *dogmatism* about clarification').

One of the most striking examples of the predominance of formal logic in the philosophy of mathematics is the way in which Brouwer's intuitionism has been 'modified' into a form of mathematics with its own alternative intuitionistic logic, and also the way in which the original *philosophical* critique of the foundational significance of formal logic formulated by Poincaré and Brouwer has been largely ignored in the logico-philosophical community.[8]

---

[6]Kitcher, P. and Aspray, W., (eds.), *History and Philosophy of Modern Mathematics, Minnesota Studies in the Philosophy of Science*, vol. XI, 1988. p. 17.

[7]The mathematician Errett Bishop explains the distance between mathematicians and philosophers of mathematics as follows: "The courses in the foundations of mathematics as taught in our universities emphasize the mathematical analysis of formal systems, at the expense of philosophical substance. Thus it is that the mathematical profession tends to equate philosophy with the study of formal systems, which require knowledge of technical theorems for comprehension. They do not want to learn yet another branch of mathematics and therefore leave the philosophy to the experts."(Bishop, E., "The Crisis in Contemporary Mathematics," *Historia Mathematica* 2 (1975), p. 507.)

[8]I am thinking of Poincaré's articles on logic and the foundations of mathematics collected in Poincaré, A., *Science et Méthode* (Paris: Flammarion, 1908) [English translation: *Science and Method* (New York: Dover,

In his lecture, von Wright mentions this critique in passing, but, as one usually does, only in passing. This indifference illustrates my earlier point, namely, that the conceptual framework that mathematical logic created leaves no room for philosophical issues that put this framework itself into question. Commentators have reacted to this critique by saying that it only shows Poincaré's and Brouwer's dislike or distaste for formal logic. But I believe that the problem of the foundational significance of formal logic was not just a matter of taste for Poincaré and Brouwer, but a serious philosophical concern. That it has been largely ignored in later philosophy of mathematics is, in my opinion, something to be regretted.

Poincaré's and Brouwer's main objection to the classical mathematician's use of formal logic did not centre on the use of *particular* logical principles such as the law of the excluded middle, but on the role the classical mathematician assigns *generally* to the use of formal logic in the construction of mathematical proofs. As Michael Detlefsen has pointed out, their critique was much more radical than what is commonly presented in the literature as "the intuitionist critique of classical mathematics," where the critique of the excluded middle is presented as the centrepiece of the intuitionist's concerns.[9] On this 'modified' view of the original intuitionist critique, it seems as though the central issue concerns the question of which logic is the true logic of mathematics (and in particular, whether the law of the excluded middle belongs to it). But the fundamental question for Poincaré and Brouwer was rather what role *any* formal logic can play in the construction of mathematical proofs.

Concerning the relationship of formal logic to mathematics, Brouwer says that "... the function of the logical principles is not to guide arguments concerning experiences subtended by mathematical systems, but to describe regularities which are subsequently observed in the language of the arguments."[10] Formal logic in this more *descriptive* sense would not have the normative, foundational role that it has been assigned in the classical view. Only in this descriptive sense could there be an intuitionistic logic in Brouwer's sense, which is therefore essentially different from

---

1952)] and some of Brouwer's early work published in English translation in Heyting, A. (ed.), *Brouwer Collected Works I* (Amsterdam: North-Holland, 1975).

[9]Detlefsen, M., "Brouwerian Intuitionism," *Mind*, Vol. 99, 1990, pp. 501-534.

[10]Heyting, op. cit., p. 108.

the recent forms of intuitionistic and constructive mathematics in which intuitionistic formal logic is taken to have essentially the same foundational significance for intuitionistic mathematics that classical logic is taken to have for classical mathematics. As Bishop points out, "Intuitionism was transmuted by Heyting from something which was anti-formal to something which is formal. When one speaks today of intuitionism, one is talking of all sorts of formal systems (studied by the logicians). That's not what Brouwer had in mind."[11]

Brouwer's early critique of the status of formal logic (which is quite independent of his later positive mentalistic doctrine that imposes *another* dogmatism about clarification) allowed him to see philosophically important difficulties that have been overlooked by the dominance of formal logic. On some of these difficulties, Brouwer made more correct observations than is generally admitted, such as when he remarks that mathematical structure is already presupposed in the setting up of the systems of formal logic and that these structures "are in no respect especially elementary, so they do not justify any priority of logical reasoning over ordinary mathematical reasoning."[12] Poincaré had already made similar points, which made Hilbert abandon his early logicist views and his original idea of a *strictly* finitary proof theory.

4. According to the received view, logic is the most general discipline so it was a quite natural step to broaden Gödel's view of quantification theory (as the underlying logic for the discourse of mathematics and science) to the status of the underlying logic for *any discourse*. Through this step, the status of quantification theory as *the* universal framework for clarification was established, and the foundation was laid for the construction of logical systems for discourses other than mathematics and science. Around the middle of the century a great number of projects for the construction of theories and formal systems started within analytic philosophy. The propositional and the predicate calculus were extended with notions central to some non-mathematical discourse and with rules and axioms that appear evident for these notions. Think of the great number of treatises within analytic philosophy that bear a title of the form "The logic of X" (e.g. the logic of induction, of modality, of norms, of preference, of belief, of decision, etc).

---

[11] "The Crisis in Contemporary Mathematics," p. 515.
[12] Heyting, op.cit. p. 73.

This genre of formal logic has been called "philosophical logic". Why was this branch of formal logic considered to deserve the epithet 'philosophical' more than the logic of mathematical discourse, which was the model for its creation? Von Wright was one of the creators of philosophical logic, but I don't find any convincing answer to this question in his writings. I think that one important reason was that there was a need to contrast this new branch of logic with the logic of mathematical discourse in a situation in which the latter study had become less philosophical and more mathematical. Gödel and his followers had created the attitude that all there remains to do in the foundations of mathematics after the incompleteness theorems is the advanced *mathematical* study of formal systems.[13] It is as though the philosophical problems and puzzles that motivated the original foundational programs *had disappeared* when the proposed programs for solving the problems had failed. This is a strange attitude because philosophical problems tend to disappear when they are solved, not when they remain unsolved. The name 'philosophical logic' for the new branch of logic in a sense gave expression to the attitude that the logic of mathematical discourse is no longer philosophy.

Another reason for introducing the name 'philosophical logic' (as well as the term 'formal philosophy') was, it seems to me, the wish to emphasize the academic affiliation of most people that are (or were) working in the field (the name might therefore have been introduced with a certain political intent). Philosophical logic is contrasted with mathematical logic, which today is a branch of mathematics, and most people working in the branch are professional mathematicians or computer scientists. If von Wright's prophesy about the continuing successful integration of formal logic into neighbouring sciences is correct, which I think it is, the epithet 'philosophical' might perhaps soon be dropped.

It has often been pointed out that one of the great philosophical achievements of early analytic philosophy was the insight that logical form does not always coincide with grammatical form (in the sense of traditional linguistic grammar). The notions of a

---

[13]Gödel commented upon the implications of the incompleteness theorems for Hilbert's program as follows: "What has been proved is only that the *specific epistemological* objective which Hilbert had in mind cannot be obtained. [...] However, viewing the situation from a purely *mathematical* point of view, consistency proofs on the basis of suitably chosen stronger meta-mathematical presuppositions ... are just as interesting, and they lead to highly important insights into the proof theoretic structure of mathematics." [Quoted from C. Reid, *Hilbert* (New York: Springer, 1970), p.217.]

proposition in the logical and in the linguistic sense do not coincide. Thus, an indicative sentence which appears to be a proposition in the logical sense, may only be of that appearance in a misleading way. *Not everything which appears to be a proposition in the logical sense is one.*

This is, of course, connected with the notion that logic is concerned with propositions as having a descriptive content that make them true or false, and in logic we are interested in the features of the proposition that are essential for its being true or false, while other features (e.g. expressive features) are disregarded. From this point of view, the logical structure of a proposition, as a complex symbol, is expressed in modern logic by the general notion of a function. (It was the model for Frege's notion of a *Begriff* and therefore a fundamental idea in his *Begriffsschrift*. The notion of a 'propositional function' is a fundamental notion in Russell's logic. The predicate calculus is a calculus of functions. In the mentioned text by Hilbert and Ackerman, first-order predicate logic is called "the narrower functional calculus".) Propositions can occur in other propositions only as arguments of truth-functions, and an 'atomic proposition' is a function of the names occurring in it (or rather, a function of objects the names signify). For a function $f(x)$ we have the rule: if $a = b$ then $f(a) = f(b)$. So if $f(a)$ is a true proposition and $a = b$ then $f(b)$ is a true proposition (extensionality). A proposition in which extensionality fails (e.g., an intensional context such as 'A believes that p is the case') is not a proposition in the logical sense. Predication is expressed by the operation of applying a function to an argument, which means that the different senses of predication that were connected with *de re* modal distinctions in Aristotelian logic disappear. They disappear as features of a proposition that are not essential for its descriptive content that makes it true or false.

Within such an extensional view, modern formal logic was designed from its beginning. To introduce modal distinctions again *within* modern logic will simply cause conceptual confusion, as Quine has argued. (That such an approach may result in *mathematically* well-defined and technically interesting formal systems and structures does not remove *this* confusion.)

In his lecture von Wright dismisses Quine's criticism of intensional logic as being merely a manifestation of Quine's "conservative bent of mind." I think that this is an unfair judgement. Quine could not have adopted a more liberal attitude to logic, allowing intensional logic while retaining the rest of his philosophical views.

It seems to me that von Wright is underestimating the extent to which (extensional) quantification theory is intimately connected to Quine's philosophy as a whole. One might say that quantification theory is for Quine as much *philosophical* logic as deontic logic is for von Wright.

Philosophical logic was made possible, it seems to me, through decayed or degenerate notions of logical form and of proposition (a development that can be said to have started already with Frege's influential paper "Über Sinn und Bedeutung"). It manifests itself in the philosophical logician's tendency to work according to the principle: If an indicative sentence appears to be a proposition *then it is a proposition* and should be 'logically analysed' as one. The problem is *how* it should be paraphrased as a proposition in a 'satisfactory' logical symbolism and *how* its truth-conditions, its semantics, should be spelt out. This approach relies heavily on verbal readings of the logical symbolism and it presupposes a kind of homogenous, 'seamless' view of language, or at least of assertoric discourse. Instead of confining the descriptive use of language to those parts of language that deal with the subject matters of science, one allows descriptive use of language to pervade all regions of discourse regardless of content. Language in general is seen as though it were 'logically and conceptually homogenous'. A 'natural language' such as English is seen as being basically a formal system, though a very complicated one.

But modern formal logic was designed from the beginning as the logic of *scientific* discourse. It was bent on the concept of truth according to which "scientific method is the last arbiter of truth" (in Quine's words). Modern formal logic is intimately connected with the secularized *Wissenschaftliche Weltauffassung* that was quite common in the late 19th century. If one thinks – as von Wright suggests – that this is a too narrow view of reality, it is not enough merely to extend it or supplement it with notions connected with more ordinary human concerns. To do so may result in new, technically interesting formal systems, but it does not take the philosophical motives and aims of the original modern formal logic seriously. To overcome the narrowness of the metaphysics of modern formal logic, a much more radical rethinking of the conceptual problems of logic and language is necessary, as Wittgenstein, the author of the *Tractatus*, was forced to realize.

Using von Wright's prophetical manner of speaking, I am inclined to say that there is indeed a sense in which formal logic will continue to be an important concern for philosophy in the future. Not, however, as an instrument for theory-construction or as a universal paradigm for clarification, but as an object of investigation within a philosophy of mathematics and of computer science that is no longer crippled by the dominance of mathematical logic and set theory. There is a need for a 'critique of pure mathematics,' a critical investigation into the notions and methods of formal logic that will make us aware of their limitations, and of the requirements, ambitions and prejudices connected with these formal methods that led to the dogmatism about clarification. Only with a more sober view of formal methods that this critique can provide, will we be able to recognize the dogmatism about clarification as a mistaken philosophical project. That will be genuinely clarifying.

Logic and Philosophy in the Twenty-First Century

Timothy Williamson

1. In "Logic and Philosophy in the Twentieth Century," von Wright claims that "logic has been the distinctive hallmark of philosophy in our era." But he judges it "unlikely that logic will continue to play the prominent rôle in the overall picture of an epoch's philosophy which it has held in the [twentieth] century."

Von Wright offers two reasons for his judgment. One is that he discerns a new mood of pessimism about civilization. The suggestion is that philosophers in the twentieth-first century will at best be too preoccupied with criticizing the dark side of Enlightenment to have much time for logic, and at worst see it as integral to what they are criticizing. Perhaps: although Gödel and Tarski proved their most philosophically seminal results in 1930s Europe, which had its own urgent grounds for pessimism about civilization.

Von Wright's other reason is this. After an initial period of creative confusion, in which modern logic was mainly concerned with foundational questions of compelling philosophical significance, since the 1930s it has settled down into a period of normal science, in which precise questions of specialised interest are answered by agreed, rigorous methods. Exaggerated hopes are no longer pinned on foundational programmes. According to von Wright, "logic thus transformed ceases to be philosophy and becomes science." One may feel that the comment presupposes an unnecessarily exclusive conception of the relation between philosophy and science, perhaps based on an over-idealized conception of science. Nevertheless, most work in contemporary logic – as represented, for instance, in *The Journal of Symbolic Logic* – is of no more interest for philosophy than any other work in mathematics. Although mathematical rigour is quite compatible with philosophical significance, the direction of inquiry in logic is now far more likely to be set by mathematical than by philosophical concerns.

Still, if logic becomes less philosophical, it does not follow that philosophy becomes less logical. I see no evidence that philosophers on average use logical or formal methods less than they once did. The recent growth of formal epistemology indicates the opposite. More generally, checking arguments by formalization is a standard tool in contemporary philosophy. Of course, such methods should not be applied blindly — they have limits and must be used with discretion and good judgment. But of what scientific method is that not true?

Von Wright concedes that "We can be certain that there will always remain obscure corners in logic too, thus assuring for it a permanent place among the concerns of philosophers." But there is a more systematic challenge to the philosophical uncontentiousness of logic than von Wright had in mind.

One aspect of the process by which logic became, in von Wright's terms, scientific rather than philosophical was that (classical, non-modal) first-order logic attained the status of 'standard logic.' Logic textbooks teach first-order logic; they rarely teach second-order logic, which is marginalized and regarded as exotic. Yet the logical systems of Frege, Russell and Whitehead and others before 1914 were higher-order. Their first-order fragments were isolated as significant only in retrospect. Although the historical details of the canonization of first-order logic are contested, surely Gödel's completeness and incompleteness theorems in 1930-1 played a vital part. They showed that while first-order logic is sound and complete, second-order logic is essentially incomplete (on its standard interpretation). In this sense, first-order reasoning can be made purely formal — 'scientific,' in a narrow sense — while second-order reasoning cannot. Later, Quine offered a notorious philosophical defence of the privileging of first-order logic. He treated second-order 'logic' as a misleading façade for set theory, the ontological commitments of the latter being more honestly displayed by its explicit first-order axiomatization. Quine also dismissed the claims to logical status of other alternatives to standard first-order logic: in particular, of extensions of classical logic such as modal logic and of non-classical logics such as intuitionistic logic.

Quine's stance has come to seem unduly restrictive. Mathematically, the specific systems to which he denied logical status are well-defined structures that can be studied in the usual way. Philosophically, it seems dogmatic and pointlessly controversial to exclude them. Some extensions to classical logic, most notably modal logic, are routinely used as background logics for philosophical discussion. Many philosophers of mathematics are now convinced that the appropriate background logic for mathematical theories is second-order: most notably, second-order arithmetic captures the structure of the natural numbers because all its models are isomorphic, whereas first-order arithmetic or any consistent formal extension thereof has models of unintended structure: they contain elements that cannot be reached by finitely many applications of the successor operation, starting from zero. Moreover, serious arguments have been given for rejecting classical logic in favour of one or other non-classical logic — many-valued, paraconsistent, intuitionistic, ... — in order to give a philosophically satisfying account of the liar paradox, the sorites paradox, metaphysical problems about infinity or the future, and so on. Even if one rejects such arguments (as I do), one cannot simply dismiss them on the grounds that no genuine alternative to classical logic is on offer. Any effective response must engage with the specifics of the proposal in question.

2. How can this anarchy of different systems be reconciled with the apparently scientific, unphilosophical nature of logic? The answer lies in the role of metalogic. All these systems are normally studied from within a first-order non-modal metalanguage, using classical reasoning and set theory. Scientific order is restored at the meta-level. Not only are the systems susceptible to normal methods of mathematical inquiry with respect to their syntax and proof theory, their model theory is also carried out within classical first-order set theory.

Modal logic is an example. The decisive technical breakthrough was the development of 'possible worlds' semantics. The central definitions of a model and of truth are in purely mathematical terms. No modal operators are used in the metalanguage, even in the clauses for the object language modal operators. In motivating the semantics informally, one speaks of a set of worlds, an actual world, and a relation of relative possibility between worlds, but that plays no role in the formal definitions. The models are abstract mathematical structures, the relevant facts about which are not themselves contingent. The technical study of modal logic has made such dramatic progress over the past fifty years by eliminating all modal considerations from its reasoning.

For 'modal realists' such as David Lewis, the modal is indeed reducible to the non-modal: quantification over worlds in a non-modal language represents the underlying metaphysical reality more perspicuously than does the use of modal operators. The actual world is merely one world amongst many, just as here is merely one place amongst many, privileged only from its own perspective. Most philosophers find modal realism hopeless; for them, this actual world has objective, albeit contingent, metaphysical privileges. Thus modal operators represent the underlying metaphysical reality more perspicuously than do quantifiers over worlds in a non-modal language. On this view, the formal model theory still plays an auxiliary role in facilitating proofs that a particular modal conclusion cannot be derived from particular modal premises. Moreover, it can be argued (using modal considerations!) that for some class of models, the formulas valid in that class exactly coincide with the formulas true on the intended interpretation under every assignment of propositions to the atomic formulas. Once such a class has been identified (using modal considerations!), it can be used to check modal reasoning. But these applications are extrinsic to the formal model theory itself, and employ it in a merely instrumental capacity.

A similar phenomenon arises for second-order logic. Its standard model theory is given in a first-order metalanguage with set theory: the second-order domain is the power set of the first-order domain.

The metatheory of non-classical logics is also normally classical. Thus continuum-valued or fuzzy logic advocated as a solution to paradoxes of vagueness, on the grounds that a continuum of degrees of truth is needed to track how vague sentences can gradually shift from true to false. It may also be proposed as part of a solution to the semantic paradoxes. A continuum-valued model for propositional logic is any function from atomic formulas to real numbers in the interval [0, 1], where 1 represents perfect truth and 0 perfect falsity. A distinctive feature of the model theory is that it computes the degrees of truth of complex formulas as a function of the degrees of truth of their constituent formulas, generalizing the two-valued truth-tables. A formula is 'valid' just if it is perfectly true in every model. Classically, we can prove that the law of excluded middle is invalid on this semantics. The mathematical argument makes no appeal to vagueness. Nevertheless, according to proponents of this model theory, the formulas it validates coincide with those perfectly true on every potentially vague interpretation of the language.

That example is typical of the usual metatheory of non-classical logic. In such cases, a classical metalogic leads from non-homophonic semantic clauses to the conclusion that some classical principle in the object language is invalid.

A tacit Quineanism seems to be operating at the meta-level. Any deviation from classical first-order non-modal logic is permitted, if it can be given a model theory in a classical first-order non-modal metalogic: be as unorthodox as you like in your object language, provided that you are rigidly orthodox in your metalanguage. This attitude may even encourage the impression that differences in logic are merely notational, or at least superficial, because we all agree on our metalogic. Since contemporary mathematical logic is largely metalogic, no wonder it uses agreed, scientific methods.

3. How stable is this combination of diversity below with uniformity above? Consider some of its Procrustean effects.

Intuitionistic logic provides one of the best studied examples. Unlike classical mathematicians who study intuitionistic logic, ideological intuitionists in the tradition of Brouwer and Heyting reject the law of excluded middle for infinite domains. The metatheory of intuitionistic logic has an infinite domain of formulas and proofs. Therefore, ideological intuitionists are committed to rejecting excluded middle for their metalogic. Taking this seriously, they have developed an intuitionistic metatheory for first-order intuitionistic logic. Soundness is unproblematic: both classically and intuitionistically, one can prove that every intuitionistically provable formula is intuitionistically valid (in a natural sense). The problem concerns completeness. Classically but not intuitionistically, one can prove that every intuitionistically valid formula is intuitionistically provable. Moreover, both classically and intuitionistically, one can prove that *if* completeness holds *then* a classically valid but intuitionistically implausible consequence follows. Thus, from an intuitionistic perspective, the completeness theorem looks false, even though it is classically provable.

Admittedly, the soundness and completeness of first-order intuitionistic logic is provable both classically and intuitionistically for other notions of a model. But they seem not to correspond as well as to the original intentions of ideological intuitionists. Indeed, one may even interpret the completeness theorem for the new semantics as *showing* its inadequacy to the originally intended meanings, given the incompleteness of intuitionistic logic on the old semantics, for if truth in all the new models entails intuitionistic provability while truth in all the old models does not, then truth in all the old models does not entail truth in all the new ones.

Recall a simpler example: continuum-valued or fuzzy logic as motivated by the problem of vagueness. For its proponents, the obvious objection to studying it in a classical metatheory should be higher-order vagueness. If it is vague whether someone is a child, it is also vague what real number best measures the degree to which she is a child. Hence vagueness infects the metalanguage too. If vagueness in the object language makes continuum-valued logic appropriate for the object language, by parity of reasoning vagueness in the metalanguage should make continuum-valued logic appropriate for the metalanguage too. Hence continuum-valued logicians should not rely on the law of excluded middle in their metatheory.

Continuum-valued logicians may reply: "One must distinguish between truth theory and model theory. A truth theory for interpreted sentences should be faithful to their actual meanings, and the problem of higher-order vagueness arises. But model theory abstracts from their actual meanings. It generalizes over all assignments of semantic values of appropriate types. A model for continuum-valued propositional logic is any function from the atomic formulas to real numbers in the interval $[0, 1]$. To generalize over such functions, one requires only precise mathematical and syntactic vocabulary; thus the problem of higher-order vagueness does not arise. One can legitimately use a classical metalogic in the model theory of continuum-valued logic for a vague language."

That response makes the gap between model theory and truth theory too wide. On a model-theoretic conception, logical truth is truth in all models. But logical truths should be true. The most straightforward way of satisfying these constraints is by having one or more *intended models*, corresponding to the actual meanings of the object language expressions: a sentence is true in an intended model if and only if it is true *simpliciter*. Since a logical truth is true in all models, it is true in the intended model, and therefore true *simpliciter*. On a degree-theoretic conception, degrees of truth in an intended model equal actual degrees of truth. If models for continuum-valued logic are the purely mathematical structures the response requires, languages with higher-order vagueness have no intended models. The responder might still hope that the model theory fulfils its instrumental purpose through some less direct way in which truth in all models implies truth *simpliciter*. But even that hope is vain. Some formulas of the object language can be proved valid on the continuum-valued semantics only given excluded middle.

Philosophically, the obvious move for the degree theorist is to use a continuum-valued metalogic. Technically, however, this move causes grave problems. It is not only that continuum-valued logic is very weak, that proving serious metalogical results in it will be very difficult, and that degree theorists have made hardly any attempt to do so. It is unclear even in principle how to work out for the first time which principles are valid in this logic, if we have to use it in the metalanguage too. For if one starts out not yet knowing the validity of any principle, equally one can rely on no metalogical principles in validitating principles in the logic. Thus one never gets started.

Similar phenomena arise for classical extensions of first-order non-modal logic. For instance, the Barcan formula (BF) in first-order modal logic says that if there could have been something that met a certain condition, then there is something that could have met that condition. Many philosophers hold that BF has actual counterexamples. Wittgenstein never had a child, but he could have. Nevertheless, on their view, there is nothing that could have been a child of Wittgenstein, so BF actually has false instances.

Kripke gave possible worlds countermodels to BF. He evaluates first-order quantification at a 'world' as restricted to a domain; different 'worlds' can have different domains. Informally, the domain is conceived as the set of things that exist in the 'world,' but this plays no role in the model-theory. To falsify BF at the 'actual world' of a model the domain of some 'non-actual' must contain something not in the domain of the 'actual world.' Formally, such models are easily described. But how does such a counterexample work on the *intended* interpretation of the object language, whose 'worlds' really are possible worlds, whose 'actual world' really is the actual world, and its domain is the set of everything that actually exists. Thus, in describing the counter-model in the non-modal metalanguage, one is committed to saying that there is something that does not actually exist. For a modal realist who thinks of actually existing as being within this particular space-time system, that may be acceptable. But most philosophers who reject BF are not modal realists. Rather, they hold that *whatever there is* actually exists in the relevant sense. Thus, in describing the counter-model to BF, they are committed to saying this: there is something that there is not. That is a contradiction. All counter-models to BF interpret the object-language quantifier at the actual world as more restricted than the quantifiers in the metalanguage. But the metaphysically most interesting readings of BF involve no such unnecessary restriction. If one of the possible worlds models provides such an intended interpretation of the object language, then BF holds. Contrary to first appearances, the model theory provides no explanation of how BF could fail on an unrestricted reading of its quantifiers.

Opponents of BF on its unrestricted reading need not give up. Rather, the natural line for them is to ascribe a purely instrumental role to possible worlds model theory. On their view, the formulas true in all such models in some class may exactly coincide with the formulas that are valid in on their intended interpretations, but not because the models capture those intended meanings. Some less direct argument would be needed for the coincidence. The intended meanings would have to be captured in a modal metalanguage. The primary standard for assessing principles of the modal metalogic would itself be modal, with no explanation in non-modal terms of BF's failure. A little work has indeed been done in developing semantic theories for modal object languages in modal metalanguages. It is a laborious business, by comparison with possible worlds semantics in a non-modal metalanguage; even very simple results are very hard to prove.

For an example involving classical first-order non-modal logic itself, consider the logic of absolutely unrestricted generality, in which the first-order quantifiers are mandatorily interpreted as ranging over everything whatsoever. The set-theoretic paradoxes make the intelligibility of such quantification controversial (I have defended it elsewhere). One can prove that for a standard first-order language an argument is truth-preserving on all such unrestricted interpretations if and only if it is truth-preserving in every standard set-theoretic model with an infinite set-sized domain. One can therefore provide a sound and complete axiomatization by adding as new axioms formalizations of 'There are at least n things' for each natural number n. Since there is no universal set, no set-sized model gives the quantifiers the intended unrestricted interpretation; nevertheless, larger models are not needed to give an extensionally correct characterization of validity on the unrestricted interpretation of the quantifiers.

Those results may seem to show that we can avoid this contentious sort of quantification in the metalanguage. But that is too quick. The reason is not just that one must make initial use of unrestricted quantification in the metalanguage to prove the soundness and completeness theorems for the logic of unrestricted quantification in the object language. As Harvey Friedman has shown, the proof of the completeness theorem for unrestricted quantification makes essential use of the assumption that there is a linear ordering of absolutely everything. This is a comparatively weak but still controversial consequence of the Axiom of Global Choice. If there is no linear ordering of everything, the first-order formula NLO saying that R does not express a linear ordering of everything is true on all unrestricted interpretations. Of course NLO is false in some infinite set-sized models, for instance where the domain is the set of natural numbers and R is their usual ordering. Thus which formulas are valid on the unrestricted interpretation is sensitive to delicate issues about the structure of everything there is. Ascent to the metalanguage does not avoid such controversy.

A feature of the example is that to generalize in the metalanguage over all unrestricted interpretations of the object language, one needs a second-order metalanguage. For a first-order metalanguage, all semantic values available for the non-logical atomic predicates already belong to the first-order domain, giving a version of Russell's paradox. This problem can be avoided in a second-order metalanguage. Atomic predicates are not assigned semantic values. Even the noun 'interpretation' is replaced by a higher-order term. Any attempt to give the semantics of the second-order metalanguage in a first-order metametalanguage reintroduces Russell's paradox. Here semantic ascent is a move in the direction of more controversy, not less.

4. Von Wright writes as though most philosophically interesting technical work in logic has already been done. The examples above hint that much of it has only just been started. To an extent much greater than is widely realized, unorthodoxy in the object language can only be fully explored and fairly assessed through unorthodoxy in the metalanguage. Sometimes the unorthodoxy is in the deductive power of the logic, sometimes in the expressive power of the language. Both types of unorthodoxy result in contentious ways of doing metalogic, for instance through unfamiliar restrictions on deduction or unfamiliar freedoms of expression. Since the motivation for the work is primarily philosophical, and the necessary techniques often have a philosophical flavour, we cannot expect the mathematicians to do it for us. We will have to do it ourselves. One of the greatest pleasures in philosophy is to imagine one's way into a radically different pattern of thinking. To watch logical differences reassert themselves in metalogic is to experience just how radical such differences can be.

The conception of metalogic as a neutral arbiter between different logics is the last refuge of the conception of logic as a neutral arbiter between different substantive theories. If the ubiquity of alternative logics undermines the conception of logic as a neutral arbiter in the object language, their reappearance in the guise of alternative metalogics undermines the conception of logic as a neutral arbiter in the metalanguage.

Once we have seen that the contentiousness of logic is radical enough to reach metalogic, we should be suspicious of any attempt to bound logic or metalogic to the insubstantive, the non-metaphysical. For example, in second-order logic there are formulas CH and NCH such that CH is logically true just if Cantor's continuum hypothesis is true and NCH is logically true just if the continuum hypothesis is false. This has been viewed as an objection either to second-order logic itself or at least to anything equivalent to the standard line between its logical truths and the rest, on the grounds that both CH and NCH are too substantive, too metaphysical, to count as a logical truth. The inevitable contestability of logic makes that objection unconvincing.

Much though we may long for such a neutral arbiter to discipline philosophical debate, we cannot always have one. Logical positivism required a clean break between logic and metaphysics, but logical positivism was wrong. Logic *is* a science, and the parts of it that overlap metaphysics are science too. Since when was science uncontentious?

www.ingramcontent.com/pod-product-compliance
Lightning Source LLC
Chambersburg PA
CBHW022007160426
43197CB00007B/309